Praise for
Some Memories of a Long Life, 1854–1911

"Written in a strong declarative style, full of anecdotes and occasional humor, the memoir conveys a sense of the historical significance of the events Mrs. Harlan witnessed.... [*Some Memories*] is very much a love story. ... But it is much more ... [it is] the deeply personal story of a girl's transformation."

—*The New York Times*

"Malvina's ear for irony ... provides gems on the private [Justice John Marshall Harlan]. [*Some Memories* is a] valuable personal look at a key figure in American judicial history."

—*Kirkus Reviews*

"Harlan was a skilled and astute observer of nineteenth-century American politics and society. Originally written in 1915, this memoir ... is a significant historical document. [Harlan] ... provides rare, insightful glimpses into Washington society during the postbellum and early modern eras, including the couple's interactions with prominent politicians, diplomats, movers, shakers, and other notables."

—*Library Journal*

"From the dusty archives where it lay forgotten for so long, [Harlan's] memoir emerges as an important social document—an accurate reflection of the manners and mores of the writer's time, place, and milieu."

—*Booklist*

"[Harlan] has a self-effacing humor. . . . Throughout her life, Harlan kept diaries and voluminous scrapbooks, and excerpts from them give her memoir an appealing immediacy. She comes across as charming and likable."

—*Columbus Dispatch*

"Compelling."

—New York *Daily News*

"Taken together, foreword, introduction, and *Memories* usefully illuminate not only the life of a pivotal American, but the manners and mores of a vanished era in Kentucky and the nation."

—Louisville *Courier-Journal*

"Her observations are honest, moving, and funny."

—*Grand Rapids Press*

SOME MEMORIES OF A LONG LIFE, 1854-1911

MALVINA SHANKLIN HARLAN

SOME MEMORIES OF A LONG LIFE, 1854-1911

Foreword by Ruth Bader Ginsburg

Epilogue by Amelia Newcomb

Afterword and Notes by Linda Przybyszewski

THE MODERN LIBRARY

NEW YORK

This work was originally published in the *Journal of Supreme Court History*, 2001,
vol. 26, no. 1. A hardcover edition was published in 2002 by Modern Library, an
imprint of The Random House Publishing Group, a division of
Random House, Inc.

Library of Congress Cataloging-in-Publication Data

Harlan, Malvina Shanklin, 1838–1916.
Some memories of a long life, 1854–1911/Malvina Shanklin Harlan;
foreword by Ruth Bader Ginsburg; introduction and notes by Linda
Przybyszewski.—2002 Modern Library cloth ed.
p. cm.
ISBN 0-8129-6744-5
1. Harlan, John Marshall, 1833–1911.   2. Harlan, Malvina Shanklin,
1838–1916.   3. Judges' spouses—United States—Biography.
I. Przybyszewski, Linda.   II. Title.
KF8745.H3 H37 2002
347.73'2634—dc21
[B]   2001057959

Modern Library website address: www.modernlibrary.com

Printed in the United States of America

2 4 6 8 9 7 5 3 1

*Frontispiece: John Marshall Harlan of Frankfort, Kentucky, and Malvina French Shanklin
of Evansville, Indiana, were married on December 23, 1856, after a two-year engagement.
The groom was twenty-three; the bride was seventeen.*

CONTENTS

FOREWORD

Ruth Bader Ginsburg

The publication of Malvina Harlan's *Some Memories* is cause for celebration.

The rooms and halls of the United States Supreme Court are filled with portraits and busts of great men. Taking a cue from Abigail Adams, I decided, when asked some years ago to present the Supreme Court Historical Society's Annual Lecture, it was time to remember the ladies— the women associated with the Court in the nineteenth and early twentieth centuries. Not as Justices, of course; no woman ever served in that capacity until President Reagan's historic appointment of Sandra Day O'Connor in 1981. But as the Justices' partners in life, their wives.

"Behind every great man stands a great woman," so the old saying goes. Yet one trying to tell the nineteenth-century wives' stories runs up against a large hindrance— the dearth of preserved primary source material penned by the women themselves.

My law clerk, Laura W. Brill, and I began our research

by collecting stories told by or about the wives of Supreme Court Justices—stories one will not find in standard accounts of the Court's part in the governance of our nation.[1] The Library of Congress aided that endeavor by furnishing us with a remarkable, yet unpublished manuscript written by Malvina Shanklin Harlan. Malvina was the wife of the first Justice John Harlan, who served on the Court from 1877 until 1911. Her manuscript was found among the Justice's papers lodged at the Library. (Malvina lived from 1839 until 1916 but she dated *Some Memories* from 1854, the year she met John, until 1911, the year he died.) The manuscript, running some two hundred double-spaced typewritten pages, was edited by hand, and there were notations in margins, both perhaps in anticipation of a hoped-for publisher. Malvina's memoir is full of anecdotes and insights about the Harlan family; politics in Indiana, Kentucky, and Washington, D.C., in the pre– and post–Civil War period; religion; and, of course, the Supreme Court.

I was drawn to Malvina's *Some Memories* as a chronicle of the times, as seen by a brave woman of the era. Malvina wrote of her adjustment as a seventeen-year-old bride, when she left the free state of Indiana in 1856 to reside with John and his parents in Kentucky, and of her feelings when her mother-in-law presented her, on arrival, with a personal slave. She strove to serve her husband selflessly, yet did not surrender all pursuits of her own, particularly the music that brightened her life. The reader is drawn into the Hayes White House through Malvina's friendship with First Lady Lucy Hayes. We learn of the extraordinary encouragement Malvina gave to her husband when he wrote the lone dissent from the Supreme Court's judgment striking down the Civil Rights Act of 1875, a measure Congress enacted to promote equal treatment, without regard to race, in various public accommodations.

I thought others would find the manuscript as appealing as I did. For many months I tried to interest a university or commercial press in publishing *Some Memories*, to no avail. Ultimately, with my appreciation and applause, the Historical Society decided it would undertake the publication, and devoted the entire summer 2001 issue of the Society's *Journal* to Malvina's *Some Memories*. On the cover is a portrait of Malvina, age seventeen, and John, age twenty-three, on their wedding day.

—

In the Supreme Court's early-nineteenth-century days, when the great Chief Justice John Marshall led the Court, the Justices lived together in one boardinghouse or another when the Court was in session, leaving their wives at home. If the boardinghouses diminished family life, they served one notable purpose—they helped to secure the institutional authority of the nascent, underfunded Supreme Court. Recent biographies of the great Chief Justice tell how John Marshall used the camaraderie of boardinghouse tables and common rooms to dispel dissent and achieve the one-voiced Opinion of the Court, which he usually composed and delivered himself—the unanimity that helped the swordless Third Branch fend off attacks from the political branches.

Although Chief Justice Marshall strictly separated his court and family life, he did not lack affection for his wife. In a letter from Philadelphia in 1797, four years before his appointment to the Court, John Marshall told Polly of his longing. "I like [the big city] well enough for a day or two," he wrote her. "But then I begin to require a frugal repast with cool water. I wou[l]d give a great deal to dine with you today on a piece of cold meat with our boys beside us & to see little Mary running backwards & forwards over the floor."

In 1832, a year after Polly's death, Marshall reflected: "Her judgement was so sound & so safe that I have often relied upon it in situations of some perplexity. I do not recall ever to have regretted the adoption of her opinion. I have sometimes regretted its rejection."

———

Sadly, Polly Marshall's letters to her husband did not survive history, but we have Malvina Harlan's vivid record of the relationship of another Supreme Court Justice and his wife in her *Some Memories*.

In commenting on her decision to marry John, a slave-owning Kentuckian, Malvina, who lived her first seventeen years in Indiana, wrote:

> All my kindred were strongly opposed to Slavery, the "peculiar institution" of the South. Indeed, an uncle on my mother's side, with whom I was a great favorite, was such an out-and-out Abolitionist that I think (before he came to know my husband) he would rather have seen me in my grave than have me marry a Southern man and go to live in the South.

On her husband's decision to join the Union Army five years after their marriage, when two children were part of the family, Malvina recalled:

That night he paced the floor until dawn, his duty to his wife and little ones and his duty to his country wrestling within him in bitter conflict. He came to my bed, and sitting beside me, he said he would leave the matter entirely to me; that he felt his first duty was to me and his children. I asked what he would do if he had neither wife nor children. He said at once, with great earnestness, "I would go to the help of my country."

I knew what his spirit was, and that to feel himself a shirker in the hour of his country's need would make him most unhappy. Therefore, summoning all the courage I could muster, I said, "You must do as you would do if you had neither wife nor children. I could not stand between you and your duty to the country and be happy."

Decades later, in 1903, the War was a not "altogether" faded memory. Malvina wrote of a dinner party that year:

There were perhaps a dozen people at the table, and my husband, being in the best of spirits, began to tell the company some of his experiences in the Civil War. He was describing a hurried and exciting march which he and his regiment made through Tennessee and Kentucky in pursuit of the daring Confederate raider, John Morgan. He came to a point in his story where he and the advance guard of the pursuing Union troops had nearly overtaken the rear-guard of Morgan's men, who had just crossed a little stream near Hartsville, Tennessee, and were being fired upon by the Union men from the opposite shore.

Suddenly, Judge Lurton [a guest at the dinner] . . . laid down his knife and fork, leaned back in his chair, his face aglow with surprise and wonder, and called out to my husband in a voice of great excitement, "Harlan, is it possible I am just finding out *who* it was that tried to shoot me on that never-to-be-forgotten-day?"

In a tone of equal surprise... my husband said, "Lurton, do you mean to tell me that *you* were with Morgan on that raid? Now I know *why* I did not catch up with him; and I thank God I didn't hit *you* that day."

The whole company was thrilled by the belated but dramatic sequel to my husband's story, as they realized afresh how completely the wounds of that fratricidal war had been healed; for there were those two men, fellow citizens of the one and united country, serving together as Judges on the Federal Bench. It was as if there had been no Civil War.

(Judge Lurton, at the time of the dinner party, served on the Court of Appeals for the Sixth Circuit; he was appointed to the Supreme Court seven years later.)

——

By the time of John Harlan's appointment in 1877, boardinghouse days were long over, and a Supreme Court appointment meant a move to Washington, D.C., for all members of a Justice's immediate family. It also meant an unpaid job for the Justice's wife.

Malvina Harlan wrote of the "at home" Monday receptions Supreme Court wives were expected to hold. The callers came in numbers. Malvina reported she might receive as many as two hundred to three hundred visitors at an "at home" Monday. These events were more fancy than plain. Tables would be spread with refreshing salads and rich cakes. Musicians were engaged so the young people might dance a waltz or two while the older folk looked on. "At home" Mondays held by Court wives continued into the Chief Justiceship of Charles Evans Hughes in the 1930s.

In 1856, when seventeen-year-old Malvina Harlan left her parents' home in Indiana to begin married life in Kentucky, her mother counseled:

> You love this man well enough to marry him. Remember, now, that *his* home is YOUR home; *his* people, YOUR people, *his* interests, YOUR interests—you must have *no other*.

Malvina valued that advice, but did not follow it in all respects. She continued to pursue her interest in music; she eventually sojourned abroad on her own; and even, after forty-seven years of marriage, spoke for the first time on a public platform.

When John became a Supreme Court Justice, Malvina developed a friendship with First Lady Lucy Hayes, nicknamed "Lemonade Lucy" for her avid temperance. This friendship yielded the Harlans more than occasional invitations to the White House. At White House evenings, Supreme Court wives did not always stand solidly, or at least silently, behind their men. Malvina Harlan tells of a dinner at which Chief Justice Waite endured some teasing by his wife, Mrs. Waite, and the First Lady for having "squelched" Belva Lockwood's 1870s application to be admitted to practice before the Supreme Court. Lockwood was persistent. She eventually gained admission to the Court's Bar in 1879—the first woman ever to do so—but only after an Act of Congress required the Court to relent. (Lockwood's case is a striking illustration that the Legislature is sometimes more sensitive to individual rights, and the winds of change, than the Court is.)

Malvina reported an episode showing that Supreme Court wives attended to more than the social side of a Justice's life. Justice Harlan was a collector of objects connected with American history. He had retrieved for his collection, from the Supreme Court Marshal's office, the inkstand Chief Justice Taney used when he penned the 1857 *Dred Scott* decision, which held that no person descended from a slave could ever be a citizen, and that the majestic due process clause safeguarded one person's right to hold another in bondage. It was a decision with which Justice Harlan strongly disagreed, an opinion overturned by the Civil War and the Fourteenth Amendment.

Chivalrous gentleman that he was, Harlan promised to deliver the Taney inkstand to a woman he met at a reception, who claimed a family relationship to Chief Justice Taney. Malvina thought the promise unwise, so she hid the inkstand away among her own special things, and Justice Harlan was obliged to report to the Taney relative that the item had been mislaid.

In the months immediately following this incident, the Supreme Court heard argument in the so-called Civil Rights Cases, which yielded a judgment striking down the Civil Rights Act of 1875, an Act Congress passed to ensure equal treatment, without regard to race, in various public accommodations. Justice Harlan, alone, resolved to dissent. He labored over his dissenting opinion for months, but "his thoughts refused to flow easily." He seemed, Malvina wrote in her memoir, trapped "in a quagmire of logic, precedent, and law."

Malvina, as I earlier mentioned, grew up in a free state, in a family strongly opposed to slavery. She very much wanted her husband to finish writing that dissent. On a Sunday morning, when the Justice was attending church services, Malvina retrieved the Taney inkstand from its hiding place, gave the object a "good cleaning and polishing, and filled it with ink. Then, taking all the other inkwells from [her husband's] study table, [she] put the historic . . . inkstand directly before his pad of paper." When Justice Harlan came home, Malvina told him he would find "a bit of inspiration on [his] study table." Malvina's memoir next relates:

> The memory of the historic part that Taney's inkstand had played in the Dred Scott decision, in temporarily tightening the shackles of slavery . . . in the ante-bellum days, seemed that morning to act like magic in clarifying my husband's thoughts in regard to the law that had been intended . . . to protect the recently emancipated slaves in the enjoyment of equal "civil rights." His pen fairly flew on that day and . . . he soon finished his dissent.

The next time my thoughts on an opinion "refuse to flow easily," I may visit the Marshal's office in search of a pen in need of absolution, perhaps the one Justice Bradley used to write his now infamous concurring opinion in Myra Bradwell's case, *Bradwell* v. *Illinois*, an 1873 decision upholding a State's right to exclude women from the practice of law:

> Man is, or should be, woman's protector and defender. The natural and proper timidity and delicacy which belongs to

the female sex evidently unfits it for many of the occupations of civil life. The constitution of the family organization, which is founded in the divine ordinance, as well as in the nature of things, indicates the domestic sphere as that which properly belongs to the domain and functions of womanhood....

... The paramount destiny and mission of woman are to fulfill the noble and benign offices of wife and mother. This is the law of the Creator.

—

Fast forward with me now to our own times. Justice Sandra Day O'Connor is serving her twenty-first year on the Supreme Court and I am well into my ninth year as her colleague. A custom that started in 1972, whenever there is a change in the Court's composition, a group photograph with spouses is taken. And prompted by *Good Housekeeping* magazine in 1957, a photograph is taken periodically of spouses only. The subjects of these photographs have changed surely beyond anything Justice Bradley or even Justice Harlan would have contemplated.

The life of a Supreme Court spouse also has changed greatly since the days of Malvina Shanklin Harlan. Spouses do not receive "at home" callers on Monday, or any day; they pursue careers or interests of their own. Adding "humanizing" variety, two of them are men. Spouses have seats in a special section of the courtroom, and they lunch together three times a year, rotating cooking responsibility. One member favored as a co-caterer is my husband, superchef Martin D. Ginsburg. The lunches are held in a ground-floor space once designated the Ladies Dining Room, but in the 1997 term, at Justice O'Connor's suggestion, fittingly renamed the Natalie Cornell Rehnquist Dining Room.

Our Chief Justice commented in a 1996 address at American University: "Change is the law of life, and the judiciary will have to change to meet the challenges we will face in the future." Change yields new traditions. A most positive one, I think, is the new tradition we are creating by the way the Justices and their partners—at work and in life—relate to, care about, and respect each other.

And I like to think Malvina Harlan would say, "That's fine."

———

In August 2001, the *New York Times* ran two feature stories about Malvina's *Some Memories*. On page 1 of a Sunday edition, the *Times* ran the wedding photograph and described the memoir. The follow-up story included several quotations from the manuscript. Indicating the power of the press, the *Times* coverage of *Some Memories* garnered the attention of diverse publishers, resulting in Random House's decision to produce this hard-covered edition in its Modern Library series.

To enhance our understanding of Malvina Harlan in her own time, the Society engaged the fine mind and hand of historian Linda Przybyszewski, a professor at the University of Cincinnati and author of the engaging biography *The Republic According to John Marshall Harlan.*[2] She carefully edited and annotated the manuscript prepublication. Shepherding the project through to completion, Clare Cushman brought to the task the same intelligence and good judgment that made a great work of the Society's recent publication *Supreme Court Decisions and Women's Rights: Milestones to Equality.*[3]

Malvina Shanklin Harlan wrote *Some Memories* four years after her husband's death, as a tribute to his public life.

Thanks to the Society's original initiative, we can read *Some Memories* for the light it casts on the life of a great lady.

———

1. The result of that effort appears in Ruth Bader Ginsburg and Laura W. Brill, "Remembering Great Ladies: Supreme Court Wives' Stories," 24 *Journal of Supreme Court History* 255 (1999).
2. See Tony A. Freyer, "Prophet of Example: A Review of *The Republic According to John Marshall Harlan*," 24 *Journal of Supreme Court History* 325 (1999).
3. Congressional Quarterly Press, 2001.

A Note on the Text

At some point, the typescript of Malvina Harlan's memoir was revised, pasted into a scrapbook, and corrected by hand. Typographical errors, simple misspellings, inconsistencies, and punctuation errors have been silently corrected. The editors have tried to identify as many individuals and incidents as possible and to confirm and correct facts.

SOME MEMORIES OF A
LONG LIFE, 1854-1911

Courtship and Marriage

One day during the late summer of 1853 in Evansville, Indiana, a small but growing town in the Southwestern part of the State—a young girl of fifteen, suffering from some slight affection of the eyes, had been confined by the physician's orders to a darkened room.

Happening at the moment to peep through a narrow crack of the almost closed window-shutters she saw a young man passing by. As she had lived all her life in that small town and was familiar with almost every face in it, she knew at once that he was a stranger.

That was sixty-one years ago; but, as clearly as if it were yesterday, she can still see him as he looked that day—his magnificent figure, his head erect, his broad shoulders well thrown back—walking as if the whole world belonged to him.

On the sixth of the following February, 1854, she was invited to take supper with the family of Dr. J. G. Hatchitt,[1] a young physician living in the block beyond her father's residence. To her surprise, as she sat talking to her hostess, a young man—with a rope to each arm, as he "played horsey" for the little nephew that was the delightful and uproarious Jehu—suddenly pranced into the room. The young girl at once recognized him as the interesting stranger who had caught her eye six months before, as she peeped through the narrow crack of her window-shutters, and whom, after the romantic style of that period, she had (to herself) called "A Prince of the Blood."

Very much amused and yet covered with manly confusion, at thus being caught by a strange young girl in the act of "playing the boy," the young man who proved to be John Marshall Harlan, of Frankfort, Kentucky, and a brother of the hostess (Elizabeth Harlan)—was duly presented to "Miss Malvina Shanklin."

His conversation during that evening greatly interested the young girl, showing unusual thought and intelligence for a youth of only twenty-one, and that night he escorted her home.

As was her custom, being an only daughter, she went straight to her mother's room to tell her "all about" the very pleasant acquaintance she had just made. She showed so much enthusiasm in her description of him that her mother,[2] after listening awhile to her girlish outburst, said, in a very dry, decided and matter-of-fact tone: "You have talked quite enough about a young man whom you have only seen for an hour or two; now, you can go up to your room. Good night."

During the next week, a daily call from this new friend gave me a new interest in life; and at the end of the week, before he left for his Kentucky home, to my great surprise he asked me to be his wife.

"Does the course of true love ever run smoothly?" Considering the strain put upon it in this case, where disenchantment might so easily have followed, I can say that for me it did.

A MISCHIEVOUS BROTHER'S PRANK

In my memory of those first days of courtship, one absurdly embarrassing incident stands out very vividly.

At that time I had three brothers[3] living—one of them my senior by three years, the other two being a few years younger. My oldest brother was a great tease and, as the only sister, I was often the victim of his harmless practical jokes.

One day, during the week of my acquaintance with the interesting young Kentuckian, my eldest brother and I were talking together near a front window of our house, which stood back quite a distance from the street. His conversation was always interesting to me—for he was my oracle; and even if my side face had not been turned toward the window, I was too much absorbed in what he was saying to have noticed the approach of any visitor. My brother, though standing where he was himself invisible from the outside, could see any one who opened the front gate; and suddenly—at a moment most inopportune for a young girl in my then state of mind—my brother, while still keeping out of sight, seized me from behind and pressed my face firmly against the windowpane, flattening my nose, and features generally, out of all shape. At the next instant, to my horror, I saw my new friend approaching the house, with a broad smile on his face, as he took in the unwilling picture at the window.

Extricating myself with a mighty effort from my naughty brother's grip, and smoothing out my features and somewhat disheveled hair (that I might, if possible, make my visitor forget the hideous picture he had just seen at the window), I entered the parlor and told him of the many similar pranks, at my expense, that had often been played by this mischievous brother, and I laughed heartily over them with my visitor.

A STYLE OF DRESS IN THE EARLY DAYS

I must mention a style of dress for young men that was in vogue in the days of our courtship—whether it was a fashion in the country at large or was confined to the West and South, I do not know.

It consisted of a dark blue dress-coat, decorated with large flat brass buttons on both sides of the front and at the waistline in the back. The buttons were a generous inch in diameter, wholly without design, the polish of the flat surface equaling gold in brilliancy. This coat was worn with a buff waistcoat and buff trousers, made of a material somewhat resembling in texture the khaki of today. This interesting fashion was not long-lived, as I remember it; but while it lasted it gave an air of its own to the young men of that day. It was used for informal evening occasions. This style of dress-suit was most becoming to my young man—the dark blue color bringing out his wonderfully clear complexion and his fine blue eyes. His beautiful sandy hair, which he wore quite long (as was the fashion of the day) he always parted on the right side, instead of the left, as did all the young men of his family, giving them a most marked individuality.

In those days early marriages were quite common, and in my case the young man urged an immediate consummation of his wishes. But the wiser counsels of parents prevailed, and for two years—during which I was at school and he at the practice of law in his father's office in Frankfort—we corresponded, an occasional visit from him making the time seem shorter.

The young man's letter to my father asking for my name in marriage was somewhat different, I fancy, from similar letters written at the present time. He said nothing whatever of the worldly or material aspects of the matter. After expressing the hope that he could make me happy, he referred my father, for information as to his character, to prominent men with whom my father was acquainted in Henderson, a neighboring town on the Kentucky side of the Ohio River.

I never heard any questions from either of my parents as to what he had in worldly goods or prospects—his character and habits being their one and only thought. Perhaps if they had known what the young wife afterwards learned, namely, that my "Young Lochinvar[4] from out of the" South had to borrow $500 from his father for the expenses of our wedding and for our start in life, my parents might have looked upon their decision as a trifle unwise and hasty.

They never had reasons, however, to regret their consent, for their relations with the son-in-law, who came to be like an own son to them, grew in respect and affection as long as they lived. My husband's pride in my mother was most marked, and many times, in speaking of her, he would say to me with great earnestness and admiration, "I want you to be just like her."

MY WEDDING

In those days, in the community in which I was brought up, the announcement of an "engagement" would have seemed somewhat indelicate; and in my case it was *not until* the receipt of an invitation from my parents, announcing simply that they would be "At Home" on December 23, 1856, and enclosing two cards tied together at the top with a tiny telltale bow of white ribbon—one bearing the name of "John Marshall Harlan" and the other the name of "Malvina French Shanklin"—*that any of the friends on either side had any idea that a marriage was in prospect.* The only exceptions were the six bridesmaids, who were pledged to secrecy. A dressmaker from New York had been smuggled into the house and was carefully hidden from view for two whole months, during the preparation of my simple trousseau. Thus bidden in the quaintly reserved fashion of those early days, a large company of our friends gathered promptly at nine o'clock on the evening of December 23, 1856, in the large front parlor of my father's house, to witness what was called a "Tableau Wedding"—which at that time was quite an innovation.

In the smaller back parlor, which was shut off by folding doors from the front room, until the great moment arrived, the bridal party of fourteen were grouped in a semi-circle facing the wedding guests—six bridesmaids alternating with six groomsmen, the Bride and Groom standing in the centre. At weddings in those early days (as I recall it) there was no "best man"—at all events, at *my* wedding the Groom (to one person, at least) was the only "best man"; so that in the semi-circle that formed our "Tableau," a brides-maid instead of a groomsman stood at the Groom's right hand, while a groomsman stood at my left.

Two of the bridesmaids were dressed in pink, two in blue and two in buff, the Bride, of course, being in white.

The Groom wore the traditional black dress-coat; but his waistcoat was of black velvet, and his neck tie, instead of being white, was an old-fashioned black stock, rather broad and fastened in the middle with a gold scarf pin. He wore a high-standing collar, with a broad opening, the slightly flaring points coming well above the line of his firm and strongly marked chin—the quaint stock and col-lar, together, giving him a dignity and maturity beyond his three-and-twenty years.

The immediate members of the two families and the of-ficiating clergyman were the only other persons in the back parlor.

When all things were ready, the folding doors were then thrown open, thus revealing the "Tableau," and the cere-mony was performed in the presence of the large company of friends who were gathered in the front parlor.

At every entertainment in those days, amateur music, both vocal and instrumental, made part of the pleasure of the occasion. And in marked contrast to the formality and conventionality of social life at the present time, I may re-call the fact that the Bride on that December night, fifty-nine years ago, was escorted to the piano by the young husband, that she might contribute to the pleasure of the evening. I had had advantages in the way of musical education that were rather unusual in those days in my part of the country, and it was not until I had sung three or four of the popular ballads of the day that I was allowed to leave the piano.

During the first week of our honeymoon (which was spent, as was the usual custom in my time, under my father's roof) three or four parties were given to us at the house of friends. Though the company on each of those occasions was substantially the same, yet our pleasure seemed fresh every time, and we made a merry week of it.

Our honeymoon was thus begun in the house where I was born—a home where love and perfect trust had always reigned supreme; and then with a young husband who had promised to love and cherish me (which promise was faithfully kept during a long and happy married life of nearly fifty-five years), I went from a home of Puritan New England and Scotch-Irish Presbyterian traditions and principles to the radically different environment that was found, during the ante-bellum days, in Frankfort, the Capital of "Old Kentucky."

A WISE MOTHER'S COUNSEL

All my kindred were strongly opposed to Slavery, the "peculiar institution" of the South. Indeed, an uncle on my mother's side, with whom I was a great favourite, was such an out-and-out Abolitionist that I think that (before he came to know my husband) he would rather have seen me in my grave than have me marry a Southern man and go to live in the South.[5]

Such was the general attitude towards the South that was taken by my family, at that time; and as I now look back upon the great changes which my marriage was to bring in my surroundings, I am all the more impressed by the wisdom of the parting advice which my mother gave me as I left for my new home in Kentucky. Her advice was practically a command, and her words were, substantially, as follows:—

"You love this man well enough to marry him. Remember, now, that *his* home is YOUR home; *his* people, YOUR people; *his* interests, YOUR interests—you must have *no other*."[6]

Knowing, as she did, how terribly I had always suffered from homesickness when away from her, she went on to say:—

"We know you will love us, as you have always done, and that you will miss us terribly; but never let your husband know that you are mourning for your girlhood's home. Never let him hear you contrasting it with your new home, to the disadvantage of the latter. Often you will have to relieve your homesickness with a good cry; but wait until your husband is out of sight and have it over and out of the way before his return, and have nothing but smiles to greet him when he comes home."

First Years in Kentucky

Following the patriarchal custom that was quite common in Kentucky at that period—in accordance with which a son brought his bride home to live under his ancestral roof—the first few years of my married life were spent in the family of my husband's parents.

The Harlan household consisted of two married sons (my husband and one other son) with their wives, one unmarried son, two unmarried daughters, and a married daughter, who with her two children spent the greater part of every summer with us.[7]

My father-in-law was then a man of fifty-seven years, but he appeared much older than one of the same age would seem in these days. He was as straight as an arrow with firm, elastic step, his head well set on a magnificent pair of shoulders. His manner was very reserved—the result of great modesty and shyness, and not from a lack of interest in those around him. He was indeed the head of his house, and his wife and children adored and revered him.

My dear mother-in-law was the moving spirit and comforter of the entire household.

The town house of my husband's family was an old-fashioned frame mansion, with spacious rooms, standing at one corner of an unusually wide and deep lot. Of their country home, on "Harlan's Hill," I shall tell later on.

MUSIC AS A MATRIMONIAL ASSET

As I looked about me in my new home, one of the first things that struck me most forcibly was the beauty of the Frankfort girls, and I wondered that my young husband had left them all, and gone so far from home to get so little. Finally I came to the conclusion that the advantages I had had in music (of which he was very fond) had something "to do with the case."

I had some talent for music, and a love for it that made me improve the opportunities given me for its cultivation. I could also read it easily. Almost from my babyhood I had been encouraged to sing, and apparently (as was afterwards explained to me by the only first-class vocal teacher I ever had) I had always used my voice "*naturally, and in no way to its hurt,*" so that, after one year's instruction by that teacher (at the "Glendale Female Seminary," near Cincinnati, where I finished my school days at the age of sixteen), I was ready to make rapid progress in my music.

My own accomplishments in music would, in these days, seem very insignificant, when classical music and skill and technique count for so much, while harmony and true feeling for music often seem lost sight of. In my young days, ballads, with their simple but often very musical accompaniments, were the staple of most of our musical entertainments.

One or two of the Frankfort girls played beautifully on the piano. And there were three or four who had as fine natural voices as I have ever heard any where; but they were without cultivation and, moreover, their vocal attainments were often unavailable, because they knew nothing of the piano and could not read music at all, learning wholly "by ear."

On the other hand, I could not only play my own accompaniments, but I sang without notes. I never left a song until it was *mine;* indeed, I never wished to see the notes again. I think it was for these two reasons that whatever talent and attainments I had in music were, in the beginning, a special attraction to my young suitor, making me (to his mind) somewhat out of the ordinary, and more and more he came to take a special pride in my music.

THE HARLAN SLAVES

In the end of the long hall extending from one side of the town house, and in the cabins at the back of the lot, lived the slaves, who had been inherited from both sides of the Harlan family. There were almost as many slaves as there were members of "the Family" and they were all carefully looked after, not only physically but morally.[8]

Among the slaves I specially remember "Uncle" Joel, who was about ninety years of age, and his wife, who was almost as old. They were cared for like two babies; and the almost daily visit that was made to their cabin, by one or more from the "Big House," kept them in good cheer and full of interest in what was going on in "the Family."

The close sympathy existing between the slaves and their Master or Mistress was a source of great wonder to me as a descendent of the Puritans, and I was often obliged to admit to myself that my former views of the "awful Institution of Slavery" would have to be somewhat modified.

Each daughter and daughter-in-law in the Harlan family had her own special maid, with whom she was most familiar; but the familiarity was never abused by the maid, and the real affection which each had for the other showed itself in many ways. The pride which the maid took in the fine clothes of her "Young Missus," though at times quite helpful, was most amusing, and the liberties the household slaves took, and the fun they had, at the expense of their owners, was often fairly ludicrous.

Imagine a "Young Mistress" getting ready for bed, and kneeling for her evening prayer, her white feet tempting the maid to stoop and tickle the pink soles—as she waited to put out Miss Sallie's light, after she retired. A sudden and vigorous backward movement of Miss Sallie's foot brought the maid to her senses; and, upon rising from her prayers, the "Young Mistress" said:—

"Luo' Ann; what did you do that for? You know that wasn't right."

"Yass'm, I knowed it wa'nt right."

"Then, what did you *do* it for?"

The maid's answer was a good illustration of what we hear, nowadays, as to the "dual nature" in man:—

"Well, Miss Sallie, it war jes' dis way;—One min' in me

say, *Doan you do it;* 'ter min' say, *Go 'long, go do it*, an' I done listen to de min' what say, *Go 'long, go do it*; but I aint gwine to do it no mo', Miss Sallie. I 'clar[e] fore Goodness, I ain't."

Their quaint drollery, and what would have been gross impertinence in a white servant, often surprised and always amused the looker-on. One of my husband's sisters, upon returning from a visit to a neighbouring town, had told us of the wonderful beauty of a young girl whom she had asked to visit her, and who was to arrive within a day or two.

When this much-heralded guest reached the Harlan home at the end of a long, hot thirty-miles ride in a stage-coach, the tell-tale streaks on her fair cheeks made it painfully evident that her colouring was not (entirely) Nature's own.

One of the maids, full of curiosity to see the beautiful visitor, dropped on her knees and peeped through a crack in the door, to get a good look at her. Contrasting her with her own "Young Missus" (whom she adored), she said to the present writer (who was equally curious and was *very* young herself, and who, as she now confesses, was peeping through a crack higher up):—"La, Miss Mallie, if *dat* gal's pretty, it mus' be unner her *cloes.*"

The darkies' fondness for large words, and the perfect assurance with which they used what seemed to them to be a new and very odd expression, was at times excruciatingly funny. One Spring, after a spell of unusually warm weather, I was about to put on a winter coat; but, remembering the heat of the day before; I asked my maid if a lighter wrap would not be more advisable. "No, Miss, it's more keener to-day dan it were yestiday. It aint so *sulky* and close, like it was."

On one occasion when I was ready for an outing, and was dressed in my "best," one of the maids said, "La, Miss Mallie, you certny does look sweet; I'd jes' like to *kiss* you." Being a new comer in the South, and unused to such familiarity from a servant, I exclaimed with much dignity, "Marie, you'd better not; if you do, I will tell your Marse John." Not at all intimidated by this threat, she gave me a resounding smack on each cheek. "Marse John," however, heard no word of complaint from me, but he laughed heartily with me over the incident.

I almost never saw a negro who did not sing, or at least have some ear for music, and very soon many of my songs were being quietly hummed by the slaves in the back of the house; they were too well trained to sing them where they could be heard.

My husband had recently become very fond of the wonderful Marse[i]llaise Hymn, and though, as it seemed to me, it needed a man's voice to bring out its dramatic strength and spirit, he insisted upon my learning it, and he often asked me for it. I used the English translation, beginning with the stirring words:—

> *Ye sons of France awake to glory.*
> *Hark, hark, what myriads bid you rise—*
> *Your children, wives and grandsires hoary;*
> *Behold their tears and hear their sighs.*

One of the maids had evidently been much taken by that glorious old War Song and very soon I overheard her singing it with the greatest gusto. Most of the words were wanting in her rendering of it, although she had caught their spirit—especially in the climax of the song,

> *To arms, to arms, ye brave,*
> *The avenging sword unsheathe.*

With a most tragic air she would sing

> *March on, march on,—*

although, to her prejudiced and partial ear, that militant command had sounded like

> *Marse John, Marse John,—*

which were the very words she always sang, uttering them with truly martial fervour; for, to her *imagination*, her "Young Master" (my husband) was the Hero that was being appealed to in the song; and she felt sure that he was quite equal to any and all demands. The concluding lines:—

> *All hearts resolved*
> *On Victory or Death—*

were always sung by her in such a dramatic fashion as to make the mere words a trifling detail that could be entirely ignored.

The care of the flowers in the front yard, and of the vegetable garden in the rear of the lot on which the Harlans' town house stood, gave the men slaves plenty of work.

Among them was old "Uncle" Lewis, and, from a side porch where we often sat in the summer, we could hear him singing as he wielded the spade or hoe, or attacked the stubborn weeds.

I can still hear a certain never-ending song that was his special favourite. At the end of each verse, he would appear to stop altogether, and then the sight of something new in the garden, or some fresh and thrilling inspiration, seemed to take possession of him, for he would suddenly launch out on another verse.

His manner of attacking each succeeding verse always led us to expect a new development in the plot of the song; but the next verse was always identical with the first and only stanza, which he never seemed to tire of singing. These were the words:—

> *I went to the ribber,*
> *And I couldn't get across;*
> *Nobody wid me but an ole blin' hoss—*
> *Up! Sangaree! Up! Sangaree!*
> *Up! Sangaree!*

"Sangaree," we learned, was the name of "Uncle" Lewis' own horse; but, although he would sometimes repeat this verse a hundred times and, each time, with an air of having made a fresh discovery, his "old blin' hoss" seemed never willing to "get up," and apparently "Uncle" Lewis never *did* get across that "ribber." The song, however, certainly did help him hoe many a row, and dig out many a weed.

THE DARKER SIDE OF SLAVERY

There was another and darker side to the question of slavery, which was forcibly brought home to our minds, every now and then.

Most of the property of my father-in-law consisted in slaves, and he felt that there was nothing for him to do but to accept the responsibility for these human souls, doing for them as best he could.

I recall one incident, however, which showed his inborn hatred for the dreadful institution of human slavery.

One Sunday morning, on his way to church, he passed in the main street a company of slaves that were being driven to the "Slave Market" in a neighbouring town. The able-bodied men and women were chained together, four abreast, proceeded by the old ones and the little "pickaninnies," who walked unbound.

This pitiful procession was in charge of a brutish white man, belonging to a class which in those days were called "Slave-drivers," because their duty was to drive gangs of slaves, either to their work or to the place of auction. Their badge of office was a long, snake-like whip made of black leather, every blow from which drew blood.

The sight stirred my father-in-law to the depths of his gentle nature. He saw before him the awful possibilities of an institution which, in the division of family estates, and the sale of the slaves, involved inevitably the separation of husband and wife, of parent and children; and the dreadful type of men which the institution of slavery developed as "Slave-drivers" seemed to my father-in-law to embody the worst aspects of the system.

My father-in-law could do nothing to liberate the poor creatures then before him; but he was so filled with indignation that any one calling himself a man should be engaged in such a cruel business that, walking out to the middle of the street and angrily shaking his long forefinger in the face of the "Slave-driver," he said to him, *"You are a damned scoundrel. Good morning, sir."* After having thus relieved his feelings, he quietly pursued his way to the House of Prayer.

To those who heard and saw him that day, there was no suggestion of profanity in his language. Like some Old Testament prophet he seemed to be calling down Heaven's maledictions upon the whole institution of Slavery.

My husband, who was then very young and was with his father on that peaceful Sabbath morning, never forgot the impression that was made upon him by his sudden indignation at the brutal and typical incident. It was the nearest thing to "Swearing" that he had ever heard from his father's lips.

SLAVERY'S BRIGHTER SIDE

My father-in-law, with his sympathy for the unfortunate race, was always quick to recognize anything like unusual ability in them. He made it possible for two of his men servants to purchase their own freedom, by giving them, each year, for several years, the money equivalent of half-a-year's hire.

One of those freedmen went to California in 1849, and was fortunate enough to "strike gold" almost immediately.[9] His "Young Mistress" (my sister-in-law, Elizabeth Harlan) received at the time of her marriage, several years later, a fine new piano as a bridal gift from this grateful quasi-member of the household!

The other negro who was thus enabled to purchase his own freedom, showed aptitude for business. He found a place as porter on the railroad running from Louisville to Lexington, and he proved himself a most valued employee of the company, and was very helpful to travellers.

THE HOME ON HARLAN'S HILL

My father-in-law had a small summer home, on what was known as Harlan's Hill—one of the lovely hills that so completely surrounded Frankfort that a local poet once described that charming little city as "A dimple in the cheek of Nature."

As the boys, one-by-one, brought their brides to the family home, or the girls their husbands, room after room was added to the rambling house, which was only a storey-and-a-half in height and one room deep. A broad vine-covered latticed porch, which ran the full length of the long-drawn-out cottage, served in very warm days as sitting room and dining room and library—for books were everywhere.

The distance from the town was not over a mile; but the road, which seemed to be Nature's own, was so steep that it made anything but horse-back riding impossible. It wound its way up a broad, rocky ridge or cliff, that was known as "Harlan's Backbone." The steep hill was no drawback to the lovely retreat, for upon reaching its summit such a picture met the eye as to make one forget the steep climb.

The pretty town, divided by the picturesque Kentucky River, whose banks were dotted with attractive homes and shaded by lovely trees; here and there a church spire, as Heaven's own sentinel, guarding from all harm and emphasizing the peace and quiet of the little town so far removed from the turmoil and stress of the world— altogether, it was a picture never to be forgotten.

The hospitality of the Harlan homes, in both town and country, was most marked. Many a party of young people, after enjoying the steep climb to the house on the hill, found such a welcome as gladdened their hearts. They felt sure that, even if the rain should come up in the evening (and I remember many such an occasion), the girls, at least, could count on comfortable housing for the night and a good breakfast in the morning, at any hour after sleep forsook them. A way was always found by my capable and hospitable mother-in-law to "make room for one more," even if the younger members of the household, both married and single, had to be put up with cots laid on the floor.

This reminds me of a story told by an old bachelor friend of the Harlan family, to the great amusement of his friends. He was a man of wealth and had a delightful home a mile or two out of Lexington. He was in the habit of giving large supper parties to his men friends. On one such occasion a very heavy rain, coming out towards midnight, made it impossible for some of the guests to return, for they had come in open vehicles. Having plenty of servants at his command, rooms were made ready for the guests.

The host, however, had to do without a bed. Calmly stretching his length on the floor of the living room, with his feet to the blaze of the huge log fire, he dismissed the young darkie who had stayed to cover up his "ole Marse."

During the night, not being altogether comfortable, the host became half awake. Between him and the dying embers, he saw what he took to be the young darkie's head. Thinking that his orders to "go to bed" had been disregarded, he quietly reached for his cane beside him and, shouting to the "young rascal" to "go to bed at once," he thereupon stoutly whacked what proved to be—*his own foot*!

The next morning when he limped into breakfast, his guests, who expressed sympathy at his plight, were regaled by the story at his own expense.

The climb up "Harlan's Hill," was attended by many laughable incidents, one of which I vividly recall.

The dear mother of "the Family" had gone to town to do some shopping. On her way home on horse-back she was caught in a severe thunderstorm. The Harlan women always stood in mortal terror of lightning. Many a time, at the faintest appearance of it, they would run for a silk skirt and would drape it over any mirror in the room—the mirror being considered a great attraction to the dangerous element.

On this occasion, my mother-in-law wore an old-fashioned steel hoop-skirt, but she found a way, even on horse-back, to adjust it so as not to be conspicuous. Terror seized her as the lightning grew more and more severe, though the rain had not yet come. The hill was too rough and steep for speed; so, climbing down from her horse, she quickly dropped her hoop-skirt and, not being able to remount, she was leading her horse with all haste, at the same time calling; first one servant and then another, for she was then in sight of the house.

As we heard her sharp cry of terror to "George, Lewis, Bob, Chance and Bet" (in turn), we quickly recognized the voice of one we all loved, and every member of the family, with quaking hearts, rushed to the front of the house, only to hear her say to the first slave that responded to her call of distress, *"Lewis, go and get my hoop-skirt, down on the hill-side."*

We made no little fun at her expense; for, afraid as she herself was of the lightning, and kind as she was to every living thing, we accused her (that, as we insisted, was the only way of explaining her action) of thinking that *"African blood was immune from the dangers of Heaven's thunderbolts."*

It became a "family joke," of good, lasting qualities, and thereafter it always provoked a laugh and teased the dear woman quite a little.

A TRAGEDY

In the autumn of 1858 (as I remember it), my husband—in his efforts to save the life of a young negro girl, the maid of one of his sisters, and the last of the children of the favourite "Black Mammy" who had cared for him when he was an infant—met with an accident that nearly cost him his own life.

It was early in October, and we were about to move down from the summer house on the hill to the town house, for the winter.

My mother-in-law, who was a very methodical and careful house-wife, had given the servants due notice of the move to town, cautioning them all to have their clothes in good order, and ready for the winter.

The care-free younger slaves, as was their wont, took no thought of time, and, after "the Family" had retired for the night, this young maid, finding herself quite behind hand in her preparations for town life, had crept into the large sitting room, where the dying embers of a good log-fire offered comfort and warmth on that cool October night.

Bringing her candle, work basket, and a few pieces of clothing for mending, she seated herself on the floor close to the fire, putting the lighted candle on the floor, near by.

Sleep overcame her, and she dropped full length on the floor. In a moment her clothes caught fire from the candle. Unconscious, at first, of the heat that would have quickly awakened one of another race, she lay twisting and turning in her sleep. Suddenly, her screams of agony awakened every member of the household and, running into the sitting room, we found the poor girl a veritable pillar of fire, or, like a wild animal making the circuit of the large room in her awful agony.

My husband, catching her with one hand as she was about to pass the door by which he entered, held her fast, and, with the other hand, tore her clothes off as best he could. His father and mother both joined him in his efforts and were badly burned, though not so severely as he was.

The excitement and terror of the moment made us lose sight of every one else except the poor suffering girl; but I can never forget my husband's muffled and agonized cry ("My God,") as he held out his poor hands to me. The left hand, with which he had gripped the girl with full strength, was seared to the bone and the right arm from the finger tips to the elbow was almost unrecognizable as belonging to a human body. He was a hero in his suffering, and with unsurpassed bravery he lay waiting until the poor girl could be relieved, though the shock to her was fatal. She became unconscious in a short time, and lived only a few hours.

The funeral service was most touching, a warm change in the weather making it possible to hold it out of doors, on the latticed porch. The old Negro Methodist Preacher who conducted the services could not read; but, with the poetic touch that seems to be inborn in so many of that race, he drew a most vivid picture, in his quaint unlettered way, of the poor girl's entrance to the "Promised Land," describing how "Mammy and Daddy, brudders and sisters were waitin' for her, showin' her de way to de house not made wid han's," and how their cry of welcome filled her heart. The hymn was "lined out," that is, the preacher gave out two lines at a time, the congregation then taking them up, singing with voices full of unspeakable pathos.

Some of the lines seemed to have been improvised. On any other occasion they would have been amusing to a white person; but on that day that smile was too near to tears to make them seem at all funny. One couplet thus improvised I shall never forget:—

> *De bowl am broken at de fount,*
> *De pitchah's bust in twain.*

The solemn service was closed by a most touching prayer, full of unction, after which a great company of servants, from our own and the neighbours' houses, followed the poor girl's body to the grave.

The great strain to my husband's nerves from the intense suffering he had endured, together with the excitement attending the girl's death, brought on convulsions which the doctor pronounced as a possible forerunner of lock-jaw, every symptom seeming to point that way. The first attack occurred on the third day, during the afternoon, when I had gone down the hill, on horse-back, with two or three of the servants, to get the town house in order, so that as soon as possible we might be within nearer reach of the doctors, our poor sufferers—my husband, his father and mother—being in a distressing plight.

I was on my way back from town, after a long and wearisome day, the servants following on foot. When about half way up the long steep hill, I saw the Irish overseer of the country house, going at a great and dangerous speed to town. Hurriedly asking him what was the matter, I was told that my husband was very ill and that he (the overseer) had been sent for the doctor.

Whipping up my horse, I quickly reached the house, to find it surrounded, as it seemed to me, the yard being full of people; for the neighbours were there in force, to give a helping hand, all being anxious to do something to relieve my husband's condition. Until the family physician could be brought from town, a country doctor had been called in and was doing what he could; but the paroxysms were most severe, and panic was seen on the faces of the entire family.

My poor husband's face was so changed as to be almost unrecognizable. He knew me, however, and in a short time he seemed more quiet. Two physicians from town soon came to his relief, and they gave him quieting potions that produced a change for the better. The burns were dressed afresh, and all excitement quieted, the family physician calling me aside to say that it was a most alarming change; but that, if perfect control could be maintained and no anxiety exhibited on the part of any one of the family, he hoped that, as nature was now beginning to do her healing work, the spasms might become less by degrees, although they would probably return before very long. One doctor was to stay during the night, and the other physician was to come early in the morning, until all danger was passed.

The day physician, an orthodox Presbyterian of the bluest type, had a conscience that under no circumstances would permit him to make even an evasive answer to my poor husband's question, "Doctor, what was the nature of the attack I had yesterday?" The doctor blurted out, "Well, John, now it is (as I hope) all over, I will tell you: it was the forerunner of what we call tetanus, or lock-jaw."

Not daring to leave my post at my husband's head, where I was doing all I could to relieve the strain of its twitching, but with my face, I am sure, blazing with anathemas upon the man who had been sent there to soothe and not to frighten my patient, I opened out on him in good fashion, almost telling him that he was "an old fool," and that he did not know what he was talking about; that the family physician had told me all about the matter before leaving that morning, and that the attack was perfectly natural, after the suffering my husband had endured. I asked him to attend to his work of dressing the burns, and I told him to "stop talking." At the moment I could have torn him limb from limb.

I had my own way and nothing more was said by that Doctor, but the succeeding paroxysms, although they proved to be lighter, made my husband believe (as he told me, later) that his old dyed-in-the-wool Scotch Presbyterian physician was *the only one who had understood his case!* After several days the danger was over, though it was a long time before the poor hands could do their work.

The scars of this accident, both physical and mental, remained with my husband throughout his life—the mental scars showing themselves in a strange fashion nearly fifty years afterwards. One evening in Washington, only six or eight years before his death, he ordered a pot of tea brought to him and, in attempting to pour it out for himself, he turned the scalding-hot tea onto the same hand that had been so cruelly burned nearly fifty years before. He was seized with such a peculiar attack, that the physician could not account for it, until I told him of the terrible accident that has just been described. He then diagnosed the symptoms as being due to a vivid "association of ideas." The memory of his suffering fifty years before had brought on what the Washington doctor called "psychic stroke," which for an hour or two made him unable to give expression to the thoughts in his mind, though his utterance was perfectly clear. It was a most unusual condition, and was very alarming to us while it lasted.

The hospitable and cordial atmosphere of my father-in-law's house made life there exceedingly pleasant for me. Our chief amusement during the session of the State Legislature was to attend the meetings of the Lower House, and some times of the Senate. An occasional evening party, or a formal supper (which, in those days, took the place of the late dinners of the present time) made the winters pass delightfully.

MY YOUNG LAWYER

My father-in-law was so much absorbed in the work of his profession and with the business problems incident to the maintenance of his large household (including his slaves), that, very early in his married life, his wife, who was an unusually efficient helpmeet in the upbringing of their children, had gotten into the habit of working out the preliminaries of all the important plans for their children before she took up such matters with her husband. It thus happened that, at the crossroads confronting my husband at the age of seventeen, immediately after his graduation from Centre College[10] at Danville, Kentucky, she had developed all the details of a plan for him which, had it been carried out, would have made his life radically different from the great career that was afterwards his.

His four older brothers (James, Richard, William, Henry)[11] having all been trained for the legal profession, his mother thought that there were already enough lawyers in the family. She, therefore, cast about for some other pursuit for my husband. Some years before, during my father-in-law's term as a Member of Congress, she had met, while in Washington, a Mr. Harlan from Philadelphia,[12] with whom a distant kinship had been traced (the Quaker connections of the Harlan family); and, at the time of my husband's graduation from college, she wrote to this Pennsylvania kinsman and through him arranged for her fifth son to be apprenticed as a clerk in some mercantile house in the Quaker City.

All the preliminaries had been arranged and she had even gone so far as to pack her son John's trunk for his fateful trip to Philadelphia. She then took up the matter with my father-in-law, telling him of the reasons that had influenced her and of the plans she had already perfected, subject, of course, to his father's approval. Without hesitation, he said that "it would never do, but that John too was to be a lawyer"; he had not named him "John Marshall,"[13] after the great Chief Justice, only to have him spend his life in the counting room of a mercantile pursuit. He said he was at once to begin his legal studies and prepare to enter his father's office. Accordingly, the youthful John Marshall Harlan was matriculated, that very autumn, in the Law School of the Transylvania University,[14] at Lexington, Kentucky, where he was graduated about 1852; so that, instead of a business career, for which he was temperamentally so unfitted, he entered upon the path which was finally to lead him to the exalted position he afterwards attained on the Supreme Bench.

One night, not long after our marriage, when my father-in-law was seated with the family at supper, he took from his pocket a clipping he had made that day from a Lexington newspaper giving a description of a speech which my husband had made at some political meeting in Lexington. Carefully unfolding the clipping and pushing his heavy gold-rimmed spectacles upon his forehead (as he was so apt to do when he wished to speak to any one near him) he passed the clipping on to me with a courtly gesture, without saying a word. I always sat next to him at the table. As might be supposed, the young wife eagerly devoured the complimentary references which the paper made to her husband's speech, in the course of which the editor described him as one of the rising young men of the State, predicting a great future for him. Looking up I said:

"Why, I knew that long ago."

"Oh, you *did*, did you?"

"Yes, I always knew it."

"Oh, *you always* knew it? Then you are not *surprised*?"

"Not at all; I am only pleased that others are beginning

to discover it." And then, after a pause, I asked, "Do you want this clipping, Mr. Harlan?"

"Would you like to keep it?"

"Yes, very much"—whereat, bidding me to keep it, he looked as pleased and proud as I felt.

Small as it was, the town of Frankfort, being the Capital of the State, had its full quota of distinguished lawyers, many of whom were older men. It was, therefore, quite necessary for my Young Lawyer, in his effort to build up his practice, to go "upon the Circuit." For the first four or five years of our married life, he was gone away from Frankfort for practically half the year, though it was only for a week or ten days at a time; so that we had to be content with what snatches of home life we could get in the intervals between.

It was a period of steady growth for him, and was just what he needed to prepare him for his future career. The contact with comparative strangers and with men of learning and standing in every profession greatly widened his outlook, giving him an experience that he would not otherwise have had. Many of these trips were made by the old-fashioned stage-coach lines, and some of them were on horseback, with saddle-bags to carry his clothes and law papers.

He was quite remarkable in the number of friends he had among the older men, so that, when he himself became an old man, the recollection of the inspiration which he had received from older men during the days of his early manhood led him always to show great sympathy and interest in young men.

In the old days, the "help-mate" idea entered more universally into the marriage relation than is now the case.

The man was not only the bread winner, but the *name*-maker for the family, and an ambitious wife felt that no sacrifice on her part was too great that would in the slightest degree make the way to the desired goal for her husband.

My Young Lawyer had a place in his father's office, with such financial returns for his part of the work as his father could give him, from time to time. There was no "partnership" in the usual sense of the word. But, considering the lavish generosity with which a home was so freely given to us in my husband's family, "without money and without price,"[15] our life was made much easier than would have been the case if he had received a regular percentage of the profits of the large practice that came to his father's office.

But there were certain limitations to which we had to adjust ourselves, limitations that called for very careful economy. In those days stenographers and typists were unknown, and lawyers, as a rule, did all their own writing and in "long hand." As a large part of my father-in-law's work in that line devolved upon my husband, he was compelled to snatch odd moments for writing out his own briefs, which was done in such a desultory fashion that a clean, continuous copy for the printer had afterwards to be made. When my husband appealed to me for assistance in this regard, my exultation of feeling, in thus being able to help him, made a large part of my happiness in those days.

I could write quite rapidly and, though not at all "up" in the language of the Law, a question now and then smoothed the way for me, so that I rarely made mistakes. And if I were asked, as was often the case, if I could have my copy of the brief ready to go to the printer, say, "tomorrow," everything else was laid aside for the task, such work often taking up the entire day. Many things in the way of outside pleasures had to be given up. And if the pressure of work in the office made it impossible for *both* of us to go to some social function and if it was thought best, when my husband was thus beginning his career, that we should be represented on such an occasion, then another sacrifice would be made, and *I* would go alone.

A BONNET AND SOME OTHER THINGS

My husband often went to Louisville on Law business. On his return from one of these trips, I saw him coming up the steps with a huge hand-box under his arm, which he had carried all the way from the big city. Somewhat surprised, I said: "Why, what in the world have you got there?" To which he replied:—"Oh, I have gone into the millinery business." The box, when opened, revealed a lovely bonnet—which in those days meant a *bonnet* indeed, fitting closely around the face and tied with beautiful ribbons under the chin. It was a lovely creation; but, alas, the lining was of pink, a colour I could never wear.

I admired the bonnet greatly, but I hinted that I might have to change the colour of the face trimming. His countenance fell and he was somewhat distressed at my criticism of his choice. Remembering that I was just about to start on my usual Spring visit with my own parents, I therefore concluded to say nothing more on the subject, for I felt sure that while visiting with my mother I could change the colour without *his* ever being the wiser—which turned out to be the case. For, during my visit to Evansville the colour was changed from pink to blue, making it most becoming; and when, upon my return to Frankfort, I wore the bonnet to church on Sunday and when a neighbour whispered in my ear, on our way out at the close of the service, "What a pretty bonnet and *so* becoming," my husband proudly said, "That was *my* choice." That was fifty years before Barrie wrote his *What Every Woman Knows;*[16] but, young as I was, I knew enough of Men's amiable weaknesses to say nothing, and I let my young lawyer-milliner think that the bonnet was *all* his choice.

It was my mother's great pleasure, during the first years of my married life, to renew my wardrobe from time to time, and during my annual Spring visit to Evansville my summer outfit was always renewed, throughout. Just before I was leaving Frankfort for one of those visits, I was calling with my husband on a neighbor, to say good-bye. The sharp-eyed hostess, having noticed the freshening up I always got on these visits to my childhood's home, allowed her tongue a little too much freedom in referring to the proposed visit to my mother, for she said in that connection, "I *thought* you were looking a little shabby."

Her tactless remark made my husband very indignant and, after we had left her house, he said, "Now, you are going to do your fixing up *before* you go home to your mother; we will have no more of such talk." I remonstrated saying, "That is absurd, for it is such pleasure to mother." But he replied, "No, I don't want you to go home, until *after* you are ready for the summer." Thereupon, without my knowing it, my husband purchased the material for three very pretty dresses of silk and silk tissue, and I had them made up at once, before going to Evansville.

My visit "home" *that* year, made quite a stir in my circle

of girl friends. They talked so much about the splendor of my apparel that my husband's reputation in Evansville ascended by leaps and bounds, marking him at once, in the minds of my own townspeople, as one of the leading young lawyers of his state, which in fact he was.

A PAIR OF SLIPPERS

My father-in-law was such a shy and reserved man that his family, while holding him in affectionate reverence, stood rather in awe of him. They were very undemonstrative in their relations to him and had never got into the habit of showing him the little personal attentions to which I had been accustomed in my own home. For some reason, I soon got to be on closer terms with him than was true even of his own children, though they loved him dearly. In this connection I must run a little ahead of my story and tell of a Christmas present I made to him in the winter before he died.

I had embroidered a pair of slippers for him which I had his shoemaker finish in secret. I wrapped them in an attractive looking parcel, tying it up with a gay Christmas ribbon, and sent it into him by my little daughter, then about six years of age. Peeping through the crack of his door, I saw and heard what followed:

My father-in-law adored the little girl and as she drew near him with my Christmas offering, he pushed back his gold-rimmed spectacles on his forehead, as she held up the package, and he asked, "What's this?"

"It is something that Santa Claus sent you."

"Oh! Who is Santa Claus?"

"I do not know, exactly; but Mama made them."

Taking the package from her little hands he carefully undid it. His grave and kindly face was wreathed in smiles as his eyes fell upon what was evidently a most welcome gift. Without saying a word, he at once took off his shoes and put on the slippers, which fit him perfectly. Taking the little girl on his knee, he said, "Tell the kind Santa Claus and your dear Mama that I like them *very* much"; at which the little tot rushed into the hall to tell me all about it,— though I had seen and heard everything.

From that time on those slippers of mine were his constant companions. Every morning, he wrapped them up in paper and took them to his office, where he wore them all day; and, bringing them home at night, he put them on as soon as he reached the house. He died the following February, and his beloved slippers, which I had had the happiness of making for him, were put upon his feet when his body was prepared for burial.

CHURCH AND SUNDAY SCHOOL

My husband's mother and sisters were members of the Presbyterian Church in Frankfort. His father, though not a church member, had a great respect for religion, and was a regular attendant at the Sunday morning services. Going as I did from a home where the Church services on Sunday, and the weekly prayer meetings were fixed and important events in my life, and belonging (as I did until my marriage) to a Sunday School Class, I naturally became interested at once in the Church home of the Harlans.

My husband wishing (as it seemed) to be always near

me, went with me to all the services of the church. Very soon I was asked to take a class in the Sunday School. The very thought of it appalled me, for I was but a child myself, being only eighteen years of age at the time. After many appeals, I finally consented to take the Infant Class.

From the start, my husband went with me to the Sunday School and he often embarrassed me by following me into the Infant Classroom. I was terribly upset at his presence, and was dumb before him. At such times, I generally fell back upon asking the children to repeat after me "The Ten Commandments in Verse"—one line being given to each. Whether the author of that "Child's Version of the Decalogue" was my own dear mother (who was somewhat gifted as a versifier), or some one else, I do not now remember; but, as the ten-lined Summary of the Commandments was a part of my own early education, I give it here as being, perhaps of interest to those who have children under their care:

> *Thou shalt have no gods but me.*
> *Before no idol bend the knee.*
> *Take not the name of God in vain.*
> *Dare not the Sabbath Day profane.*
> *Give both thy parents honour due.*
> *Take heed that then no murder do.*
> *Abstain from deeds and words unclean.*
> *Steal not, though thou be poor and mean.*
> *Make not a willful lie, and love it.*
> *What is thy neighbour's do not covet.*

Some of the older teachers, noting my husband's regular attendance at the Sunday School, prevailed upon him to take the place of Superintendent, and afterwards they persuaded him to take a class of young ladies.

From that time on and throughout his entire life, in any church with which he was connected, my husband always taught a Bible Class. At the time of his death, he presided over a large class of middle-aged men in the Sunday School of the New York Avenue Presbyterian Church in Washington.[17] It is still called the "Harlan Bible Class." After his death its members gave, as a memorial to him, a substantial contribution to the work of the Presbyterian Alliance, and they have shown in many other ways the grateful and affectionate remembrance in which they held him.

CHOIR AND MUSIC CLUB

For many years I served as the organist of the Church in Frankfort. The choir was made up of volunteers, and was said by some to be the finest in the State. My husband was always ready to stay at home with the little ones, so that I might be at my post for the "Choir Practice." He took the greatest delight in the pleasant things that were said of the music, for I was not only organist, but was also the Choir-mistress.

A "Music Club" was evolved out of the Choir Practice and, after the gay season was over, this Club met regularly every Thursday night at the different houses and created a new interest in music in the little town. On one session it gave the Contata of "Esther, the Beautiful Queen," before a crowded house, the soloists being largely from our own choir.

My husband was always ready to have me avail myself of every opportunity to hear fine music. When an organization from New York, called the S[ä]ngerbund,[18] was to give a week of concerts in Louisville, he insisted upon my joining a party of six or eight ladies, with an equal number of gentlemen, that went down to Louisville to enjoy a week of music; he was unable to go himself.

I had never heard so large a chorus before, and I well remember what a new and wonderful thrill it gave me to hear that volume of men's voices giving with so much expression some of the old German Chorales. As ticket holders we were entitled to attend the afternoon rehearsals, as well as the more formal evening concerts.

With the tremendous nervous strain the unwonted musical experience put upon me, I was unable to sleep. During the night after the second concert, I got to thinking of my two little children,[19] whom I had left at home with my husband; and, though his mother lived near-by, I felt sure that he would need me and that something terrible had happened. I made up my mind to give up the rest of my week of music, and I started for Frankfort the next morning on the 6 o'clock train, taking my husband completely by surprise, a few hours later. I found the children in excellent health and that he had been giving them all the care they needed. He laughed at me for my foolish weakness; but, all the same, he was glad to see me.

MY FATHER-IN-LAW'S POLITICAL VIEWS

At the time of my marriage, my father-in-law, the Hon. James Harlan, was one of the leading lawyers in Kentucky.

He had served for two terms as Attorney General of the State.

He was such an earnest believer in the principles of Constitutional Law laid down by the great jurist who was practically the first Chief Justice of the Supreme Court of the United States, that he named his fourth son (my husband) "*John Marshall*," little dreaming that he would, one day, sit upon the same Bench.

In this connection, I may quote from an autobiographical letter written by my husband in July, 1911—a little more than three months before he died—to his son, Richard:[20]—

My father was an ardent admirer of John Marshall, and held to the views of constitutional construction which that great jurist embodied in the opinions delivered by him as Chief Justice of the Supreme Court of the United States.

He was equally ardent in his opposition to the views of constitutional law which were supposed to be, and doubtless were, entertained by Thomas Jefferson.[21] Marshall, my father always contended, held to views which, all concede, would give to the country a government that would be supreme and paramount in respect to all matters entrusted to the General Government, its powers, however, to be so exerted as not to infringe upon the rights which remained with the People of the several States, which had never been surrendered or granted, expressly or impliedly, to the National Government.

My father adhered firmly to these views and opposed to those maintained by Jefferson, because he believed that Jefferson's views were based upon a narrow, literal construction of the words of the Federal Constitution which, in time, would so minimize the functions of the Government intended to be established by that instrument as to place the National Government so completely at the mercy of the States that it could not accomplish the objects of its creation.

He regarded "Jeffersonianism" (speaking generally) as an evil that needed to be watched and overcome. He was therefore a life-long opponent of the Democratic party, the leading statesmen of which always seemed to take pride in saying that that party was founded by Jefferson, and that they avowed their purpose to engraft "Jeffersonianism" upon our system of government.

Throughout his entire life, my father was bitterly opposed to the accomplishment of any such purpose. Hence he became a follower of Webster and Clay[22] and he fairly gloried in being a Whig.

At the Philadelphia Convention of 1848 when the followers of Clay were so bitterly disappointed at their idol's failure to receive the Presidential nomination—my husband's father represented the Whigs of the Ashland district. And when the majority of that Convention had voted in favour of General Zachary Taylor[23] as the nominee, and it was moved to make that nomination unanimous, the motion failed of adoption because there was *one* vote against it, though only one—that of James Harlan, of the *Ashland* district. Such was his devotion to the great Whig chieftain that he voted "No," preferring to go down to defeat with the Clay flag still flying.

His action was so gratifying to the Whigs of the Ashland

district that upon his return to Kentucky they presented him with a massive silver pitcher as a souvenir of his loyalty to their beloved leader.

Mr. Clay's own feelings toward his devoted follower and lieutenant were indicated in the directions he left that after his death his favourite cane should be given to my husband's father. That cane is still in our possession. It is the same cane, by the way, which appears in the full-length engraving of the "Great Commoner" that is very familiar to collectors of political portraits of that period and which was to be found in many Whig households throughout the country in the early days. In the picture Mr. Clay, in the quaint dress-coat habitually worn by statesmen of that period, is standing by a table, against which leans this very cane, in full view. Its head is a knob of stone (or rather of petrified wood, beautifully grained) and is very curious.

MY HUSBAND IN PUBLIC LIFE

Very early in his life, my husband began to take part in public affairs.

In April, 1851 (four years before my marriage), Governor Helm, with whom my husband was a great favourite, appointed him as Adjutant General of Kentucky. He became thereby *ex officio* a member of the Governor's staff and the Chairman of the Board of Trustees of the two Military Schools of the States—the Kentucky Military School near Frankfort, and the Western Military Institute at Drennon Springs. This appointment was a great compliment to a young man not yet eighteen years of age.

Among the duties of his new position was that of going

with the Governor on his yearly visits to the Kentucky Military School. The Adjutant General was the "Officer of the Day" on the occasion of the Governor's review of the cadets at this special, annual military drill. My husband has often told me how hard it was, at the age of eighteen, on the occasion of his first review of the cadets, to keep a solemn face when he was receiving the formal salutes that were given to the "Officer of the Day."

At the Commencement exercises in June 1851, my husband met James G. Blaine,[24] who was then a professor at the Drennon Springs Military Institute.

As a bit of fun, the young people about Frankfort, on account of this new position, gave my husband the rather large title of "General," which made a youngster of eighteen feel very top-heavy.

My husband must have held this office during the next administration, for Morehead[25] was Governor when we were married (in 1856) and I think he was Adjutant General during Morehead's full term. I vividly recall the great pride I took in going with him to the annual "Parade Days" at the Military School near Frankfort.

In 1855, he had his first experience in public speaking; for, at the country-seats in the mountain district, he addressed public meetings on behalf of Charles Morehead, the American Party's candidate for Governor; and in 1856,[26] shortly before our marriage, that party selected him as one of the Electors-at-Large for Fillmore and Donelson.[27]

In 1858, at the age of twenty-five, he was elected County Judge of Franklin County; and in 1859 he was selected, by what was then called "The Remains of the Old Whig Party of Kentucky," as a candidate for Congress in the Ashland District. His opponent, Wm. E. Simms[28] (afterwards the Kentucky representative in the Confederate Senate) was returned as elected by only 6% majority. Upon careful investigation, my husband became convinced that he himself had been really elected by a majority of more than 500 and that he had been cheated out of the election by fraudulent and illegal voters who had been brought into the district from Covington and Cincinnati. His party friends raised a fund of $10,000 to defray the expenses of a contested election; but he afterwards concluded not to make the contest.

Had he gone to Congress at the age of twenty-six, his entire public career might have been different.

In the Presidential campaign of 1860, my husband was appointed as one of the electors on the Bell and Everett ticket,[29] whose platform was "The Union, Constitution and the Enforcement of the Laws." That ticket carried that State and my husband cast his vote in the Electoral College for Bell and Everett the Union candidates for President and Vice-President.

To quote here from my husband's autobiographical letter already mentioned:[30]—

Lincoln's candidacy for the Presidency in 1860 had aroused bitter hostility among the people of the slaveholding States, particularly in the States south of Kentucky. Many public men in the South and some further North declared that Lincoln's assumption of the office of President would be resisted, if need be, by force. But the supporters of Lincoln —indeed, substantially all the people in the non-slaveholding States—insisted upon the right of the American people to have their own choice for the

Presidency, when expressed in the legal mode. They insisted (as Mr. Lincoln himself had always done) that there was no purpose whatever to harm the South, or to do anything that was not authorized by the law of the land.

But the men who were afterwards the leaders of the Rebellion would not accept these disavowals and they succeeded in getting the public mind in the South into such a condition of frenzy that the application of force to prevent Lincoln's acting as President was openly planned. And when Lincoln's election was settled by the popular vote in November, 1860, the work of Secession began. During the closing months of Buchanan's Administration[31] and before Lincoln's inauguration in March, 1861, State after State passed an "Ordinance of Secession." The Southern Confederacy began to be organized and it forbade the exercise, within its limits, of any authority not in harmony with the Secession scheme.[32]

The county literally trembled at the possibility of war between the Unionists and Disunionists.

In January 1861, the Governor of Kentucky (Magoffin), who was Southern in his sympathies, proposed to the Legislature that it pass a resolution called for a State Convention to determine "the future of Federal and inter-State relations in Kentucky." That resolution was avowedly a preliminary to the passage of an "Ordinance of Secession," and as the majority of the men then in control of the State Government were strongly inclined to favour the South, the outlook for the Union cause in Kentucky was very dark.

During those critical days in January, 1861, when that dangerous resolution was pending before the Legislature, a group of "Old-line Whigs" and other loyal men (including

my husband and his father) fairly haunted the lobbies of
the State House, doing what they could to stiffen the backs
of the men opposed to Secession. My husband and a few
others of the younger men actually slept in the State
House during several all-night sessions when that dangerous resolution was being discussed.

The only thing which the opponents of Secession could
unite upon was to offer a substitute resolution in favor of
Kentucky's remaining "neutral" in the armed conflict that
threatened the country.

Their efforts were finally successful, though it was only
by a hair's breadth. The final vote on the substitute being a
tie (47 to 47), the Lieutenant Governor (who was the presiding officer at the joint session and who was a Union
man) cast the deciding vote in favor of the substitute, and
the danger was averted for the time being.[33]

To quote again from my husband's autobiographical letter:—

At last, the actual crisis came. On April 12, 1861 (five
weeks after Lincoln's inauguration), the flag of the United
States floating over Fort Sumter (a fort of the United
States in the harbour of Charleston, South Carolina) was
fired upon without cause, thereby defying the authority of
the Union. The purpose of the extreme men of the South
was to provoke a war that would ultimately disrupt the
Union.

Then the people, in the non-slaveholding States, and
the Union men in the "Border States" of Kentucky and
Missouri,[34] felt that any more efforts to keep the peace
and prevent bloodshed was useless. They felt that the time
had come when further forbearance was out of the ques-

tion. They rose as one man and resolutely determined that the rightful authority of the Union should be maintained over every foot of American soil, cost what it would in men and money.

My father, as might have been expected, publicly declared at the outset that he had adhered to the Union, and he favoured the punishment of every man who resisted its lawful authority. No amount of persuasion could carry him into the ranks of the Seceders, although he was surrounded by men who sympathized with the Secession and who opposed the application of force to maintain the Union.

I agreed with my father thoroughly and, although I did not vote for Lincoln, my position was well known. As an Elector on the Bell and Everett ticket, I had stood for "the Union, the Constitution and the Enforcement of the Laws." I was regarded by the "rebel" leaders as a "traitor," because of my opposition to Secession and because I had announced that the National Government was under a solemn duty to save the Union, if need be, by armed force.

At that time Kentucky was in a peculiarly embarrassing position. Her business interests were immediately with the South, and her people were connected with the people of the South by the ties of kinship. Many families were divided on the Union question, and the idea that a man should go into battle against near kin in the ranks on the other side, and either kill his own kin or be killed by them—was not an agreeable thought.

When, after Fort Sumter was fired upon, President Lincoln called upon the Governor of the loyal states for volunteers, Governor Magoffin of Kentucky telegraphed the President that:—*"Kentucky would furnish no troops for the wicked purpose of subduing her sister Southern States."*[35]

That truculent telegram, and the narrow majority of one against the resolution that had squinted at Secession, gave the impression to the country that Kentucky was not only merely "neutral" but that it was even trembling upon the verge of rebellion.

That impression, however, was a mistaken one, for, at a Congressional election held in February, 1861, the anti-Secession candidates carried nine out of ten districts. And in August, an election of one-half of the State Senate, and of *all* of the House of Representatives, resulted in a Union majority in the Legislature of 103 to 31. Moreover, the records show that Kentucky sent over [50,000] white troops into the Union army, as compared to only [between 30,000 and 40,000] troops for the Confederate army.

REMOVAL TO LOUISVILLE

By the beginning of the year 1861, it had become evident that a fearful crisis was before the country and that the Border States were in peculiar danger. The next election for Congress was near at hand. It was generally believed that the Ashland District could not be carried against the Democrats unless my husband were the opposing candidate. He felt that if he remained in the district he could not well refuse to accede to the wishes of those who had stood by him so valiantly in 1859. But, as he was devoted to his profession and did not wish to give his life to politics, he determined to take himself out of the race and avoid all embarrassment, and at the same time get a larger field for the practice of his profession, by removing to Louisville, which he did in February, 1861. He formed a partnership with Judge Wm. F. Bullock,[36] a much older and very prominent lawyer in that city.

But he soon found himself more deeply involved than

ever in the political issues that were agitating the country. To quote again from his autobiographical letter:[37]—

> Some of us thought that the time had come when positive action should be taken, at Louisville, by those who were Union men. A private meeting was held, at which James Speed,[38] myself and others were present. We concluded that the people needed to be educated as to the value of the Union, in itself, as well as to the danger that would come to Kentucky, as a Border State, from armed conflicts between great armies occupying its territory. We raised a little money and hired some bands of music, for a local campaign of education. During the months of May, June and July 1861, there was hardly an afternoon when, standing upon some dry goods box on the sidewalk as my platform, I did not address a street audience on behalf of the Union.
>
> During that period an armed volunteer company was formed by Union men in Louisville, mainly for self-protection. We intended to let the violent men on the Confederate side know that we were not to be imposed upon or intimidated. The company was named the "Crittenden Union Zouaves"[39] and became a part of the Louisville "Home Guards"; and I was chosen as its Captain.

At the time, we were boarding at the National Hotel on Jefferson Street. My two little children and I were necessarily left alone much of the time. However, we were never out of my husband's thoughts, and he did everything he could to make us comfortable and happy.

HISTORY MADE BEHIND THE SCENES

During the first half of 1861, the Union cause in Kentucky hung in the balance.

While the Kentucky Whigs (who had generally been in the ascendancy in the State) were all determined to keep Kentucky in the Union, yet they were not quite ready to accept the more radical views of the Northern Whigs; and still less were they ready for the more progressive positions of the new Republican Party, whose key note was opposition to Slavery.

The great masses of the Kentucky people were opposed to secession, and the overwhelming majority of the whites were willing and ready to fight for the Union but they were slow in reaching the point where they would have been willing to fight for the freedom of the negro.

The crowning proof of Lincoln's wisdom during these critical days was the way in which he kept the question of the Union constantly in the foreground and carefully nursed the devotion to the Union in the two Border States of Kentucky and Missouri by resisting the demands of the Abolitionists of the North for the immediate emancipation of the slaves. *"He held his long purpose like a growing tree."*[40] He kept the problem of emancipation in the background, biding his time until 1865, when that question became ripe for solution. In this way he kept the two great Border States of Kentucky and Missouri in the Union, thus making them buffers between the contending armies of the North and South.

But there was a time—especially during the critical first

half of 1861—when many of the best men in Kentucky were "halting between two opinions," and when events threatened to move too rapidly for some men to keep up with them. Conspicuous among that group of men was George D. Prentice,[41] the editor of the *Louisville Journal,* which was the chief organ of the Whigs of Kentucky and the South.

Mr. Prentice belonged to a type of Journalist that does not exist at the present time—the journalist with a special personal following.

Besides Mr. Prentice, the most conspicuous journalists of that type were Horace Greeley[42] of the *New York Tribune,* Henry J. Raymond[43] of the *New York Times,* Samuel Bowles[44] of the *Springfield Republican,* and Joseph Medill[45] of the *Chicago Tribune.*

In these days, men did not ask how the newspapers just named stood on the questions at issue; it was always "What does Horace Greeley, or George Jones or Samuel Bowles or Joseph Medill say?" This was especially true in Kentucky, where men read the "Louisville Journal" in order to find out "how George D. Prentice stood."

Mr. Prentice was born in Connecticut, of sturdy Puritan stock. Within a few years after his graduation from Brown University, and his admission to the bar, he went into journalism and soon became the most influential Whig journalist in New England.

In 1830 at the age of twenty-eight, he was sent to Kentucky by the Connecticut Whigs to prepare a life of Henry Clay, for campaign purposes. While there, he was persuaded to remain, for the purpose of establishing a new Whig daily in Louisville; and in November of that same year the *Louisville Journal* was started, with Prentice as its first editor.

By birth and education, and from his close affiliation from his youth up with the Whig party, Prentice was therefore strongly opposed to Secession; but his social relations in Kentucky were chiefly with people of Southern sympathies, and, greatly to his sorrow, his two sons joined the Confederate army, their mother (as indicated by at least one of Mr. Prentice's biographers) becoming strongly sympathetic with the Southern cause, although she was a native of Ohio.

In spite of all these hostile tendencies, Mr. Prentice had warmly supported Bell and Everett, the standard bearers of the temporary "Conservative Union Party"; and upon their defeat in November, 1860 (as stated by one of his biographers), he "recognized no other course but to accept and, if necessary, to support the Republican Union administration of Lincoln", and he strenuously resisted the efforts made by the Southern leaders to secure the Journal's powerful influence in behalf of the Confederacy.[46]

But there was a brief period in the early part of 1861, shortly after Lincoln's inauguration, when events seemed to Prentice to be moving too rapidly in regard to the Slavery question and, suddenly, his editorials began to take on an uncertain sound.

The Union men of Louisville became somewhat alarmed. My husband (who at the time was Captain of the Home Guard stationed in that city) telegraphed to his father to come to Louisville at once and to bring with him ex-Governor Letcher,[47] Colonel John Mason Brown[48] and other "old-line" Whigs of strong Union sympathies—all of whom were warm personal friends of Mr. Prentice.

Fortunately for the Union cause (and for that great editor, personally), Mr. Prentice had been taken sick and was confined to the house for a time. On the very day of the arrival at Louisville of the Union leaders from Frankfort, an editorial by Prentice squinting dangerously at the Southern side was actually standing in type, ready to appear in the next morning's issue.

At that time, Mr. Walter N. Haldeman, who was a strong Union man, was the proprietor of the *Journal*. His sentiments were strongly shared by the City Editor and the Business Manager of the paper, Mr. Paul Roberts Shipman,[49] who afterwards won a distinguished place for himself as a journalist and a writer on public questions. He is still very much alive, in spite of his more than fourscore years, having been for a long time an honored resident of Edgewater, N.J.

At the time of which I write Mr. Shipman was a young man of about my husband's age, both of them being under thirty.

In the emergency created by Mr. Prentice's sickness at such a crisis in the history of the country, Mr. Haldeman put "Captain Harlan" and Mr. Shipman in charge of the editorial policy of the *Journal* and, for about two weeks, these two young men overlooked everything that went into the paper.

The type of a very uncertain article was redistributed and the editorial was not used, being replaced by another that was prepared by "Captain Harlan" and Mr. Shipman; and that editorial was taken by the readers of the *Journal* as Prentice's. In order, however, not to excite suspicion, the soldier-editor and his able journalistic colleague restrained themselves, for the time being, from making the *Journal* take *too* strong a position. They simply shifted its rudder a few points nearer to the Pole Star of the Union.

After a day or two, there appeared another editorial (which was also taken by the public as one of Prentice's) pointing a little more strongly toward the Union side. This was followed up by several other editorials, each a little stronger than the preceding one, until, at the end of the ten days or two weeks, "Captain Harlan" and Mr. Shipman had (anonymously) committed the paper, and its great editor, to an out-and-out support of the Union.

Meanwhile, the contingent of Frankfort Whigs had called every day to see Prentice. They filled the atmosphere of that sickroom with Union sentiments. They were with him constantly, that his other friends with Southern sympathies could not get at him.

What Prentice thought of the subtle and gradually increasing changes in the editorials which Kentucky and the whole South were attributing to him, or what theory he had as to who was responsible for them, I do not know.

But, by the time he recovered his health and returned to his post in the "Journal's" office, the paper had been irrevocably committed to the Union side.

Meanwhile, Prentice's brief period of wavering had passed and his own opinions had become irrevocably fixed in favor of a vigorous support of the Republican Union administration.

It was in no way discreditable to Mr. Prentice that he had passed through a short period of "thus halting between two opinions." There were thousands like him in the Border States—good men and true—who, after a brief period of hesitation, became ardently loyal to Mr. Lincoln's policies; and from that time on, and throughout the war, no man in the country did nobler work for the Union than was done by George D. Prentice. Indeed, at the age of sixty, he shouldered his musket, as a member of the Volunteer Home Guard for the protection of Louisville during the temporary Confederate occupation of Kentucky.

This episode was only one of the many cases when great events have turned upon the influence exerted "behind the scenes;" and I have always been specially proud of the part my husband thus played in the secret history of those epoch-making days.

Enlistment in the Union Army

Coming to me one day, about night fall, my husband said that he would have to go out with the Home Guard, that night, as the "rebels" were threatening the city.[50] As he could not think of leaving me alone with my little ones, he insisted upon taking me to the home of his law partner for protection. We started almost immediately; but at every corner we found the troops drawn up in line, and though ordinarily it [would] have taken us only fifteen or twenty minutes to reach Judge Bullock's house, we were more than one hour on the way. Evidently the Bullocks had gone to bed, for we found the house darkened. My husband rang the bell and, in response to Judge Bullock's inquiry from the upper window, he explained the situation, and said that he could do nothing else but bring his little family to him for his care.

Judge and Mrs. Bullock were delightful people of the old Southern type, and we were taken in most hospitably and were made to feel very much at home.

That night, which was dreadful enough in itself, was a most horrible one for me. My dear host and hostess were alone in the house. Their son (an only son, I think) had enlisted in the Confederate army (though his parents were Union people) and he was then in the far South. Added to my own anxiety was the agony I heard expressed in dear Mrs. Bullock's tears and prayers throughout the whole night.

On the next day but one my husband returned. The immediate cause for alarm for the city being over, we went back to the hotel. That night he paced the floor until the dawn, his duty to his wife and little ones and his duty to his country wrestling within him in bitter conflict. He came to my bed, and sitting beside me, he said he would leave the matter entirely to me; that he felt that his first duty was to me and his children. I asked him what he would do if he had neither wife or children. He said at once, with great earnestness, "I would go to the help of my country."

I knew what his spirit was, and that to feel himself a shirker in the hour of his country's need would make him most unhappy. Therefore, summoning all the courage I could muster, I said, "You must do as you would do if you had neither wife nor children. I could not stand between you and your duty to the country and be happy."

My husband, therefore, decided to enlist at once in the Union Army.

He issued an address, or proclamation, which was published in the *Louisville Journal*, in which he stated his purpose to raise and command a regiment of infantry, and inviting young men from any part of the State to join it. I quote here the latter part of that proclamation:

And now I appeal to my fellow-Kentuckians to come forward and enroll themselves for service. Their invaded State appeals to them. The cause of human liberty and of republican institutions everywhere appeals to them. All that is most glorious in human government is now at stake, and every true man should come to the rescue.

The time, fellow-citizens, has come and even the unpatriotic and the selfish should hasten to take up arms for the common defense of their State and Country. Every consideration of enlightened self-interest calls us to the field. If our enemies triumph, all our trades, all our professions, all our avocations of whatever character, all our possessions of every description, become valueless. To save ourselves and our families from ruin, not less than to save our State and our Country from degradation and shame, we must rally now where the National Flag invites us.

Come, then, let us gird up the whole strength of our bodies and souls for the conflict, and may the God of Battles guide home every blow we strike. For one, I am unwilling to see the people of my native State overrun and conquered by men claiming to be citizens of a foreign government. I cannot be indifferent to the issue which an unnatural enemy has forced upon Kentuckians.

My husband's regiment was quickly raised, and was mustered into the service of the State in October, 1861; and in November it was mustered into the service of the United States at Lebanon, Kentucky, as the 10th Kentucky Volunteer Infantry, and became a part of the division of General George H. Thomas.[51]

As soon as my husband had begun recruiting for his regiment, I went to my own father's home, having a most exciting trip on the boat between Louisville and Evansville. A great many Southerners were fleeing homeward. Among them I found an own cousin of my husband, whose welcome to me was that she felt "disgraced" that any one of the Harlan name should be "enrolled in the Yankee Army."

Two beautiful women, both of them friends of my husband, were also on the boat. They were going to Bowling Green to join their husbands, who were in the Confederate Army. One of them was the wife of a close friend of my husband's—indeed, he had been one of the groomsmen at her wedding. The word went around from the Captain, and was only whispered from one person to another, that the husbands of both those women had been killed in a fierce battle near Bowling Green (those poor women being ignorant of it at the moment); and that the Confederate Army had evacuated the town and had gone further South. We were all in the same frame of mind in those bitter days, and though those two women were (as I suppose we all were at the time) unreasonable and some times fiercely forgetful of right feelings for others, yet such was the sympathy that was afterwards shown to them by every one on board as soon as the news of their loss spread among the passengers, that I am sure that those sadly stricken women had nothing to complain of as they looked back on that dreadful journey.

I went to my father's home, and was separated from my husband for several long months. I heard from him, however, every day, for it was our invariable custom throughout our lives to send each other daily letters whenever we were separated.

RETURN TO FRANKFORT

On February 23, 1863, my father-in-law, the Hon. James Harlan, who had been twice elected Attorney General of the State, suddenly died. I quote once more from my husband's autobiographical letter:[52]—

My father's death was on every account an unspeakable calamity to the family, even if looked at only from the standpoint of business. At the time he died my father had the largest practice of any lawyer in Kentucky and the support of my mother and the family depended upon the right handling of the business left by him. My three oldest brothers were dead, and my only remaining brother had become incompetent for business.[53] I was connected with my father in business and alone knew of what was necessary to be done in order to preserve from loss or waste what he had fairly earned by hard work in his profession. So, in every just sense, I was compelled to return to civil life. This was the view of all my brother officers, including General Rosecrans[54] and his Chief of Staff, Gen. James A. Garfield.[55] My letter of resignation, addressed to General Garfield, Chief of Staff, was as follows:—

Lavergne, Tenn.
March 2nd, 1863.

Brigadier General Garfield,
Chief of Staff Army of the Cumberland,
Murfreebore, Tenn.

General:

I hereby tender my resignation as Colonel of the 10th Kentucky Volunteer Infantry.

I am not indebted to the Government of the United States, nor have I any Government property in my possession. I have not been absent any time without leave nor are there any charges against me which can affect my pay. I have been paid to January 1, 1863.

It is my due to my Superior Officers—to those with whom I originally entered the service, and to the cause in which we have alike laboured for nearly sixteen months, that I should state explicitly the reasons which have induced me to take this step.

The recent sudden death of my father has devolved upon me duties of a private nature which the exigencies of the public service do not require that I shall neglect. Those duties relate to his unsettled business which demands my immediate personal attention.

I deeply regret that I am compelled, at this time, to return to civil life. It was my fixed purpose to remain in the Federal army until it had effectually suppressed the existing armed rebellion, and restored the authority of the National Government over every part of the Union. No ordinary considerations would have induced me to depart from this purpose. Even the private interests to which I have alluded would be regarded as nothing, in my estimation, if I felt that my continuance in or retirement from the service would, to any material extent, affect the great struggle through which the country is now passing.

If, therefore, I am permitted to retire from the army, I beg the Commanding General to feel assured that it is from no want of confidence either in the justice or ultimate triumph of the Union cause.

That cause will always have the warmest sympathies of my heart, for there are no conditions upon which I will consent to a dissolution of the Union. Nor are there any concessions, consistent with a republican form of government, which I am not prepared to make in order to maintain and perpetuate that Union.

I have the honor to be, General,

> Very Respectfully,
> Your Obedient Servant,
> John M. Harlan,
> Colonel Commanding
> 2nd Brig. 3rd Div.
> 14th Army Corps.

Quoting again from my husband's own account of that period:—

Before my resignation was put into the hands of General Rosecrans, and without its being generally or publicly known that I intended to return to civil life, President Lincoln had sent my name to the Senate for Brigadier General. As soon as I became aware of this fact, I wrote to Senator Crittenden informing him that I had or soon would resign, and requested my nomination as Brigadier General to be withdrawn. He complied with my wishes, and, hence, there was no confirmation.

This closed my career in the Union Army. But immediately upon my return to Kentucky the suggestion was made that I should be nominated for Attorney General at the Union Convention, then soon to assemble to make nominations for State officers to be selected at the approaching State election in August. The suggestion was not disapproved by me, principally because if elected I would be required to remove to the capital of the State where my father lived at the time of his death, and where I was compelled to be in order to wind up his business and estate. I was elected Attorney General by more than 50,000 majority, and went to Frankfort to reside.

At this time my husband was just a little over thirty years of age. He performed the duties of the office of Attorney General for the full term of four years.

Although his nomination as a full Brigadier General had been withdrawn (as above stated), yet, inasmuch as he was an Acting-Brigadier-General at the time of his resignation from the army, he became popularly known throughout the State, from that time on, as "General Harlan."

Under the law, my husband's mother, who was his idol, was entitled only to one third of her husband's estate. She had always had ten or twelve slaves at her command, and my husband felt that it would have been cruel to leave her with the few servants that would ordinarily have fallen to her in the division of the Estate. In addition to the feeling he had as to her comfort, my husband, having been brought up with those servants in the peculiarly close relations that existed between Master and slaves in the case of the best type of Slave-holders in the South, had a real affection for his father's servants. He would not bear to think of them falling into other hands through the barter and sale of human beings that was then still in vogue. Promptly, and without a thought of himself and of the burden he would have to carry, he therefore made himself responsible to the Estate for the value of the rest of those slaves, and he actually paid for them *after* Lincoln's Emancipation Proclamation had set them free.[56]

A "REBEL" ATTACK ON FRANKFORT

In 1864, while my husband was practising his profession, and while there was still a fear of invasion by the Confederates, great excitement was caused, one morning, by the news that one of the near-by hills, the view from which commanded the little town, was threatened by the "rebels."[57] Every citizen with Union sentiments shouldered his gun, even ministers of the Gospel being among the number. We were then living in a little house quite near my husband's office, in the very heart of the town.

That night, the Home Guard, with cannon and musketry for the defense of the Capitol, stationed themselves on the hill that was threatened. My husband's widowed mother was in her summer home, Harlan's Hill, directly opposite the one on which the Union troops had gathered. To his horror, and only in the nick of time, he observed that the cannon, which was being managed by the Captain of the Volunteer Artillery, was so aimed that its charge would have gone directly through the Harlan summer home. At that time, my mother-in-law was there alone, with her servants and one daughter. In the twinkling of an eye, my husband turned the cannon's mouth from the point of danger, and while the Confederates were pouring up the hill on his mother's side of the river, he felt that he had saved her from great danger and, perhaps, from death.

The engagement was very short, the "rebels" finding the heavy and unexpected artillery fire too much for them, and, though many of their officers lingered long enough to get a good breakfast at the hands of my dear mother-in-law, they soon disappeared altogether.

For two or three years the life in Frankfort was most unsettled and full of anxiety.

A TALE OF TWO COOKS

After my father-in-law's death, the household slaves became the property of my mother-in-law, so that when we went to housekeeping, we were obliged (as the custom then was) to hire them by the year. A certain young couple who were leaving Kentucky, and who felt sure that freedom for the slaves was near at hand, sold us a very good cook for One Hundred Dollars, a year's hire.

She was a woman of decided ideas as to her own importance. Being very much older than I was, she bitterly resented the mildest suggestion I could make as to her preparation of certain dishes. On one occasion she said to me:

"You don't know nuthin' 'bout cookin'. I allus done it dis way foh Miss Eddie." To which I replied, "But you are working for *me* now and not for Miss Eddie, and you must do it *my* way." With a look of scorn she said again, "I jus' tole you, you don't know nuthin' 'bout cookin'." Once or twice, taking me by the shoulders, she actually put me out of the kitchen and locked the door.

This sullen, vindictive temper was very rare among slaves, and, as I had never seen any such example of it in my mother-in-law's household, the situation became very uncomfortable and almost terrifying, and we concluded to give "Aunt" Fanny her freedom.

The matter of filling her place was a difficult one, for a good slave-owner never forced good servants to hire themselves to any household that was objectionable to the servant. Being in despair, after several unsuccessful attempts to get a successor to "Aunt" Fanny, I asked an old family servant, "Aunt" Emily, who was a favourite with us all, why it was so difficult for me to get a cook. With a look on her face of mingled amusement and sorrow (lest she might hurt my feelings) she said, "Ole Fanny done gib you such a bad name, Miss Mallie, dat it's gwine to be hard fer you to get a good cook. She say that Marse John is a puffect gen'l-man, but dat *you*'se nuffin but a She-Debbil"—which (to me) was a new and rather startling aspect of my character and disposition.

As good luck would have it, however, there was a certain man in the neighbourhood, whose wealth consisted mainly in slaves, and who thought that the only way to save his property was to "run his negroes South." Among them was an old "Mammy" who was breaking her heart at the thought of being separated from her husband ("George") who belonged to another slave-holder. She had therefore been permitted to sell herself to any one in the neighbour-hood for a year's hire ($100). Having heard that I was look-ing for a cook, she came to me to apply for the place. As she walked, she rolled from side to side, like a ship under full sail in a rough sea; but there was such a mild look on her face, as she appealed to me to take her and as she told me with tears in her eyes what it would mean to her to leave "George" behind her, alone, that I determined to close the bargain and we bought her for One Hundred Dollars, her husband, George, afterwards joining her. She was most grateful and said, "I done know Marse John ebber since he was lil'l boy, and I'm sure you'all will be kine to me."

It was a most fortunate purchase, and "Aunt" Char-lotte's[58] devotion to us, and her prayers for us and our chil-dren (of which I shall tell, later on) are among my sweetest memories of those old days.

OUR TIN WEDDING

About 1865 (nine years after our marriage), my father bought us quite a large house in Frankfort, known as "The Hewitt House."[59] It occupied a large lot at the corner of the Main Street and the small side street that formed the Northern (?) boundary of the Capitol Square.

The lower storey of this house was only one room deep, the rooms being very large and opening onto a latticed porch in the rear, with six or eight steps leading to a gar-den. The part next to the house was planted with flowers, in back of that was a kitchen garden. The house had a frontage, however, of four rooms facing the Capitol Square. The fourth room led to a passage-way to the kitchen, which was the first room in a long-drawn-out ell at the Eastern (?) end of the house, the ell having been added to, from time to time, according to the needs of the former owner, who was a slave-holder.

In this house we gave our first large "entertainment"—in the celebration of the tenth anniversary of our wedding. I well remember how anxious my dear mother-in-law was that the party should be worthy of the young married people of the family, and, although *she* did all the managing and the superintending, *I,* as the hostess, was given all the credit. That was her generous way of coming to the rescue of every member of the family.

The presents we received at our "Tin Wedding" were very numerous, supplying us with tin-ware of the finest quality for years to come. I must mention one present—a tin fan made to order, the sticks cut in a fancy design and strung together with blue ribbons. A very pretty French clock was given us by the congregation of the Presbyterian Church.[60]

The occasion was considered quite a brilliant one, and we were congratulated on its success.

In this connection, I recall an experience which emphasizes the very close and affectionate interest which the servants of that time had in the affairs of their Master and Mistress.

At the time of our "Tin Wedding" we had several visitors in the house. After I had gone to bed, I remembered that I had failed to give explicit orders for the next morning's breakfast. I therefore slipped down to the kitchen door through the passage-way, to speak with "Aunt" Charlotte. Reaching the door that led from the kitchen to her bedroom, I heard her voice lifted in prayer—old "Uncle" George (her husband), I had no doubt, was kneeling with her. She prayed for every member of the family by name, especially asking that the little boys and "all the chillen" might be a comfort and blessing to their Father and Mother. I quietly stole back to our own room, telling my husband as I closed the door, that I did not care whether we had any breakfast or not, so long as there were such prayers going up for us from the kitchen.

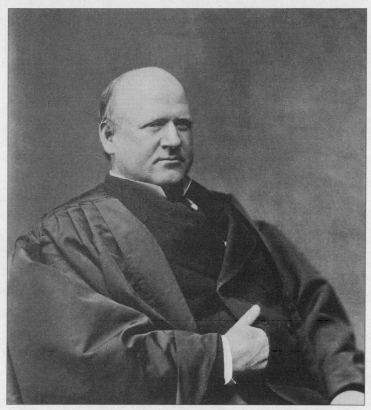

Justice John Marshall Harlan. Initially from a slave-owning family, Justice Harlan came to condemn that practice. His landmark dissent in *Plessy* v. *Ferguson* (1896) denouncing segregation inspired Thurgood Marshall's arguments in *Brown* v. *Board of Education* (1954).

Malvina Shanklin Harlan. Malvina Harlan penned this memoir of her life with Justice Harlan. One of her children tried to get it published, and the stamp of Paul S. Reynolds, the literary agent, appears on the first page of the typescript. However, it was only published in 2001 by the *Journal of Supreme Court History,* after being found among some Harlan family papers in the Library of Congress.

Justice Harlan was born on June 1, 1833, in this "Old Stone House" near Danville, Kentucky.

This engraving of Harlan's hometown of Frankfort, Kentucky, was made in 1841, when the future Justice was eight years old.

The daughter of Kentucky farmers, Eliza Shannon Davenport Harlan (left) married James Harlan (right), a lawyer who became a Whig Congressman and the Kentucky attorney general. In addition to John, whom they named after Chief Justice John Marshall, the couple had three daughters and four sons.

Robert James Harlan (1816–97) was born a slave, and for a long time was believed to have been the son of James Harlan. He lived in James Harlan's household until 1848. Being only seven-eighths white in ancestry, he was refused admittance to the local public school. So he was taught the elements of education by James Harlan's older sons and also received financial support toward the purchase of his freedom. In 1849 he traveled to California where he made a fortune in the Gold Rush, and then settled in Cincinnati to pursue a distinguished career in business and politics. Robert James Harlan and John Marshall Harlan remained friends and political allies throughout their lives.

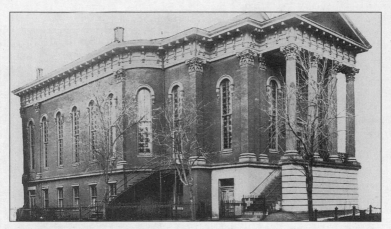

The New York Avenue Presbyterian Church in Washington, D.C., where John Harlan was an active member. In 1896, he organized a Sunday school class for men, which he taught until his death in 1911. According to Malvina, in 1915 it was still referred to as the "Harlan Bible Class."

HENRY CLAY.

James Harlan, Malvina's father-in-law, was such a devout supporter of Henry Clay and the Whig party that Clay left Harlan his favorite cane in his will.

John Harlan was a Union officer during the Civil War, raising his own regiment, the 10th Kentucky Infantry, in September 1861. When his father died in early 1863, he resigned his commission to take over the family law practice.

Benjamin H. Bristow was Harlan's law partner and closest political ally. Their rivalry for a seat on the Supreme Court ultimately cooled their friendship.

In 1877, Chief Justice Morrison R. Waite swore in Rutherford B. Hayes as President, after an election that was so close that a fifteen-member bipartisan commission was appointed to decide the contest and to avert civil war. One month after his inauguration, Hayes appointed five men, including Harlan, to form a "Louisiana Commission" to investigate conditions in that state that had resulted in two rival state governments.

Lucy Hayes (pictured with her husband), with whom Malvina Harlan became friends. Malvina would often visit her at the Executive Mansion at eleven or twelve o'clock for an informal chat. On Sunday nights, the Harlan family regularly stopped by the White House after church for hymn singing, and Edith, their eldest daughter, would play the piano.

John Maynard Harlan, the youngest of Malvina's three sons, ran unsuccessfully for mayor of Chicago in 1897 and 1905 and lost a bid for governor in 1920. His son, John Marshall Harlan II, was appointed to the United States Supreme Court in 1955, to become the second member of the Harlan family in this position. He never attained the national political prominence that both he and his father expected.

When Justice John Marshall Harlan was having trouble formulating a dissent in the Civil Rights Cases, Malvina placed on his desk the inkwell Chief Justice Roger B. Taney had used in 1857 to pen the notorious *Dred Scott* decision. The Civil Rights Cases legal briefs had not mentioned *Dred Scott*, but Harlan's dissent did.

The Supreme Court Justices heard argument in the
Old Senate Chamber throughout Harlan's tenure.

President Benjamin Harrison appointed Harlan to the Bering Fur Seal Commission to settle the dispute among Canada, the United States, and Great Britain over seal-fishing rights in the Bering Sea. Malvina accompanied her husband to Paris in 1893 with their daughter Ruth and their granddaughter Edith Harlan Child (whom they raised after her mother, Edith, died tragically young). The Harlan women traveled to Italy with the wife and daughters of Senator John Tyler Morgan of Alabama (above), who served with Harlan on the Arbitration Tribunal.

While in Paris for the arbitration meeting, the Harlans were received cordially at the Palais de l'Elysée by French President Marie François Sadi Carnot (left) and his wife (right). Malvina found that the palace "did not compare with our much less pretentious, but far more stately and impressive, Executive Mansion, with its spacious and beautiful grounds."

In 1897, Justice Harlan summered in Murray Bay, a resort in Pointe-au-Pic, Canada, on the St. Lawrence River. There he took up golf, which, according to Malvina, "was a radical change in his habits of life, for up to that summer he had never indulged in any out-of-door diversion as a relief from the constant strain of his exhausting professional labours."

William Howard Taft spent his summers in Murray Bay and socialized with the Harlans. At his birthday party in 1904, Taft, then Secretary of War, invited Malvina to dance the Virginia Reel. She initially refused because of his reputation for being an excellent dancer, but relented when she saw Mrs. Taft lead her husband out on to the dance floor.

In 1906, Justice and Mrs. Harlan (above, left) visited Lake Forest College in Illinois, where the Justice gave a series of talks on government and the Constitution. Their son, Richard Davenport Harlan (above, right with his wife, Margaret, and left), was the president of the college from 1901 to 1905, when he left for Washington, D.C., to do administrative work at George Washington University.

In 1908 Justice Harlan (with top hat, holding a cane) and his old friend Augustus E. Willson, the governor of Kentucky (standing to Harlan's right) paid a visit to the Law School of Transylvania University in Lexington, Kentucky, their alma mater. It had been unusual for Harlan to go to law school, as most aspiring attorneys in the 1850s apprenticed in law offices.

Garfield Memorial Hospital, which was Harlan's chief interest in Washington outside of his judicial duties and his church work. During the last years of his life, he was the president of its Board of Directors. The hospital has since been demolished.

This photo of the Justices was taken in 1911, the year Harlan died. He is seated second from left, with Oliver Wendell Holmes, Jr., seated to his right and Chief Justice Edward Douglass White, Joseph McKenna, and William R. Day seated to his left. Standing from left to right are Willis Van Devanter, Horace H. Lurton, Charles Evans Hughes, and Joseph R. Lamar.

Attorney General James C. McReynolds hosted a luncheon for Justice Harlan in New York a few weeks before the Justice's death in October 1911. McReynolds, who would join the Supreme Court in 1914, drove Harlan to see Grant's Tomb in the afternoon, an experience that so impressed the Justice that he insisted on returning the next day with his wife.

"The wakening in the morning to find him gone is heartbreaking," wrote Malvina upon the death of her husband after nearly fifty-five years of marriage. She survived him by five years, dying in 1916.

Final Removal to Louisville

As the opportunities at Frankfort for developing my husband's practice were very meagre, he concluded to take up his residence in Louisville again, to which place we moved permanently in November, 1867. He formed a partnership with Judge Newman,[61] a much older man than himself, who brought a good practice of his own to the new firm of "Harlan & Newman." ... I do not remember the exact date, but it must have been in 1868 or 1869 that General Benjamin J. Bristow[62] joined the firm, whose title was then changed to "Harlan, Newman & Bristow." During General Grant's second Administration (1872–76), General Bristow was appointed to the office of Secretary of the Treasury in Washington. About that time Judge Newman died, and the firm's title was changed to that of "Harlan & Bristow."

Augustus E. Willson,[63] then a very young man, had been taken into the office as a clerk. He was so highly esteemed by the members of the firm that, during General Bristow's

Administration of the Treasury Department, he was given a very responsible position in that Department, ultimately returning to my husband's office, and being taken finally into the firm as a junior partner. Between my husband and Mr. Willson there grew up the affection that one finds between an older and a younger brother. Upon General Bristow's retirement from the firm in 187[6], its title was changed to that of "Harlan & Willson."

Mr. Willson afterwards (in 19[07]) became Governor of the State and, in his efforts to solve the difficult problems that confronted him during a very troubled period in the history of the State, he made an enviable record for himself.

A BELATED BRIDAL TOUR

In the early days of my married life my husband nicknamed me "Old Woman." But the unromantic title was very sweet to my ears, because it was always accompanied by a look and a tone that meant much to me at that period. He had taken me into his life when I was still a child, having little or no confidence in myself and no knowledge of the world. His nick-name helped me, therefore, to take myself at his own estimate;—for he looked upon me as having the judgment and experience that only years can bring.

One day, early in the summer of 1868, when we were living at Louisville, he came home and, with a joyous light in his eye and a pleasant ring in his voice, he said to me:

"Old Woman, I am going to New York tomorrow and

you are going with me. Our expenses will be covered by the retaining fee that has been promised. We shall see New York, Philadelphia and Boston together and we shall call it our Bridal Tour, as we have never had such a trip together. So, get your things in your trunk, for we are to take the morning train."

"But," I said, "I am not ready for such a trip; I haven't the clothes."

"No matter," was his reply, "we'll get ready *after* we get to New York."

So off we went on our belated Bridal Trip, leaving the four little ones in the care of my sister-in-law.[64]

We went first to New York, where we stopped at the Fifth Avenue Hotel, which was then at the height of its popularity.

Business visits and shopping rounds were attended to each day; but, between times, we managed to get in a little sight-seeing. Our means of transportation were the omnibusses universally used in those days, and they were crowded from morning until night.

Almost every time we got into a 'bus, some lady would ask in a very courteous manner, "I beg your pardon, but are you not from the South?"

The question was put to me so often that it began to get on my nerves. Looking about me in the 'bus, I could see no man who, in my estimation, compared in any sense with my husband, with his splendid carriage and figure, and his handsome face; and my own attire, simple as it was, seemed to me quite neat and inconspicuous. I therefore determined to find out *why* every one seemed to take us for Southerners. So, the next time the question was asked, I courteously put a counter-question, saying:—"I beg your pardon, but *why* do you think that we are from the South?"

My pride was restored by the reply, for the reason given for the guess as to our locality was:—

"Because the gentleman with you got up to give his seat to a lady. They don't do that here in New York."

Few people from our part of the country ever went to New York in those days without crossing over to Brooklyn to hear the great preacher, Henry Ward Beecher.[65] Kentuckians were generally good judges of oratory, as their State at that time had some of the most noted orators of the day.

My husband and I had both been somewhat prejudiced against Mr. Beecher. For at that time there was current a witty saying in which mankind was thus summed up:—

"There are *good* people and *bad* people and—*the Beechers!*"

I shall never forget our trip across the river on that Sunday. The ferry boat was crowded and as we neared the Brooklyn pier we espied a very kindly man, whose speech at once marked him as an Englishman, and we asked him if he could tell us the shortest way to Plymouth Church. We were told by him to follow the crowd, as with few exceptions they were all on their way to hear Mr. Beecher. Our Englishman offered to help us to secure good seats. We followed him closely and soon found ourselves in the gallery of the spacious building.

I shall never forget Mr. Beecher's beautiful prayers, nor his reading of the Lessons. His prayers seemed to be the natural talking of the human heart to our Heavenly Father, and his simple, and at times dramatic, reading of a very trite passage of Scripture lighted it up with a new meaning.

His sermon, and the service as a whole, caused our prejudices to vanish like dew before the sun, and to the end of Mr. Beecher's life my husband and I greatly admired and respected him as one of the greatest of Americans and we never failed to hear him whenever we had an opportunity.

Campaigns for the Governorship

In 1868 my husband had identified himself with the Republican party, and he voted for Grant[66] at the Presidential Elections of 1868 and 1872.

In response to the urgent call of the Republicans of Kentucky (though he had no hope whatever of being elected) my husband made two campaigns for the Governorship of Kentucky—one in 1871 and the second in 1875. He proved to be a real leader, increasing the vote of the party, especially in the second campaign, far beyond the hopes of the most sanguine.[67]

The two campaigns were made at a great sacrifice to his professional career, for he was, first of all, a *Lawyer,* devoted to his profession, giving himself heart and soul to his work.

He greatly enjoyed the two campaigns, however, especially on account of the opportunity it gave him to know more of his State and its people. The sturdy mountaineers, in particular, became a most interesting study to him. He predicted a great future for them, because of the opportunity for education that was then opening to them and the new ambitions that seemed then to be stirring in them.

At that time, political campaigns in Kentucky, and through the other portions of the South, were a great contrast to the campaigns of today. The opposing candidates travelled together from place to place and generally on horseback, dividing the time as to the speaking—one candidate having the opening and closing speech at one town, while the other had the opening and closing speech at the next town. These joint debates occupied from three to five hours, the people from the whole surrounding country coming on horseback and in wagons and buggies to attend the meetings. These joint debates were an important means of political education for the masses of the people. The friends and adherents of both candidates would listen respectfully to both speakers, who would often be interrupted by questions from the audience which were answered by the speaker in a perfectly good-natured way.

The candidates always stopped at the same hotel or way-side inn. They took their meals together with the utmost good fellowship, although each day, after dinner and supper, they would on the platform fiercely attack each other and each other's political party.

They had to put up with all kinds of inconveniences, frequently occupying the same room, and quite often the same bed. A very amusing story arose out of one such experience, and the opposing candidates often laughed together in after years as they recalled it.

One night after a long day's ride(in the course of which they had participated in joint debates at two places—one in the afternoon and the other in the evening—they not only had to room together, but were compelled to occupy the same bed! After trying vainly to settle themselves comfortably for the night my husband, whose sense of humour was always keen, remarked solemnly to his opponent. "Of one thing, my friend, there can be no doubt—the *next Governor of Kentucky* is in this bed tonight."

Whether this incident occurred in the first campaign, when the opposing candidate was Preston [H.] Leslie,[68] or in the second, when Mr. J. B. McCreary[69] (afterwards a member of the U.S. Senate and now [in 1915] Governor of the State for the second time) was the Democratic candidate, I do not now remember.

The story got out, however, and was afterwards somewhat added to by one of the Democratic newspapers which asserted that my husband's remark as to the "*next* Governor of Kentucky" was followed by a terrible crash, my husband's side of the bed dropping down and tumbling on to the floor, while the candidate who really became "the next Governor" quietly resigned himself to pleasant dreams.

It was a good "story"—but those last touches in it were taken from a journalist's imagination.

After those two exciting and laborious campaigns my husband returned, each time, to the practice of his profession with a new interest and ambition in building up his law practice.

The Presidential Campaign of 1876

The Kentucky Republicans, at their State Convention in the Spring of 1876, named my husband as a candidate for the nomination to the Vice-Presidency at the approaching National Convention that was to be held at Cincinnati in June of that year. But, inasmuch as an influential group of Republicans in different parts of the country, who had been opposed to Grant's Administration, were strongly advocating the nomination of General Bristow as the Republican candidate for the Presidency, my husband did not permit the movement for himself to go any further, but, as the Chairman of the Kentucky delegation to the Cincinnati Convention, he loyally stood by his former partner.

After several ballots had been cast, a "dark-horse" was brought forward in the person of Rutherford B. Hayes,[70] then the Governor of Ohio. As the ballotting progressed, it became apparent that Mr. Blaine (who was a political enemy of General Bristow and therefore unacceptable to most of the Kentucky Republicans) might be the winner and that there was no chance for the nomination of Bristow. Therefore, as Mr. Hayes had developed unexpected strength in the Convention, the Kentucky delegation, after careful deliberation, cast its vote for Governor Hayes at the crucial moment, and he was nominated for the Presidency.

It was a most exciting campaign, the worst trouble being in the South, especially in Louisiana, Florida and South Carolina. At the close of the polls in November, both parties claimed the victory, each charging the other with gross fraud, especially in the States just named.

The result was so close and the feeling throughout the country became so intense, that, in order to avoid the civil war that was being threatened over a contested Presidential Election, a special Act of Congress was passed, providing for an "Electoral Commission" of fifteen, which was to decide the whole matter. The Act named five Senators (three Republicans and two Democrats), five Members of the House of Representatives (three Democrats and two Republicans) and four Justices of the United States Supreme Court—the four Justices being empowered to name a fifth member of the Court as the fifteenth member of the Commission.

The case was discussed before the Commission by able lawyers on each side; the returns from each State were canvassed and the "Electoral Commission," by a divided vote of eight to seven, reported the election of Mr. Hayes, who thereupon took the Oath of Office on March 4, 1877.

THE LOUISIANA COMMISSION

In April 1877, one month after his inauguration, President Hayes appointed five men (who afterwards came to be known as "The Louisiana Commission") to visit that State for the purpose of investigating the conditions that had developed there since the November election—conditions which had resulted in two rival State Governments—and to report their recommendations to the President.

The Commission consisted of Mr. Wayne MacVeagh of Pennsylvania,[71] ex-Governor John C. Brown of Tennessee,[72] Judge Chas. B. Lawrence of Illinois,[73] General Joseph R. Hawley of Connecticut,[74] and my husband.

At my husband's urgent request, I had planned to go with him to Louisiana; but, after the Commission had received its instructions from the President and just as we were leaving Washington, I decided that I could not, with any peace of mind, be absent so long from my children. Whereupon my husband telegraphed to our eldest son, Richard (who was then eighteen and who had begun at even an earlier age to take a keen interest in political affairs), to join the party the next day, at Louisville, on route to New Orleans. My son was allowed to be present at all the sessions of the Commission, and he watched with a keen and intelligent interest the kaleidoscopic changes that took place in the political situation in that State, during the month or six weeks spent there by the Commission. He has furnished me with the following account of the exact part that was played by the "Louisiana Commission":—

In December 1876 the Returning Board of Louisiana—consisting of the officials duly authorized under the State Law to canvass the votes for the Presidential Electors, and also for the rival candidates for the Governorship and the State Legislature—met in New Orleans for the purpose.

A Committee of the prominent Northern Republican leaders (including, among their number: John Sherman of Ohio[75] and, as I remember it, Wm. E. Chandler[76] of New Hampshire) went to New Orleans to watch the counting of the votes for the Presidential Electors. This group of Northern Republicans were nick-named by the opposition Press as "The Visiting Statesmen."

The Returning Board, after canvassing the votes for the Presidential Electors, certified the election of the men pledged to Mr. Hayes.

Whatever may have been the influence exerted by "the Visiting Statesmen," in regard to the decision rendered in December, 1876, by the State Returning Board in favor of the Hayes Electors, the part played by those Northern Republican party leaders should not be confused (as certain political writers have often done) with the mission that was undertaken in April 1877, by the non-partisan "Louisiana Commission." That Commission had nothing whatever to do with the question as to whether Mr. Hayes or Mr. Tilden had carried Louisiana. *That* question had been settled in December 1876 by the State Returning Board, whose decision had finally been ratified (in February and March, 1877) by the "Electoral Commission" appointed by Congress.

But the same Returning Board that had awarded Louisiana to the Hayes Electors had awarded the gubernatorial election to Mr. Packard,[77] the Republican nominee, who had taken the oath of office in January and had begun to act as Governor of the State. Shortly thereafter, the adherents of Mr. Nichol[l]s,[78] the Democratic candidate for the Governorship (who had claimed the election), forcibly seized the State House and had set up a rival Legislature consisting of the Democratic legislators who had run with him on the same ticket.

Thus, when Mr. Hayes was inaugurated as President, there were *two* rival Governors and *two* Legislatures, each claiming the allegiance of the citizens of the State. This condition of affairs threatened civil war in Louisiana.

Gov. Packard called upon President Hayes to send the Federal troops back to Louisiana, in order to support the Packard Government. President Grant had withdrawn the troops from the South, *before* the November election. Mr. Hayes (most wisely, as was generally believed at the time) declined to accede to Governor Packard's request. Instead of the troops, he sent the so-called "Louisiana Commission."

That Commission, however, was not appointed under any Act of Congress (though I am under the impression that, later on, an appropriation was made by Congress for the purpose of paying its expenses) and as the Commission was of an extra-legal character, no power nor authority was given to it by the President. They were simply his personal representatives, who were asked as public spirited citizens to examine into the conditions then prevailing in Louisiana, and to report to the President any recommendations as to the best method of peaceably adjusting the affairs of that disturbed state.

Their task was a very difficult one, for feeling ran very high throughout the State. All that they could do was to ask the representatives of the two warring factions to appear before them and present their views and claims, and vent their grievances.

As things turned out, the local situation settled itself during the Commission's stay in Louisiana. For, although the Commission gave no advice to either side, yet, while the Commission was still in session at New Orleans, those members of the Legislature who had "recognized," and had been acting with Governor Packard, began—one by one, and then by twos and threes—to desert to the rival Legislature, which had "recognized" Mr. Nicholls, and, finally, the remnant of the Packard legislators went over in a body to the rival Legislature—most of the Democratic legislators resigning all claim to their seats. So that, *before* the Commission left New Orleans, practically all of the legally elected legislators "recognized" Mr. Nicholls as the Governor of the State, and (whether justly or not) the Packard regime disappeared from view.

The Louisiana crisis therefore settled itself, without any action whatever, or even advice, on the part of "the Louisiana Commission."

Appointment to the Supreme Court

At the very beginning of his Administration, Mr. Hayes had my husband in mind for a place in his cabinet as Attorney General. This position was finally given to General Charles Deven.[79]

Mr. Hayes then offered my husband his choice of any of the first-class diplomatic positions; but he was such an intense American that he could not bear the thought of being out of his native land for four years, and he therefore was unwilling to accept Mr. Hayes' offer. With new zeal he then gave himself to the practice of his profession.

Before the meeting of Congress in the fall of 1877, Justice David Davis[80] resigned his position in the Supreme Court and was elected by the Illinois Legislature to the Senate of the United States.

In August 1877, Mr. Wayne MacVeagh, who in the course of his services on "The Louisiana Commission" had the opportunity of forming a good estimate of my

husband's character and ability, wrote the following letter
to President Hayes:—

August 21, 1877

My dear Sir:—

You will remember that you did me the kindness at one
time to talk with me about a vacancy on the Bench of the
Supreme Court, and as to the weighty considerations of
public interest which you desired to consult in filling it.

I therefore venture to say that I have also endeavored to
consider the subject from the same high ground; and that I
cannot resist the conclusion that you are wrong in the tendency that you first expressed to fill it from one of the extreme Southern States.

I certainly need not protest that I am wholly free from
prejudices against that section of our common country, or
that I would have the slightest desire to keep alive the bit-
terness of the Civil War; but in view of the political history
of the country for the thirty years preceding the Rebellion,
as well as of the sixteen years since, I cannot divest myself
of the conviction that if a lawyer of unquestioned ability, a
statesman of comprehensive views and a thoroughly sound
Republican can be found living in the more Northern
States of the South, it is safer to offer him the position.

I believe General Harlan of Kentucky meets all the re-
quirements, and that you could not possibly do a wiser or
better thing for the country as well as for your Administration, than to offer him the existing position.

If another vacancy occurred during your term of office,
I could reconcile myself far more easily to the appoint-

ment of a gentleman from the cotton-growing States, because there would be less likelihood of too many vacancies occurring during the next Administration, in case it was Democratic. In other words, if your successor should unfortunately happen to be a Democrat, he would be very likely to fill the vacancies which occur with through going Democrats.

I therefore earnestly hope that you will see your way clear to offer the present vacancy to General Harlan and to await another opportunity before going further South.

> Yours very truly,
> Wayne MacVeagh.
> To the President.

On September 29, 1877, (five weeks after the receipt of the foregoing letter), President Hayes wrote a private and personal letter to the late Wm. Henry Smith,[81] formerly the President of the Associated Press and a close personal friend of Mr. Hayes. Many years afterwards, Mr. Smith gave that letter to my son James. It contained the following postscript with reference to the vacancy on the Supreme Bench, which indicates the estimate which the President then made of my husband:—

Confidentially and on the whole, is not Harlan the man? Of the right age, able, of noble character, industrious, fine manners, temper and appearance. Who beats him?

Thereupon, early in November, 1877, President Hayes sent my husband's name to the Senate as the successor to Justice Davis on the Supreme Court.

He was then only forty-four years of age. As his chief interest and activities had always been along the lines of the legal profession, and as he had never taken any active part in politics—excepting in his two campaigns for the Governorship of Kentucky, and in the brief part he played in the effort to nominate General Bristow—he was very little known outside of his own State; and there was at first some opposition to his appointment to the Bench, on the part of a small group of Senators. One of the New England Senators was at first specially prominent in his opposition to my husband's confirmation, and it hung fire for some time.

Senator Beck,[82] though a Democrat, was a warm admirer of my husband, and he led in the fight for his confirmation. He predicted that if he was confirmed he would, within five years and in spite of his youth, rank with the most learned and wise on that great tribunal of Justice.

I well remember the circumstances under which my husband received the news of the success that attended Senator Beck's staunch support.

It was on Thanksgiving Day, which my husband, as usual, spent at home with his family, and we had attended the Thanksgiving Service at the College Street Presbyterian Church. After lunch—as he was, naturally, somewhat restless because of the way in which his nomination was hanging fire in the Senate—his three boys urged him to join them in an impromptu game of foot-ball which took place upon a common in the outskirts in the city. With great glee they afterwards described to me the way in which their father had played "full-back" on their side, and how everyone had "stood from under" when he advanced, with great deliberation and dignity, to kick away the ball whenever it threatened their goal.

When my *four* "Boys" (for my husband was always a boy along with his three sons) returned, late that afternoon, to our Broadway home—tired and happy, and hungry for their Thanksgiving Dinner—a telegram was waiting for him, informing him that on that very morning "the Senate had unanimously confirmed his nomination as an Associate Justice of the Supreme Court of the United States."

The head-line in one of the Cincinnati papers of the next morning ("Harlan's Thanksgiving") was an accurate description of the mingled happiness and pride with which we sat down to our family dinner that night. The unconscious prophesy embodied in my husband's baptismal name, "John Marshall," was to be fulfilled, for he was to sit on the august tribunal whose far-reaching opening chapter had been mainly written by the great Chief Justice of that name.

My husband took the oath of office, and his seat on the bench, on December 10, 1877.

In those days, the ceremony connected with the induction into office of a Justice of the Supreme Court was of such interest as to draw a large crowd. Mrs. Hayes,[83] wishing to witness the ceremony, came for me in her carriage and sat beside me in the Court room.

To our great amusement, one of the newspapers of the next morning, after speaking in a most rapturous way of Mrs. Hayes, described me as "the *Fiancee*" of the new Justice. French was not used in those days as much as it is now, and the reporter on that occasion, considering himself a master of the French language, thought that *"fiancee"* was the word that expressed my status. I certainly was as proud, that day, as the most recent of *"fiancees"* could possibly have been.

After his very active life as a lawyer, I was filled with some apprehension lest the quiet life of a Judge might be irksome and monotonous, and I endeavoured in every way possible to make the change a desirable one.

To my great joy, however, my husband became more and more absorbed in his judicial work. The veneration he had for the high place to which he had been called, filled him more and more with an intense ambition to be worthy of it; and while he never reached his own ideal for that position, yet his opinions, even in the earliest years of his services on the Bench, won for him, in the judgment of the legal profession, a high place among the great men that have sat on the Supreme Court of the United States; and the friends who had begun to mark him out for a brilliant and influential career in politics, soon came to think of him as "the right man in the right place."

It was not long before his brothers of the Court (many of whom had been on the Bench for years and were looked up to and revered by the whole country) came to think of him as their equal in every way, although, in the intimacy of the Conference Room, they called him "The Boy of the Court," he being very much the youngest man on the Bench at the time of his appointment. Indeed, with the exceptions of Joseph Story (who was only [32] years old at the time of his appointment) and of Justice [William Johnson] (who was also appointed at the age of [32]), my husband was the youngest man ever appointed to the Court.[84]

As the years passed on, and one after another of his colleagues died or resigned, he soon became (in 1897) the Senior Justice.

I am under the impression that he sat with a larger number of the appointees to that high place than any other man that was ever a member of the Supreme Court, having had the following men as his colleagues, from the time of his appointment in 1877 to his death in 1911:—

Chief Justice Waite, Chief Justice Fuller, the present Chief Justice (White), Justices Clifford, Swayne, Miller, Field, Strong, Bradley, Woods, L.Q.C. Lamar, Gray, Blatchford, Peckham, Shiras, Brown, Moody, Holmes, McKenna, Lurton, Day and Lamar[85]—twenty-four (?) in all.[86]

With the exception of the great Chief Justice, John Marshall (who sat on the Supreme Bench for 34 years, 5 months and 5 days) and of Justice Stephen J. Field (who served for 34 years, 6 months and 10 days), my husband's term of service in the Court was much the longest in its history, having been 33 years, 10 months and 3 days.

Early Washington Days

As I had had the care of a large family for many years and knew nothing of the ways of the new place to which we had come, I determined to take a rest from housekeeping for a while. Accordingly, we took a suite of rooms at Mrs. Rines' boarding house on Twelfth Street—a well-ordered establishment that for years had been patronized by many well-known Senators and Congressmen with their families.

The social life among officials in Washington at that time was most exacting in regard to "calls." For many years Monday afternoons had by common consent been set apart (and such is still the case) as the day when the wives of the Supreme Court Justices were "at home." During our first years in Washington, my eldest daughter, Edith, and I were ready for visitors on Monday afternoons as early as two o'clock and we often had as many as two or three hundred visitors.

A table spread with all kinds of dainties, including salads and rich cakes, was the rule at most houses, on such occasions. Also (what would seem rather unconventional in these days), if one's daughter (as was the case with mine) were at all accomplished in music she was often called upon to do her share in the entertainment of visitors. Dancing, too, was sometimes a part of these afternoon receptions. It was not of the tango variety, but was the more graceful and dignified waltz of those earlier days, and it was participated in only by the young, while the older, married people and grandmothers were generally quite content to be on-lookers.

At these afternoon receptions, punch, at most houses, had practically taken the place of tea and was freely indulged in by both sexes—sometimes to such an extent as to produce anything but a pleasant impression. Mrs. Hayes, with her very strict ideas on the subject of Temperance (which she very quietly and decidedly maintained during her husband's Administration) had a marked influence upon this unwholesome practice; and, within a comparatively short time, Washington Society yielded to her gentle sway and acknowledged the wisdom and good taste of her example.[87]

MRS. HAYES' POPULARITY

How general was the respect, admiration and affection for Mrs. Hayes may be shown by a remark that was made to me at a White House dinner by a prominent Democratic Senator. Said he:—

"I have the greatest respect for Mrs. Hayes' stand on the Temperance question—though I will confess that we sometimes long for 'the cheering glass' at these long dinners; but I would really feel sorry for her successor, even were she a Democrat, as I am, I would almost feel willing to have Hayes re-elected, so that we might have *Mrs.* Hayes in the White House for another four years."

The next moment, however, the Senator hailed with delight what came to be nick-named "The Life-saving Station," which came midway in the dinner, in the shape of a small cup of frozen "Roman Punch," of which, by the way, dear Mrs. Hayes always partook; and some good-natured comment was occasionally made as to the distinction which *she* seemed to draw between "eating" intoxicants and "drinking" them.

A story that came to me in a direct way may explain her seeming inconsistency. A well-known caterer (who was a veritable "institution" in Washington at that time and who supplied such articles at many of the dinners) assured Mrs. Hayes, with the cleverness of a true Frenchman, that he could produce the "Rum flavour" without using *rum.* The truthfulness of his boast may well be doubted; but, relying on the art of the culinary alchemist, the gentle lady believed him and was satisfied.

That Democratic Senator's willingness to elect Mr. Hayes for the sake of continuing *Mrs.* Hayes' Administration at the White House reminds me of another story that was told me by a friend who had hired two Irishmen to put in a load of coal. From her open window she heard them talking politics. The "second term" was freely discussed and the question was put by one of them as to whether Mr. Hayes would consent to run again. Remembering the pledge contained in Mr. Hayes' letter of acceptance, the other answered, "No, he does not believe in Second

Terms." "Never moind," said the other. "If we can get Mrs. Hayes' consint, we will run *her* in, any how."

I specially remember the beautiful floral decorations at that dinner. The tables were works of art. The State dining room, with its long table—in the centre of which was a large plateau or mirror (an historic piece)—was a perfect bower of roses. In the middle of the table, on this lake-like mirror, was a huge swan made of white flowers resting on an island-bed of Jacqueminot buds.

On either end of the table was a device, in pastry, showing the Coats-of-Arms of all the leading nations; and there were confections and ices of every shape and description. One of them was the British Lion, which, as the evening wore on, hung its head with a melting and sentimental manner that would be hard to reconcile with its steadfast and determined attitude in this year of our Lord (1915), when it is not only standing for British rights, but for "the freedom of Europe" and perhaps of America—for which we give it all honour.

In the vestibule, the Marine Band made beautiful music throughout the evening and at eleven o'clock the company dispersed, bringing to a close what (to me) was a most memorable and brilliant affair.

MY FIRST "DIPLOMATIC RECEPTION"

I well remember the first "Diplomatic Reception" we attended at the White House. The invitations were from 8 to 11 P.M., and, as it was not considered good manners to keep the President waiting, nearly all the company were there promptly by 8 o'clock. The President and Mrs. Hayes, with the Cabinet, received in the great East Room, assisted by several ladies of the Supreme Court.

The Diplomats entered according to their rank—a matter which to those not versed in the intricacies of Washington official etiquette would often be a very knotty problem. Ambassadors, as a class, out-rank Ministers while within a given class the rank is determined not by the relative importance of the various countries (which would often have been an insoluble problem) but by the date of a given Diplomat's appointment to the Washington post.

After the Diplomats, came the members of the Supreme Court, Senators and Congressmen, with their wives and daughters, until the East Room was filled to overflowing.

Many of the toilettes were magnificent, Mrs. John Jacob Astor Sr.[88] of New York being fairly ablaze with diamonds. It is said that, on that occasion, she wore $800,000 worth of diamonds; she was called "The Diamond Queen." At that period, however, the greater majority were simply dressed and one could feel quite comfortable in one's "black silk." In those days, the "square neck" was as near to the full *decollete* as fashion demanded, and it was worn generally by the older women.

THE WHITE HOUSE DURING THE HAYES' ADMINISTRATION

During the Hayes' Administration, the White House was a most perfect home, in the truest sense of the word. In the life of the Executive Mansion at that period there was very little formality and ceremony.

At that time in Washington, friendly and informal visits

were always made in the forenoon and those who were (or who like myself had come to be) close, personal friends of Mrs. Hayes would often "run in" at 11 or 12 o'clock for a little visit with her. Quite frequently in the forenoon my husband, on his way to the Court, would take me as far as the Executive Mansion and leave me there for friendly chat with Mrs. Hayes.

On Sunday evening after church, we often "stopped in" at the White House and found our way to the "Green Room" on the second floor, where, with perhaps eight or ten other visitors, we would spend the rest of the evening in singing the old-fashioned hymns, my oldest daughter, Edith, playing the accompaniments and adding to the pleasure of the occasion by the beauty of her rare voice. One of Mrs. Hayes' favourite hymns was "Come Ye Disconsolate," and her evident enjoyment of it, as expressed in her sweet voice, still warms my heart as I think of it.

In this connection, I may tell a little incident that occurred during the Garfield Campaign (1880) which showed the womanly tact that made Mrs. Hayes such a power in her husband's career.

A noted Glee Club from Cleveland, Ohio, which was making a tour of the country, singing "campaign songs," gave an informal concert at the White House one evening, about a hundred guests (of both political parties) having been invited to hear them. After giving several of these songs, the Club sang a very long one containing references to the current "Campaign" stories, which, as in this day, was founded more upon malice than upon fact. As the song approached dangerously near to its well-known climax (which would have greatly offended the Democrats present on that occasion), we all held our breath, wondering how the unpleasant incident might be avoided. Whereupon, our hostess, tactfully interrupting the song (yet without appearing to do so), gracefully moved across the room, carrying one of the many baskets of beautiful flowers which were about the room, and presented it to the leader of the Club. She thanked him in her sweet voice for the pleasure which the Club had given her guests and expressed her own appreciation of the good music. And thus the objectionable verse was never reached.

General Sherman,[89] who stood at my side and who was apparently agitated at the thought of what had been threatened, drew a long breath and leaning towards me whispered in my ear, "no one but Lucy Hayes could have done that."

The informal dinners in the small dining room at the White House at that time were most delightful. Although the table easily seated eighteen or twenty people, the company never numbered more than twelve or fourteen. General conversation was the rule on these occasions and the good cheer and flow of soul was abundant.

On one such occasion, when my husband and I were present, Chief Justice Waite was the guest of honour, his wife sitting at the right of the president on the other side of the table.

The evening paper of that day had given an amazing account of a young woman (Belva Lockwood) applying for admission to practice before the United States Supreme Court.[90] It was an unprecedented proceeding at that time, and the people of Washington generally were laughing in their sleeves over it. The Newspaper, in giving an account of it, said, "*The Chief Justice squelched the fair applicant.*"

The company that night at the White House was much

amused by the story. Mrs. Hayes, turning her laughing face to the Chief Justice, asked, in a tone of mock sympathy, "Mr. Chief Justice, *how do you look when you squelch people?*" The Chief Justice feeling the suppressed mirth of the company present (for every one was listening for his answer), replied with a funny look of embarrassment on his face and a shrug of his shoulders, *"Why, I do not know, I'm sure."* Whereupon, Mrs. Waite, sitting opposite and speaking *sotto voce* and pretending to shake, as if from some rather terrifying memories, said under her breath. *"I do"*— whereat the whole company, which was still eavesdropping, broke out in delighted laughter; and the kindly Chief Justice looked somewhat teased.

AN UNCONVENTIONAL RECEPTION

I recalled one unique occasion in my first few years in Washington that would today be considered altogether too unconventional.

My oldest daughter and I were invited to receive with a most charming woman, Mrs. Charles Nordoff,[91] the wife of a very prominent journalist of that period. We were asked to bring our embroidery, and also our *cups and saucers.* When I asked, "Do you really mean us to bring our cups and saucers," Mrs. Nordoff replied:—

"Oh, no, *you* are boarding too and haven't any more pretty things than *I* have; but I want our table to look pretty and I am asking some of my friends who are housekeeping to bring their own cups and saucers."

How many did so I never knew, but her table certainly looked very pretty that day.

Many of the ladies including my daughter and myself brought their fancy work and, as the afternoon wore on, all who could do so were asked to "entertain" the visitors, in one way or another. Miss Goode, a daughter of Representative Goode of Virginia,[92] who had a lovely voice, and my daughter Edith, were asked to sing. Miss Vinnie Ream,[93] the well-known Washington sculptress, also sang to her own harp accompaniment.

But the finishing touch to the interest of the afternoon was a recitation by the wife of General Lander, a most gifted and charming woman who, as Miss Davenport (one of the famous Davenport sisters of England), was formerly a well-known actress.[94] As the wife of General Lander she had made for herself a very high place in the esteem and affection of the cream of Washington Society.

Mrs. Frances Hodgson Burnett[95] was one of the receiving party that afternoon, and to her surprise (and, for a time, to her great confusion), Mrs. Lander's recitation was taken from *That Lass o' Lowrie's,* the well-known novel of Mrs. Burnett's, which had been published only a short time before.

The scene that was recited was the description of a terrible mine explosion. The hero of the story, bleeding and torn and perhaps dying, is brought up from the mine, his betrothed waiting for him at the mouth of the shaft. The scene was most touching and, under Mrs. L[a]nder's tender and skillful touch, was very affecting, many of the company being moved to tears. Mrs. Burnett, unable to hide her emotion, left the room until she could command herself.

The tribute thus paid by one gifted woman to another

was most interesting and made an incident that could never be forgotten by those present.

COUNT DE LESSEPS

During the winter of 1880, Count de Lesseps[96] visited Washington and everybody began to brush up their French, so that they might be able to talk to him. In spite of his seventy-odd years he was hale and hearty, and his head was well covered with white hair, which softened his sunburned complexion. He was short of stature and strong in figure and was as full of life and fun as a boy. Though he and his wife were much feted during their stay, very little of his Panama Canal stock was taken up, as the President and the Members of Congress, sticking closely to the Monroe Doctrine, were not inclined to lend American aid to a canal that was to be controlled by Europeans. The Count professed to approve of this course, though the Charter of the Company which he represented was far from being in accord with it. As history has proved, he was probably a better diplomatist than engineer.

AN AMUSING GIBE AT AMERICAN IMPERIALISM

We had our newspaper fun in those days, as now, and political celebrities came in for their full share of criticism and good-natured railery. In an old scrapbook I made at the time, I have come across the following amusing extract from a little pamphlet entitled *The Coming Crown,*[97] which came out when General Grant was being talked of as a candidate for a "third term" and which in the event of his nomination would probably have had a wide circulation. The extract is as follows:—

From the Court Journal,
Washington, September 1, 1882.

His Imperial Majesty, Emperor Ulysses I, accompanied by the Empress, Crown Prince Frederick, and a numerous suite, arrived at the Palace yesterday, after the close of a visit to the Duke of Pennsylvania at his palatial residence, Cameron Hall, in Harrisburg.

His Imperial Majesty, we are glad to say, is in the best of health. The Imperial Escort consisted of a Battalion of the Guards and two Companies of the Household Cavalry.

Lord Henry Watterson[98] of Kentucky, who has been on a long official visit through the Southern portion of the Empire, where his services in the establishment of the Imperial Government have been crowned with such signal success, is expected to arrive in town tomorrow, and we understand that, in consideration of his brilliant political achievements, His Imperial Majesty has been graciously pleased to create his lordship, *Marquis of Bourbon.*

To those of us who knew and admired the genuine democracy of "Marse Henry" and his lifelong dislike of all "fuss and feathers," and especially to those who knew of his strong opposition to Grant's Administration, the ironical title of *Marquis of Bourbon* was most amusing.

AN EVENING WITH MR. AND MRS. SIDDONS

I remember a specially interesting evening which we spent about this time at the house of Mrs. Clafin, the wife of ex-Governor Clafin of Massachusetts,[99] where I met the famous Mr. and Mrs. Siddons,[100] the grandson of the still more famous actress of the previous century. He was then an old man of eighty years. His wife, forty years younger, was a beautiful and accomplished woman. During the evening they gave several interesting scenes from the standard plays—two scenes from *The School for Scandal,* one scene from *Macbeth,* and others from plays less familiar to our modern stage.

Their best piece of elocution, that evening, was Bishop Herber's familiar missionary hymn, "From Greenland's Icy Mountains"[101]—which was given in a very original way, both Mr. and Mrs. Siddons taking part in it, he reading some interpolated verses from a poem that was unfamiliar to me and she responding alternately with a verse of the familiar hymn.

Using the same metre employed by Heber, the (to me) unknown poet first expressed the cry for the truth that was sent up by the people of some mountainous country—a cry as strong and awful as the heights themselves. This was recited by Mr. Siddons, after which his wife's beautiful voice responded with the first verse of the hymn, "From Greenland's Icy Mountains."

Mr. Siddons next recited another verse of the poem, voicing the cry of the far-off heathen isles to the people of the Christian lands—a prayer that those who were blinded by ignorance and superstition might be able to see—after which Mrs. Siddons recited the second verse of the hymn,

> *What though the spicy breezes*
> *Blow soft o'er Ceylon's isle.*

Then, through Mr. Siddons, the unknown poet voiced the appeal for light from the peoples dwelling in the darkness of heathenism, after which Mrs. Siddons responded with the moving words:

> *Can we, whose souls are lighted*
> *With wisdom from on high,*
> *Can we to men benighted*
> *The lamp of life deny?*

And, last and most glorious of all, Mrs. Siddons uttered the voice of all Christendom,

> *Waft, waft, ye winds his story,*
> *And you, ye waters tell*
> *Till like a sea of glory*
> *It spreads from pole to pole.*

Mr. Siddons gave some interesting reminiscences, among which was a thrilling account of the great Mrs. Siddons' first appearance as Lady Macbeth. He also told an amusing story of how Kitty Stevens became the Countess of Sussex.

My Lord of Sussex, hearing her sing "Robin Adair" at some drawing room, was so moved by the quality of her beautiful voice, that he asked her "*upon what terms he would be allowed to hear her sing that 'heavenly song,' every day, as long as he lived"*—thinking, of course, that in reply she would ask for a round sum of guineas as a yearly income. Instead of which, the audacious and beautiful actress asked for his card and wrote upon it, "*The Countess of Sussex,*" whereupon he finally married her.

Our Massachusetts Avenue Home

Early in 1881—after two or three years "boarding" (a way of living to which we had been wholly unaccustomed)—we took a house at 1623 Massachusetts Avenue, where I had the pleasure of having my family all together during the vacations of my sons, the two older ones, Richard and James,[102] being then at Princeton College and John Maynard[103] being at a private school in Washington.

AN INSPIRING INKSTAND

Vividly associated in my mind with our Massachusetts Avenue home is an interesting episode that formed the closing chapter in the story of a certain historic inkstand, which played an unexpected, dramatic, and inspiring part in one of the most important of my husband's numerous "dissenting opinions."

My husband was always profoundly interested in places

and objects connected with the history of the country; and for that purpose, during his first years in Washington, he made numerous visits of discovery to the different portions of the beautiful Capitol building that for more than a century had housed the Congress and the Supreme Court of the United States. He found much to interest him, not only in the hall (now known as the Statuary Hall) where the House of Representatives sat until 18[57] and in the old Senate Chamber (now the Supreme Court Room) that had resounded to the eloquence of Calhoun, Clay, and Webster, but in the numerous small objects that were associated with the great men of the past.

One day during (I think) his second or third year in Washington, in the office of the Marshal of the Supreme Court, he spied a very old-fashioned and unique inkstand. At each end of the little wooden inkstand (which rested on four small balls, one at each corner, answering as feet) was a small inkwell, covered with a metal top. Between the two wells was a small glass jar or box, with a perforated top, that contained the sand which in the early days did the work of our "blotters." Across the front of the stand the wood was hollowed out into a little groove for the pen-holders.

The quaint little inkstand had about it such an air of mystery and history that my husband asked the Marshal[104] for its story. He learned that it had belonged to Chief Justice Taney[105] and that it was the one constantly used by him in his judicial work. Those innocent wells had furnished the ink with which he penned the famous Dred Scott decision,[106] which, more than any single event during the agitation over the Slavery Question in the ante-bellum days, had served to crystallize the antislavery feelings in the Northern States.

My husband's interest in Taney's inkstand was so marked that the Marshal asked him if he would like to have it. My husband answering most eagerly in the affirmative, the Marshal at once wrapped up the historic little inkstand and gave it to my husband, who put it in his coat pocket and brought it home as a great treasure.

One evening, shortly after we had moved into our Massachusetts Avenue home, we were present at a large evening reception. My husband was engaged in conversation with a very charming woman, the wife of Senator George H. Pendleton of Ohio.[107] Though I took no part in the conversation, I was near enough to hear it. They had been exchanging views about the many interesting things that were often found in most unexpected places about the Capitol, and my husband was telling her about the treasure-trove upon which he had once stumbled in the Marshal's office.

Mrs. Pendleton's interest was most marked, and, after hearing a minute description of the inkstand and the part it had played in the epoch-making decision in the Dred Scott case, she exclaimed,

"Mr. Justice, I would so love to have that little inkstand. Chief Justice Taney was a kinsman of my family." (I think he was Mrs. Pendleton's great-uncle.)

My husband's feeling for women was so chivalric that without hesitation he promised to send her the little inkstand the very next day.

At that time, his invariable rule was to work very late at night. Even after a reception he generally went into his study for an hour or more of work before going to bed.

After he left me that night for his study, I began to think

of the promise he had so rashly made to Mrs. Pendleton. Knowing as I did how much he prized that historic inkstand, a strong impulse took possession of me and I thus argued it out to myself:—

"Why should he give that inkstand away? He values it more than it is possible for any woman to do, for he appreciates the part it played in the history of the Nation. I won't let him part with it."

Whether that impulse came from above or from the Evil One may perhaps be best answered by the *third* chapter of my story of the Taney Inkstand. I confess, however, that during the secret part which I played in the *second* chapter, my conscience somewhat troubled me, for I never hid anything from my husband.

Next day, his much-enjoyed morning nap (which the children and the servants knew must never be disturbed) gave me my opportunity—one which the events of several months later will show to have been most opportune, not to say providential; for I think I was instrumental thereby in adding a real glory to an already historic inkstand, making it to my children a very precious heirloom.

Going that morning to my husband's study on the third floor while he slept, I found the treasured inkstand hidden away under an accumulation of law papers, briefs, and opinions, and I carried it away to my room and hid it among my own treasures.

In due time his nap was over and the day's work begun. Among the first things he thought of was the promise he had made the night before to Mrs. Pendleton. A search for the little inkstand proved unavailing and all his questions to me were met with an "evasive answer" which headed off suspicion. He wrote a note to Mrs. Pendleton telling her of the inexplicable loss of the inkstand, but that, as soon as he could find it, he would keep his promise.

As time went on he forgot all about it and I took good care that the inkstand should remain hidden.

A few months afterwards, the Court decided the famous "Civil Rights" case,[108] involving the constitutionality of the Act of 1873, which was introduced by Charles Sumner[109] for the purpose of assuring civil rights to the Negroes throughout the Union.

As all lawyers know, the Court declared the Sumner Act unconstitutional, my husband alone dissenting.

His dissent (which many lawyers consider to have been one of his greatest opinions) cost him several months of absorbing labour, his interest and anxiety often disturbing his sleep. Many times he would get up in the middle of the night in order to jot down some thought or paragraph which he feared might elude him in the morning. It was a trying time for him. In point of years, he was much the youngest man on the Bench, and standing alone as he did in regard to a decision which the whole country was anxiously awaiting, he felt that, on a question of such far-reaching importance, he must speak not only forcibly but wisely.

In the preparation of his dissenting opinion, he had reached a stage when his thoughts refused to flow easily. He seemed to be in a quagmire of logic, precedent, and law. Sunday morning came, and as the plan which had occurred to me in my wakeful hours of the night before had to be put into action during his absence from the house, I told him that I would not go to church with him that day. Nothing ever kept *him* from church.

As soon as he had left the house, I found the long-hidden Taney inkstand, gave it a good cleaning and polishing, and filled it with ink. Then, taking all the other inkwells from his study table, I put that historic and inspiring inkstand directly before his pad of paper; and, as I looked at it, Taney's inkstand seemed to say to me, "*I* will help him."

I was on the lookout for his return, and met him at the front door. In as cheery a voice as I could muster (for I was beginning to feel somewhat conscience-stricken as I recalled those "evasive answers" of several months before), I said to him:—

"I have put a bit of inspiration on your study table. I believe it is just what you need and I am sure it will help you."

He was full of curiosity, which I refused to gratify. As soon as possible he went to his study. His eye lighting upon the little inkstand, he came running down to my room to ask where in the world I had found it. With mingled shame and joy I then " 'fessed up," telling him how I had secretly hidden the inkstand in the early morning after his impulsive promise to Mrs. Pendleton, because I knew how much he prized and loved it, and felt sure it ought really not to go out of his possession. He laughed over my naughty act and freely forgave it.

The memory of the historic part that Taney's inkstand had played in the Dred Scott decision, in temporarily tightening the shackles of slavery upon the Negro race in the ante-bellum days, seemed that morning to act like magic in clarifying my husband's thoughts in regard to the law that had been intended by Sumner to protect the recently emancipated slaves in the enjoyment of equal "civil rights." His pen fairly flew on that day and, with the running start he then got, he soon finished his dissent.

It was, I think, a bit of "poetic justice" that the small ink-stand in which Taney's pen had dipped when he wrote that famous (or rather infamous) sentence in which he said that "a black man had no rights which a white man was bound to respect,"[110] should have furnished the ink for a decision in which the black man's claim to equal civil rights was as powerfully and even passionately asserted as it was in my husband's dissenting opinion in the famous "Civil Rights" case.[111]

MY ELDEST DAUGHTER'S
MARRIAGE AND DEATH

My oldest daughter, Edith, was the life of our household, helping me in all my social duties. She was a girl of rare qualities, kind of heart, and with gracious and winsome manners. In her own very quiet and sensible way, she had keenly enjoyed our life in Washington.

She was a kind of mother to the other children, always speaking of her brothers as "my boys" and exerting upon them (without any conscious effort) a sweet and tender influence for good.

She had become engaged to Mr. Linus Child[112] of Worcester, Mass. As the wedding was to take place in the Autumn of the year in which we took the Massachusetts Avenue house, we determined to spend the entire summer in Washington. It was the year of Garfield's assassination,[113] and, while for that reason, the summer was a quiet and sad one, we always looked back to it with joy and gratitude, as it was the last summer we had together as an unbroken family.

My daughter's marriage ceremony took place in the New York Avenue Presbyterian Church on the evening of October 20, 1881.[114]

Her feelings as to the sacred associations of the House of God were so strong that she did not wish anything in the way of decorations for the wedding that did not naturally belong there. To her the ceremony of marriage partook of the nature of a sacrament, and she wished nothing brought into the occasion that would make it in any way a mere social function. I remember how she particularly wished that the Communion Table, from which the Lord's Supper was dispensed, should not be moved from its accustomed place simply for the sake of making more room for the bridal party.

The young women with whom she had worked in the Sunday School and in the "Sewing Class" were very anxious to decorate the church with a display of plants and flowers; but she objected, although (after a visit from the Pastor, Dr. John R. Paxton,[115] who expressed the great desire of the people of the church that the church should look unusually pretty on such an occasion) she finally said they might put a few flowers on the reading desk on which the great pulpit Bible rested; but she would hear of nothing more than that.

She also had her own ideas as to the bridal party, and insisted it should be confined entirely to the immediate members of the two families. Her father, to whom she was devoted, was not only to go in with her and "give the Bride away," but he must stand at her left side throughout the ceremony. I went in with the groom and stood at his right, while her three brothers and Mr. Child's three brothers were grouped on either side, making a bridal party of ten.

I heard not a few people speak of it as the most impressive and lovely *church* wedding they had ever seen, the family feature giving a touch to it that struck many as being rather unusual.

Thirteen months later, on November 12, she died in Chicago, where Mr. Child had begun the practice of law.[116] Her body reached our Massachusetts Avenue home on November 14 (her birthday), and the next day her coffin was carried in and out of the New York Avenue Church by the same six brothers and brothers-in-law who had stood near her at her wedding ceremony, together with two cousins who had been devoted to her all through her life.

She left a dear little girl three months old, another Edith, who was to us as dear as one of our very own. She lived with us until her own marriage to Erastus Corning of Albany, New York, which took place in the Spring of 1906, the ceremony being performed in the same church in which her mother had taken her marriage vows.

OUR SOJOURN IN ROCKVILLE, MD.

After our daughter's death, our Massachusetts Avenue home was so changed to us that we felt we must give it up. Moreover, as my husband felt the need of additional economies in order to complete the education of our three sons (who were together at Princeton at that time), we decided to move out into the country. Accordingly, we went to Rockville, Maryland, which is sixteen miles from Washington. We found very comfortable quarters in the house of a Southern gentlewoman, who, although she had never taken "boarders," was willing to turn over a large part of her house to our family. We took our own cook with us, putting her under the supervision of the house-keeper, and we were much more comfortable than we would otherwise have been.

Thus, for two years my husband became a "Commuter," taking the tiresome thirty-two miles ride in and out, six times each week. Three times a week, however, he remained in town until the mid-evening train, in order to teach his class at the Law School of what is now the George Washington University[117]—a position which, in spite of the arduous work it entailed, he felt compelled to retain, as his judicial salary was not large enough to provide for the education and maintenance of our surviving five children and our granddaughter.[118]

A HOME OF OUR OWN AT LAST

We stayed in Rockville for two years and on our return to Washington we moved into a new house which we had built in Euclid Place, on the property whose purchase was engineered by our three sons, who seemed determined upon our securing a permanent home that should be our very own.

For twenty-eight happy years we lived together in the house on University Hill, finding it more and more true, as the years rolled by, that "an old home is like an old violin, because the music of the past is wrought into it."

My husband came to be very fond of the place, greatly enjoying the work of improving it by planting trees and shrubs from time to time; and I can remember with what great joy, on our return from our summer residence in Murray Bay, he would always look up at our house on the hill at Euclid Place, as we neared it, saying, "Oh, it is *good* to be home again."

Sunday Entertainments

Sunday "entertainments" (which I regret to say have now come to be so common an occurrence in "Society" at the National Capital) were almost unknown when I first came to Washington; so that when, during the Cleveland Administration, we were invited through a personal note to take an "informal dinner" on a Sunday evening, at the home of the Attorney General,[119] we were greatly surprised. But as the Attorney General was the head of the Department of Justice, whose functions were so closely related to the Supreme Court, my husband thought that we would have to go. When I said that it would be just "like other dinners—a formal, ceremonious, and full-dress affair," he replied, "Oh, no; the Attorney General would not invite *me* to a formal dinner on a *Sunday* evening, and we must go"—which we did. But as it was just as I had predicted, for we sat down to a large, formal dinner of eighteen or twenty covers; and I was glad that my suggestion that we should go in "full dress" had been carried out.

The next winter, quite early in the season, the second invitation to a Sunday evening dinner was received from the same quarter, being extended, as before, in a personal note from the wife of the Attorney General.

The answering of social invitations was, of course, my province. But, remembering how uncomfortable my husband had been on the former occasion (which had been the only Sunday invitation of that nature that we had ever accepted), I said to him, "You must answer this invitation in your own way"—which he proceeded to do. He wrote, however, to the Attorney General himself, and, after thanking him for his kind invitation, he said that a standing engagement which he had to meet his Pastor every Sunday Evening at the Church service would make it impossible for him to accept the invitation to dinner.

The Attorney General must have told the story of that note, for the tale of my husband's "*standing engagement for the Sunday Evening Service*" has since been repeated many times in Washington as an evidence of his keeping to the old-fashioned ways of the Fathers—which ways, as he always contended, had made our Nation what it is in the eyes of the world. The divergence from those ways distressed and alarmed him to the very close of this life, for he felt that the removal of the barriers that protected Sunday as a "Day of Rest," and as a day specially sacred to the strictly home life, spelt danger and decadence for the coming generations.

WINCHESTER AND THE HARLAN KIN

In 1885, we went to Winchester, Frederick County, Virginia, to spend the summer. We were taken in as boarders by a most charming Southern gentlewoman (Miss Funston), a representative of one of the "Old Virginia" families.

My husband was always interested in meeting new people and learning about the history of communities which he had visited. Going to the Winchester County Clerk's office, he therefore asked permission to look over the records of the earlier generations.

He had always been told that his ancestors on both sides had come from "somewhere" in the Virginia of colonial days; but, as his genealogical information had gone no further than that, he was all the more delighted, in examining the oldest records in the Clerk's office, to find copies of a number of deeds containing not only the family name of Harlan, but also many of the Christian names (some of them very quaint and unusual) that were common in the Kentucky branch of the family. The County Clerk told him that, while there were none of the name then living in Frederick County, there were a number of Harlans still living in the adjoining county of Berkeley, in West Virginia.

My husband immediately determined to go on an expedition in the hope of finding some of his kindred. Hiring a good horse and buggy and taking a small valise with him, he started out on a journey of three or four days. It was a modern instance of "Japhet[h] in Search of his"—Cousins.[120]

The driver seemed well acquainted with the country, and at the end of his first day's drive they arrived at a small town near Martinsburg, West Virginia, called by the poetic name of "Falling Water." And, "lo and behold," in a very attractive old farm house not far from Martinsburg, he stumbled upon his own *second cousin*, George Boyd Harlan,[121] whose immediate family had lived on that farm for three or four generations.

To his great pleasure, though not at all to his surprise (for hospitality was always a Harlan trait), my husband was met with an open-armed welcome. The two cousins became deeply interested, at once, in all that each had to say of the traditions that had been handed down on both the Virginia and Kentucky sides of the family.

What little history my husband had known of the Kentucky branch of the family was quickly told:—

That before the Revolutionary War, two brothers, James and Silas Harlan, had started from "somewhere" in Virginia with Daniel Boone: that, going down the Ohio River, and up the Kentucky in their canoes, they had pushed westward through the forests; and that, at Blue Licks Springs, in 1782 (where a bloody battle was fought with the Indians under the command of a renegade white named Simon Girty) one of those brothers, Silas Harlan (for whom Harlan County was afterwards named) was killed, along with a son of Boone;[122] and that the other brother, my husband's grandfather, was the founder of the Kentucky line.

My husband's family knew nothing of the whereabouts or character of the Virginia home of those two members of Boone's expedition. The missing links of that story were now supplied by my husband's newly-found cousin, who told him of the tradition that had been handed down in the Virginia family.

Three or four generations before, two of George Boyd's great-great-uncles, not finding enough "elbow room" on the ancestral farm of 4,000 acres, had suddenly disappeared, leaving word that they had gone with Daniel Boone, the famous Indian trapper and explorer, who had passed through the "Old Virginia" country on his way to the West. That was the last the Virginia family ever heard of these two boys, except the rumours that Boone's little company went in canoes down the Monongahela and into the Ohio, and then had disappeared into the unknown West.

In fighting the Indians, and in clearing the forest and in founding a new State, those venturous spirits of the early days were too busy to write home; and in this way the Virginia and Kentucky branches of the Harlan family had completely lost touch of each other, until that day when my husband, at the end of that buggy ride from Winchester, stumbled upon the cousin who still held 300 or 400 acres of the original estate of 4,000 acres.

———

The two cousins then proceeded to exchange all that each knew of the still earlier history of the family.

As both had always been told, the first Harlans in this country were Quakers; indeed, they were *Irish Quakers.*

That last statement, however, would seem to be a contradiction in terms, when one contrasts the spirit of "Donnybrook Fair"[123] with the peaceful tenets of the "Friends." The family was really of English origin, having been driven out of England at the time of the early persecution of the Quakers. They remained for two generations in Ireland, long enough and in sufficiently large numbers to be described by American genealogists as "Irish Quakers." Among them were the common ancestors of the Virginia and Kentucky Harlans, and they settled first in Pennsylvania. Later, some of the name pushed down to Virginia, where they seemed to find it necessary to give up their Quaker ideas and turn Presbyterian, so that they could fight the Indians.

My husband learned from his West Virginia cousin that for several generations the Harlan family had been represented in the Eldership of the Presbyterian Church; and also that, as far back as the oldest inhabitant could remember, some one of the family had been a teacher in "The Little Red School House" that meant so much to the country people of bygone generations.

My husband's cousin had in his possession the original parchment deed of the ancestral estate of 4,000 acres that had been sold to their common ancestor by Lord Fairfax. The boundaries of the tract were indicated in the quaint fashion of those early days. The line started, we will say, from "a white birch," at a certain point, and continued for so many rods at a certain angle, to "a walnut tree," or "a hickory tree"—each tree being blazed—and so on.

The survey upon which this deed was based was undoubtedly the survey that was made by the youthful engineer who afterwards became the "Father of his Country" and whose first important job at the age of [15] was the work of surveying the vast estates of Lord Fairfax, with whom the young George Washington was such a prime favourite.[124]

I must tell, here, of an amusing incident connected with this visit to George Boyd Harlan.

The Virginia cousin, who like my husband was a great reader of the Bible, had made use of a very striking phrase which aptly illustrated a certain matter under discussion. My husband asked him the origin of the quotation and was told that it came "from the Bible." Very emphatically, my husband replied that that was not in *his* Bible. Thereupon, the Good Book was brought out and searched; but the Virginia Harlan could not find the phrase and the Washington cousin, as he made his adieus for the return trip to Winchester, boasted somewhat humorously as to his superior knowledge of the Scriptures.

But, immediately upon his return to Winchester, he consulted that Concordance and found that the quotation *was* a Scriptural one. He wrote at once to his Virginia cousin, and backed down in the laconic confession, "I find that *my* Bible is the same as *yours*."

European Experiences

Coming home one day in the spring of 1892, my husband told me that President Harrison[125] had sent for him that morning and, after a pleasant talk, had told him that he wished to appoint him as one of the American representatives on the Arbitration Tribunal[126] that was to meet during the next winter, to settle a controversy that had arisen between Canada and the United States in regard to the Fur Seal Fishing in the Behring Sea,[127] and to provide regulations for the proper protection and preservation of the seals habitually resorting to the Pribilof Islands.

Knowing that long periods of time were generally consumed in such controversies, my husband, after acknowledging the great honour which the President wished to confer upon him, said at once that he could not think of leaving his family for so long a time. "But," said the President, "I do not wish you to leave your family; you must take them with you." This put a different light on the matter and my husband told the President that he would talk the matter over with me.

Our eldest son, Richard, was then abroad in search of health for his wife, our second daughter (Laura)[128] being with them. The proffered appointment not only made it possible to give our youngest daughter the advantages of European travel, but opened up to my husband and myself the opportunity of seeing something of the Old World— an opportunity we had always longed for, but had never had. My husband, therefore, concluded to accept the position and, having rented our Washington home to Mr. Justice Brewer,[129] we sailed for France on August 6, on the French liner "La Touraine," taking with us our daughter Ruth[130] and our little grand-daughter, Edith Harlan Child.

The voyage was uneventful, the weather fine, and the water smooth; and, although my daughter and I did not feel sure enough of ourselves to go to the table, but had our meals on deck, we did not suffer at all until the fifth day, when a storm overtook us and then for a day and a half we kept to our rooms. My husband and little grand-daughter proved to be good sailors and never missed a meal. At 8 o'clock on Sunday morning, August 14, we landed at [Le] Havre, finding ourselves indeed in a strange land, as none of us spoke French. We went direct to Paris and after a stay of a few days, we left (on August 13) for Schaffhausen Falls, where my son Richard and his wife and Laura were to meet us; and 4 o'clock the next afternoon found us a re-united family in the Old World, so new and strange to my husband and myself. After a few days near those beautiful Falls of the Rhine, we went to M[ü]rren, by the wonderful Br[ü]nig Pass.[131]

I shall never forget the overwhelming impression made upon me and, especially, upon my husband, by the sublime mountains through which we passed.

From his window on one side of the carriage, he drank in the wonderful scenery, while I looked out, awe-stricken, at the wonderful scenery on the other side. To my son and his wife, we must have seemed like two children; for my husband kept calling to me "come and look" at the scenery on *his* side, while I kept calling to him to "come and look" at the marvels on my side.

He was always very shy and undemonstrative in expressing his feelings. But on this occasion the sight of the sublime in nature, such as he had never seen before, overwhelmed him. His eyes filled with tears and he was too much moved to speak. All he could say was to stammer, "This looks like the Gate of Heaven."

After settling us at M[ü]rren, my son left us for America on August 27, from Southampton on the Hamburg-American liner, "Normannia." His trip proved a most eventful one. Cholera broke out in the steerage and second cabin, and for two weeks he was held in quarantine in New York Harbour and on Fire Island. Our anxiety can be more easily imagined than described. Cholera was raging in Hamburg and all Europe and, afterwards, New York were thrown into a panic. Our fears, however, were soon allayed by telegrams from New York and the incident proved to be no more than a vexatious and trying delay of our son's plans.

MONTREUX

The excitement attending the Cholera scare confined us to Switzerland for our summer travels and we finally settled down in a very comfortable *pension* at Montreux, Switzerland. Here my husband left us, sailing for home on September 21st, for having learned that the Arbitration Tribunal would not begin its sessions until late in the Winter (as the records in the case had to be translated into French), he considered it his duty to return to Washington and do his work in the Supreme Court for the months of October, November, and part of December.

In the Montreaux *pension* we had a very disagreeable and rather amusing experience with a Prussian Army officer. He occupied the room next to mine, the two rooms being separated by double doors which were by no means sound-proof. He was prone to turn night into day, and in his home-comings in "the wee sma' hours" of the morning, he often disturbed us by singing and stamping around his room. The annoyance was so great that my husband, before he left, had said to us that if such disturbances continued I must find rooms elsewhere.

A piano had been moved into our sitting room for the children's practice and although they were scrupulously careful never to use it before nine in the morning, his "High Mightiness," the Prussian Captain, objected very strenuously to their forenoon practice. Because of the exalted view he took of his position as a Captain in the German Army, he seemed to think that *we* should be as *quiet* during the day as *he* was *noisy* at night, and forthwith, out of revenge, he began deliberately to make such a row every night as to become unbearable.

Having stood it for several nights, each night bringing something more and more to complain of, we determined to put a stop to it. Taking the English-speaking head-waiter with us as our interpreter, we went to the office of the proprietor and told him that the noise must stop, or we would leave the house. He promised to speak to the "Herr Hauptmann" and also to move me to another room as soon as he could.

The Captain *was* spoken to, but, that night, in order to vindicate his dignity, he out-did himself in annoying and disturbing us. Coming in at about two o'clock in the morn-ing, he began in a very loud key to whistle a jingling air, over and over again. Next, he would sing it at the top of his voice. Then he hammered awhile with a very heavy stick, and either tripped, fell or jumped as hard as he could, for the whole floor shook, after which he ended the perform-ance with a loud guffaw.

I was on the point of ringing my bell until someone should come up from the office. But fearing to rouse the house, I decided to wait with as much patience as I could muster until the morning, when I went again to the propri-etor and told him that I could no longer stand those an-noyances from such a vulgar, drunken fellow. He promised that rather than let our large family go, "Herr Hauptmann" should leave. What he said to him in private must have been to the point and for a few nights we were allowed to sleep in peace. Our bumptious neighbour seemed to re-gard us with a certain respect; it was evidently a new expe-rience to him to have three women plucky enough to dare to complain of *him*—an Army officer in the service of the Kaiser.

But his chastening at our hands was not yet complete. After a few nights of quiet, he came in at half-past one in the morning, declaiming (as if to an audience) something that evidently amused him greatly, for he was seized with violent laughter. For ten minutes he made night hideous,[132] until I began to be alarmed lest he might be crazy.

Hearing him about to go out in the hall and still laughing very loudly, I put my finger on the bell button and held it there, while the bell rang out, long and loud, in the stillness of the night. I determined not to take my finger off that button until some one came from the office.

The sound of the jangling bell had an effect upon the Captain's befuddled brain that was fairly magical. I heard him dash across the floor of his room and jump into bed and he was quite quiet as a mouse—not only that night but ever afterwards.

The old *concierge* finally answered my summons. With eyes standing out in fright and speaking under his breath, he asked me what was the matter. In as loud a voice as I could muster, I said, "That man next door is making such a noise that it is impossible to sleep, and it must be stopped." The old fellow said in his broken English, "I tell him in ze morning," and then he disappeared.

The next morning, in a tone loud enough for the "Herr Hauptmann" to hear at the next table, I told the English-speaking head-waiter that we intended to *"ring the Captain to sleep every night, if he made it necessary."*

My determination to do this had its full effect, for we had no further trouble from the Prussian Captain during our stay, except that, whenever he passed us in the dining room, he attempted most insolently to stare us out of countenance. It was evident that, in *his* world, "the Frau" was compelled to know her place and to keep it.

ITALIAN TOUR

The wife and daughters of Senator Morgan,[133] the other American representative on the Behring Sea Arbitration Tribunal, arrived at Montreux the last week in October, on their way to Italy and they were very anxious to have me join them for that trip. Though I felt sure that my husband would wish me to go, yet in his absence it seemed at first impossible for me to decide such an important matter for myself, for I had always looked to him for advice and guidance. Realizing, however, that I should never again be so near to Sunny Italy, I took my courage in both hands, and decided to go. This exhibition of independence was so new and surprising to my daughters, that they called my Italian trip "Mother's Revolt."

I decided to take my daughter Ruth as my travelling companion, and we arranged to join the Morgans at Lausanne, the time of our departure being fixed for the 1st of November. My daughter Laura and my daughter-in-law, Mrs. Richard Harlan, and grand-daughter, Edith Child, remained in Montreux for a few weeks longer, after which they went to Paris to select our quarters for the winter.

On the (for me) eventful November morning (when, for the first time, I was to take an important journey without my husband) we were to take the 10:20 train to Lausanne, changing there for the train to Geneva, and thence to Venice.

After tugging up a hill to the Montreux Station we were met with the discouraging news that the 10:20 train had been taken off that very day, the next train leaving at 12:30 and reaching Lausanne only twenty minutes before the arrival of the train for Geneva. It was provoking in the extreme as I had wished to have time in Lausanne to buy circular tickets from Cook's.

Going home to the *pension,* I gave a good lecture to the stupid old concierge whose business it was to keep up with all the changes in the time-table. He argued with me that the station-man did not know and that the train was still running. For all the impression I could make on him I might as well have spoken to a stone wall. I went up to my room to wait and in a few moments he came running out of breath, screaming in his broken English (which he thought was of the best variety, for he aired it on all occasions), "The *Station* is going by. Look, Madame." Nothing would do but that I must go to the front window, from where I could hear a train passing, but could see nothing. I learned afterwards from my daughter-in-law, who took pains to inquire, that the train in question must have been a freight train and that there really was no 10:20 train on that day.

At Lausanne, Mrs. Morgan and her daughters joined us. They were most delightful travelling companions, the two Southern girls, with their fund of stories and quaint humour, making the time pass most pleasantly. After a fleeting glimpse of Milan and Verona, we went to Venice.

I shall not attempt to describe my impressions of that wonderful city where the sound of horses' hoofs are never heard, nor speak of the matchless works of art that are the pride and glory of Venice.

The picture that especially stands out in my memories

of Venice is Titian's "Assumption of the Virgin Mary."[134] I got my first glimpse of it at the end of a long corridor leading up to it; but the guide, as if to emphasize the wonder of it, led us through a side passage and suddenly brought us in awed silence before that immortal symbol of Universal Motherhood. The picture was so exactly what my imagination had painted that I felt for the moment that I had seen it before and was loath to leave. I had just the same feeling on my first visit to Westminster Abbey; it was as if I had grown up under its very shadows. I suppose we have all had these curious feelings at times, in which we seem to live over again the experiences of a former existence, and I sometimes wonder if that is what Life Everlasting may mean.

One morning in Rome, my daughter and I found ourselves locked fast in our room and we had to get the chamber maid to let us out through Mrs. Morgan's room—an experience which made me think of "Il Papa" locked up in the Vatican (though *he* could get out easily enough, if he chose to do so).

On December 17, we left Rome for Pisa, arriving late at night and spending the next day in seeing the curiously interesting Campo Santo and the wonderful Leaning Tower, where Galileo made those experiments with the pendulum which led him, in the face of Rome's threat of ex-communication, to assert that "the earth still moves." Although the tower had been standing fourteen feet out of the perpendicular for 600 hundred years or more, I will confess that I was afraid to add *my* weight to the down side, for fear that it might be the "last straw on the camel's back;" and so neither Ruth or I made the ascent.

I had been warned by my daughter-in-law about the

beggars in Italy that would meet us at every turn, with hands outstretched for pennies, and having acquired "a most frugal mind, though on pleasure bent,"[135] I double-knotted my purse strings (as my daughter put it) and arriving in Paris with so large a surplus in my half of the Letter of Credit, that my daughter accused me of leaving in my wake a mob of beggars wailing with disappointment.

BACK TO PARIS

We arrived in Paris on December 22, my husband rejoining us on Christmas Eve, after a stormy voyage, and we settled ourselves in a pleasant suite of rooms at the Hotel Lafond on the *rue Tremouille,* Senator Morgan and his family also taking rooms there.

Accompanied by Mr. T. Jefferson Coolidge,[136] the American Minister to France, my husband called very promptly on M. Carnot, the President of the Republic.[137]

A day or so later an invitation came to us through Mr. Coolidge, putting the President's Box at the Grand Opera at our disposal, which my daughters and I made use of, accompanied by Mr. Coolidge's daughter and Lieutenant Rodgers. The Opera was *Salammbo*,[138] by _____, and was new to me. As the Grand Ballet was the first ballet I had ever seen, I will confess that, to me, at the tender age of fifty summers, it was quite a shock. The thirty or more dancers were attired in garments (so-called) of such gauzy texture as to suggest nothing more than a butterfly's wing. But it was certainly very beautiful and I must admit that, in spite of my inherited feelings of disapproval, I was greatly entertained by it.

The next few weeks were taken up in receiving and returning numerous calls both official and personal.

I remember being greatly amused by an English maid who answered our ring at the door of Mrs. X., an American lady living in Paris. The maid evidently felt herself quite at home with the French language; for, in response to my question as to whether "*Mrs. X*" was "at home," she glibly replied:— "No, Madam; *Madame* X is out *sorting*"—that was as near as that cockney maid could get to the French verb, *sortir.*

In due time I went with Mrs. Sears to call on Madame Carnot at the Palais de l'Elysée, the "White House" of the French Republic. To my mind it did not compare with our much less pretentious, but far more stately and impressive, Executive Mansion, with its spacious and beautiful grounds.

Lackies in livery stood, two and two, in every doorway we passed through [in] order to reach the *Salon* where we found eight or ten people seated in a semi-circle, with Madame Carnot in the centre. We were announced in stentorian tones by the French majordomo, who ignoring the "H" in my name called me "Madame 'Arlan." Madame Carnot rose and came forward to meet us half way, being very cordial in her greeting. Her English was quite broken and we were, perforce, confined to a very few words, while I was emboldened to air the little French I knew, the lady next to me (I learned afterwards that she was the wife of the Minister of Justice) helping me out most politely.

THE BEHRING SEA ARBITRATION TRIBUNAL

The Arbitration Tribunal was composed of a very unusual body of men.

Baron de Courcelle,[139] the Chairman, who for several years was the French Ambassador in London and who spoke our language perfectly, was a most courtly and charming man. I greatly enjoyed the occasions when I met his wife socially, although our conversation was carried on in the two languages, each of us fearing to venture on unfamiliar ground. Both of us, however, understood enough of what each other said, so that an interpreter was unnecessary.

Lord Hannen[140] and Sir John Thompson[141] represented the English and the Canadian interests, while Senator Morgan and my husband represented the United States. The two Arbitrators from the neutral countries being the Marquis de Venosta of Italy and Mr. Gram of Norway.

Lord Hannen was a most delightful old man, reminding me in many ways of Justice William Strong[142] of our Supreme Court, who was one of our dearest family friends. As the months went by, my husband and Lord Hannen became very warm friends, their friendship being afterwards kept up through occasional letters, until Lord Hannen's death in 1894.

We found Mr. and Mrs. Gram to be so much like Americans that we felt at home with them from the very beginning, and, during the many years that passed after our meeting, the two families never lost interest in each other.

My husband's American colleague Senator Morgan had been a friend of some years standing. Their daily work on the Behring Sea Tribunal drew them closer together on account of their common interest in their country's welfare, and their admiration and respect for each other grew steadily.

The advocates of Britain's and Canada's case, Sir Charles Russell[143] and Sir Richard Webster[144] (afterwards Lord Alverston), were well matched by the lawyers who represented the American side, Mr. Edward J. Phelps[145] of Vermont, Mr. James C. Carter[146] and Mr. Frederick R. Coudert[147] of New York, whose brilliant pleas for our case made us very proud of them as representatives of the American Bar.

The morning Sessions of the Tribunal were largely attended every day, the wives of the Arbitrators and lawyers in the case counting it as the day's greatest pleasure to be present at the hearing.

QUEEN VICTORIA'S THRIFT

In this connection I may repeat a story told to me by Mrs. Phelps, which brings out Queen Victoria's proverbial thriftiness in an amusing way.

While we were in Paris Mrs. Phelps made a visit to London, and was present at the ceremony connected with the dedication of (as I recall it) The Albert Memorial. As Mr. Phelps had recently been the American Minister at the Court of St. James, she was given a prominent place, not far from the Queen.[148] She found her looking unusually well and she especially noticed the Queen's bonnet as being very becoming in shape and style. Turning to one of the ladies-in-waiting (with whom she had rather pleasant and close relations), Mrs. Phelps commented upon Her

Majesty's fine appearance. She especially admired her beautiful bonnet, saying it must have come from "Madame X," who was the fashionable court milliner at that period. Greatly to Mrs. Phelps' surprise and amusement, the Lady-in-waiting, under cover of a carefully raised hand (so that none but Mrs. Phelps might hear such a "Lese Majeste"), replied, "No, indeed; a suggestion that it might be ordered from Madame X. did not appeal to Her Majesty, and *I* made that bonnet myself this morning."

A RECEPTION AT THE PALAIS DE L'ELYSÉE

I quote from my diary the description of a reception given to the Arbitrators at the Palais de l'Elysée on February 2nd.

We started very promptly, hoping to get ahead of the crowd; but, as every one else had done the same thing, we found ourselves in an almost never-ending line of carriages coming from both directions in the Champs Elysées. We went at a such a snail-like pace that, after sitting in our carriage for half an hour and becoming chilled, we got out and walked to the Palais, as many others did. We made our way into the Court without any trouble, as only one carriage at a time was allowed to drive in.

After entering the large vestibule of the Palais, we found ourselves in the crush of people and with great difficulty we reached a place where we were to check our wraps. When we tried to reach the stairway, we found a solid wedge of humanity blocking the way and as the presentations were made very slowly, at the top of the stairway, we resigned ourselves to a long delay. But Mr. Jay, one of the Secretaries of the American Legation, spying my husband's tall figure and bald head, came toward us with the Directeur.

He made way for us and we were taken up a narrow passage screened off from the main part of the broad stairway by flower pots, one on each step, and by a row of French soldiers on the other side, who stood so motionless that I thought at first that they were wax figures.

Our rapid progress through the throng seemed to rouse the spleen of some of the long-suffering people on the stairway, and we had to endure some rather cross looks and many a French shrug of the shoulder. My daughter, Laura, heard one lady say in French, "these foreigners, they are everywhere."

In less than two minutes we had been piloted through the crowd and were introduced to President Carnot, in loud tones, as "Monsieur Justice and Madame 'Arlan," and were soon safely landed in the Diplomatic Salon, where we stayed for a few minutes, after which we joined the procession passing through the various rooms.

It seemed strange to be in such a jam and yet hear our own language spoken only now and then. It was a motley crowd, much more so than we ever see at the White House. I suppose it was made up largely of the middle-class people of the officialdom, for the *noblesse,* and the old aristocracy of the Fauberg St. Germain, had little in common with the rue St. Honoré.

One thing that especially struck me was the awe-stricken and almost breathless whispering of the people to each other, as they passed through the rooms. Apparently they were afraid to speak out loud. This was more noticeable when there were only a few people at a time.

The Palace was magnificent, one corridor, which was hung with the finest Gobelin tapestry,[149] being especially gorgeous. I did not see the ball-room but my daughters described it as being about the size of the great East Room at the White House. There was a small room where refreshments were served for the Diplomats and the families of the Arbitrators. The large Supper Room, elsewhere, was for the crowd. We got back to our hotel about one o'clock, having to walk a block and a half before we could get the carriage."

———

The next day, with Mr. Coolidge and Mr. Sears, we called on Madame Ribot, the wife of the Minister of Foreign Affairs.[150] By birth she was a Chicago woman, but, after a residence of twenty-seven years in Paris, she had become thoroughly French in sympathy and in tastes. French ladies, as a rule, receive guests in a fashion that greatly conduces to stiffness, the hostess sitting in the centre of a circle of callers. But, on that afternoon, Madame Ribot, in a most natural and easy manner and entirely without effort, succeeding in interesting her callers in each other. Two ladies, who sat at quite a little distance from her and who were evidently unacquainted, were introduced to each other by their hostess in such a tactful way as to make them feel very much complimented.

MY HUSBAND'S LONDON HOLIDAY

Taking advantage of the recess in the proceedings of the Arbitration Tribunal, my husband and our son Richard went over to London early in February, where they spent a delightful ten days together.

My husband greatly enjoyed a dinner that was given to him by the American Minister, Mr. Robert T. Lincoln[151]— at which were present all of the leading lights of the British Bench and Bar, including Lord Chief Justice Coleridge,[152] the Lord Chancellor, the Master of the Rolls (Lord Esher),[153] Sir Francis Jeune, Lord Justice Bowen[154] and Lord Morris[155] of the Irish Bench.

The Hon. James Bryce[156] gave him an informal dinner in the Parliament Building, and there was also a small dinner given to him by Mr. Frederick Huth Jackson, one of the Governors of the Bank of England.

A RADICAL'S TRIBUTE TO QUEEN VICTORIA'S TACT

At a dinner given to my husband by Lord Chief Justice Coleridge, my son Richard, after dinner, had a conversation with Lord Coleridge and a young English Barrister which is worth recording because of the extraordinarily frank expression of Lord Coleridge's personal opinion of Queen Victoria, and especially of the Prince Consort.

My son, pointing to a splendid bust in the upper hall (which he recognized as one of Oliver Cromwell), asked Lord Coleridge the name of the sculptor. "Oh," said Lord Coleridge, "that is a replica from the life-sized statue of the Protector that was made by Isaac Bell,[157] in the early years of Queen Victoria's reign." And, then turning to the young barrister, Lord Coleridge fairly took my son's breath away by saying: "As you know, *I was never a great admirer of the Queen;* but," continued Lord Coleridge, "I must say that the Queen was always a perfect lady, in her consideration for other people's feelings."

And then to illustrate the Queen's kindness of heart and her rare tact, Lord Coleridge told the story of a visit which the Queen made to Mr. Bell's studio, just after he had finished his great statue of Cromwell.

The sculptor had received a message from the Queen saying that she was coming to his studio. He was very much perturbed, because the most conspicuous object in it at the time was that statue of Cromwell. It was not feasible to take it out and his first idea was to cover it up. But, realizing that the Queen would be certain to ask what was under the sheet, he made up his mind to leave the statue undraped, and let the Queen take his studio as she found it.

When the Queen's eye fell on the statue, she at once put the sculptor at his ease, by expressing her great admiration for this last proof of his genius and she astonished him by saying:—"Mr. Bell, we must put that statue on the Embankment."

When Lord Coleridge had finished with his charming illustration of the Queen's rare tact, my son innocently asked whether the statue had been put on the Embankment. Lord Coleridge replied: "Bless your soul, no; why, there is not a public statue of Cromwell in all England."

That was a fact in 1893; but, since then, I believe that a statue of Cromwell has been put in the St. Stephen's Hall in the Parliament Buildings.

And, then turning to the young barrister, Lord Coleridge gave another proof of his radicalism by saying:—*"I suppose we have that miserable Prince Consort to thank for that"*—

referring to the Toryism which the Prince Consort endeavoured to instill into the mind of the young Queen.

On February 13, during their London visit, my husband and son had the rare good luck to hear the great speech, of more than two hours in length, with which Gladstone[158] introduced his last "Home Rule Bill."[159]

A DINNER AT THE BRITISH EMBASSY

One of the most interesting and unique entertainments I have ever attended was a dinner given in Paris by Lord Dufferin,[160] the British Ambassador, in honour of the British Arbitrators and Counsel in the Behring Sea case. By an interesting coincidence the dinner was given on the evening of Washington's Birthday.

On arriving at the British Embassy, we were ushered into a large vestibule where we left our wraps. Lackeys innumerable (with powdered hair, knee breeches and blue livery) stood about—here, there and everywhere, two at almost every door. In stentorian tones the majordomo called out our names as we entered the main *salon*, where we were received most graciously by Lord and Lady Dufferin. Lord Dufferin was a most courtly Diplomat, and Lady Dufferin, his junior by several years, charmed us by her rare simplicity and cordiality.

Lord Dufferin took me out to dinner, greatly to my surprise, for I had heard that on such occasions the French representatives always claimed, and were given, precedence over everyone else. Baron De Courcelle, the French Arbitrator, was, however, given the first place at Lady Dufferin's right, while, my husband sat at her left, taking out

Madame _____, a grand-daughter of one of Napoleon Bonaparte's great Generals.

I give here a description of the dinner from a diary which I kept at that time.

The British Embassy was once the Palace belonging to Princess Pauline of Borghesi, sister of Napoleon I.[161] At the time I saw it, most of its furnishings were just about as she left them. It was bought for the British Embassy by the Duke of Wellington after the Battle of Waterloo, and had ever since been the residence of the British Ambassadors. Wellington himself occupied it and, altogether, it was so full of historic interest that I would have liked to look into every nook and cranny of it.

In its arrangement and plan it is not unlike the White House, though it is much less imposing, while the bizarre tone of its colouring and furnishing detracts much from its elegance. The woodwork was very ornate, being in white or light coloured tints, with a great deal of gold; and the gilt furniture was upholstered in bright red satin damask.

A great wood fire blazed in the room in which we were received and the walls were lined with countless mirrors, the chandeliers being of crystal. And there were many curious bits of old furniture and ornaments.

The dining table was as wide as the "State" table at the White House, but on this occasion it was not so long, only twenty-four being seated at it. The wood work in the dining room was of black oak or walnut; but on account of the light tinted walls the effect was not as somber as might have been expected.

The table decorations were of rare and curious interest, consisting largely of the glass, silver and gold objects that had been given to our host in the different countries to which he had been sent as the British Ambassador, or Governor General. There were as many as six elegant *repousse* silver cases in which were the documents extending the Freedom of the cities to which he had been sent on various missions during his diplomatic career. Their shape reminded me of the cylindrical tin tubes that contained my boys' college diplomas. They lay upon narrow, red velvet cushions, or rests, and they made a brave show.

Glittering at each end of the table was a huge gold tinselled necklace, in the form of a rope, as large around as my wrist and long enough to reach the waist of a tall man, and ending in a diamond-shaped pendant. Each necklace encircled a magnificent inverted gold bowl, which rested on a rack of most beautiful open-gold work.

There were also four or five heavy silver trowels with which Lord Dufferin had officiated at the laying of corner stones.

A Tale of Spurs and Roses

Most curious of all, and very incongruous as table ornaments, were six or eight spurs, the heel pieces of which were made of heavy silver, the spurs themselves being of gold. Sharing the honours with the spurs and evidently connected with them in some way, were some gold roses, the petals of which were worked out in such perfection as to take away altogether the metallic effect. The three leaves and the stems upon which the rose lay were raised upon a base of gold about a third of an inch thick.

With true American curiosity I questioned my host

about the many beautiful things which I saw, and the tale he told of the roses and the spurs was most interesting.

The Dufferin estate lay side by side with that of his wife's family; but formerly the Dufferin land, at a certain point, cut off a corner of the other property. It was considered wise by both families to straighten out the line; but, as a trade in money would have offended the feelings of all concerned, it was agreed that, at Christmas and birthday anniversaries, a spur (the symbol of one house) and a rose (the symbol of the other house) should be given in payment for the land thus transferred.

There were also huge beaten silver bowls, or jardinieres, filled with lovely flowers, and innumerable smaller vases of glass and silver. And we were served on silver plates.

Some Historic Candelabra

On the table were three old-fashioned candelabra, whose history is worthy of record.

Lord Dufferin told me that they had originally belonged to one of the Bonapartes, probably to Princess Pauline Borghesi, the sister of Napoleon I. Lord Dufferin had first seen them, and greatly admired them, at a dinner given in that very palace, in the time of the Second Empire, by "Prince Napoleon" (known more generally by his nick-name, "Plon-Plon"), the cousin of Napoleon III.[162] Lord Dufferin knew the Prince quite well and was with him for several days at a hunting party at which time he gave the Prince a very handsome rifle.

A few years after, when the Second Empire was on its last legs, Lord Dufferin was passing through Paris. Looking in the newspaper one morning, he noticed the advertisement of a sale of the household and personal effects of "Prince Napoleon"; and Lord Dufferin told me, with a twinkle in his eye, that he said to himself;

"Now, 'Plon-Plon' is just the fellow to sell my rifle, if he is in need of money. I will go to the auction and buy it back."

Lord Dufferin proceeded to do so and, with the rifle, he also bought in those three candelabra, which he afterwards took to India when he was made Viceroy, and they adorned the Vice-regal table on all State occasions.

In the course of time the son of "Plon-Plon," when travelling in India, was invited to dine with the Viceroy and Lady Dufferin, when he sat under the light of his own ancestral candelabra. And, finally, the intersting tale of the candelabra was rounded out by their return, for the time being, to the very same Palace in Paris where they originally belonged.

One of the candelabra was so odd that it is worth describing. It stood on a gilt plateau about four feet long and slightly raised from the table. On each corner was a horseman in silver and gilt.

The standard of the candelabrum itself was square and quite large, perhaps six inches at the base and about four feet in height, tapering to a point. At irregular intervals there extended arms of uneven length, upon which were supported small gilt canoes, with oars crossed in the middle. At the end of the canoes were sockets for the candles. The whole effect was more odd than beautiful, though it was in perfect keeping with the old Palace.

These candelabra, I may add, were made of such gilt as we rarely see now-a-days.

RETURN FROM EUROPE

After the final adjournment of the Behring Sea Tribunal, my daughter and I, with my grand-daughter, went to Aix les Bains, my husband going to Buxton, England, as a quiet place where he could prepare his opinions in the case. He found very homelike quarters in the home of two English spinsters, who were most kind to him.

Having finished the preparation of his opinions he seized the opportunity for a trip he had always wanted to make in Scotland, his great desire being to visit the Island of Iona, which many scholars declare to have been the early, historic home of the Presbyterian Church of Scotland. But fierce winds and bad weather, and the near approach of our day of sailing, made the trip impossible, and my husband, after a brief visit in Edinburgh, got only as far as Oban. At this latter place he had his first sight of a regiment of kilted Highlanders, marching behind their pipers. The sound of the bag-pipes, the swing of the kilts, and the martial bearing of the regiment as it swept by him, so completely lifted him out of himself, that he threw his judicial dignity to the winds and, before he knew it, he found himself marching at the side of the pipers, block after block!

He joined us at Liverpool just before our sailing, much refreshed by his hurried and interesting trip to Scotland.

After our fifteen months of stay in Europe (very little of which, however, had been spent in travelling), it was most interesting to see my husband's joy at being again in his own country and with his own people. Our trip abroad had been an experience that my husband and myself had never dreamed of having; for any chance of seeing the Old World we had always thrown to our children, giving each of them every opportunity that presented itself for travel. We had never thought to cross the ocean ourselves and, but for the opportunity offered to my husband of serving his country on the Behring Sea Tribunal, we would never have gone.

We returned to our own land just in time to see the wonderful Chicago Exposition,[163] after which my husband resumed his work on the Bench with new vigor and interest.

MURRAY BAY

After trying Halifax and Montpelier, Vermont, as summer resorts (the chief charm of the latter place being the care of our little grand-daughter Lysbeth Harlan, whose mother and father were spending that summer in Europe), we decided to spend the summer of 1897 on the lower St. Lawrence, at Pointe-au-Pic, in the Province of Quebec— or "Murray Bay,"[164] as it is more generally called.

My son Richard and his wife, having been there for the summer of 1896, had found it so attractive that they had taken the responsibility of deciding our next summer's plans for us, and they even went so far as to engage a cottage large enough for both our households, feeling sure that they could prevail upon us to try that delightful Canadian summer resort. They had no difficulty in doing so, and quite early in June of the following year (1897), my two daughters and I went to Murray Bay as the advance guard, my husband remaining behind for a course of lectures which he had agreed to give to the "Summer Law School" of the University of Virginia.

The cottage thus chosen for us by my son nestled among the spruces on the cliffs overlooking the majestic St. Lawrence. It was large enough for our double household of seven, consisting of my husband, myself, our two daughters and little grand-daughter (Edith Harlan Child) and my son Richard and his wife.

Shortly after his arrival at Murray Bay, sometime in July, my husband was persuaded to learn the game of golf, which was, and still is, the chief diversion among the men visitors at Murray Bay. It was a radical change in his habits of life, for up to that summer he had never indulged in any out-of-door diversion as a relief from the constant strain of his exhausting professional labours. It proved to be a most healthful pastime for him, both mentally and physically. His love for the game grew upon him steadily, and during the next fifteen summers which he spent at Murray Bay his interest in it never flagged.

As my son Richard was the one who persuaded my husband to take up Golf, giving him his first lessons, he is better qualified than I am to tell the story of how his father became interested in "The Ancient and Royal Game." [This story was never added.]

Our first summer at Murray Bay proved to be so satisfactory that my husband and two of our sons (Richard and John Maynard) took a three years' lease on *Maison Rouge,* the cottage belonging to the Hon. Edward Blake[165] of Toronto, who at that time was a member of the British Parliament, representing one of the Irish constituencies.

Our household during our first summer at *Maison Rouge* (1898) was an experiment which I fear would have been hazardous in some families. In addition to my husband, myself, two daughters and our grand-daughter (Edith Child), there were under the same roof our two sons, Richard and James, with their wives and mothers-in-law, our third son, John, with his wife and little daughter—fourteen people in all.[166] The mother-in-law of our third son, with her unmarried daughter, was compelled to find rooms in a near-by boarding house; but they spent much of their time at *Maison Rouge*.

A friend of my son-in-law (Linus Child), visiting Murray Bay for that summer, was asked on his return to his home in Massachusetts if he "had made the acquaintance of the Harlans while at Murray Bay." He answered in the affirmative, but with note of surprise in his voice:— "Oh, yes, but it was the *funniest* household you *ever* saw. Why, every time you turned round, you met a mother-in-law."

Notwithstanding the risky experiment of mixing so many mothers-in-law and other kinds of "things-in-law"—our *Maison Rouge* household had lovely times together for two seasons, with no friction or jarring incident to mar the harmony of our happy days together.

Murray Bay became so attractive to us as a summer home for our family that at the end of the second summer in *Maison Rouge*, my son John Maynard took a long lease on a new cottage for himself. Next year, Richard's wife bought a beautifully wooded tract of land and built a cottage for herself, which she named Tamarack Top—because of the feathery larches that abound in the woods behind her cottage.

My husband and I remained, meanwhile, in *Maison Rouge* until 1902, when we moved into a cottage of our own, which we built on the land adjoining Tamarack Top. Its very location—a sunny meadow on the high bluff or brae—led me to call our permanent summer home "Braemead," a name that seemed natural to the Scotch-Irish blood which I inherited from my dear father.

From its lovely verandahs, we could see the majestic St. Lawrence and the far off opposite shore, sixteen miles distance; the beautiful curve of the bay into which the Murray River empties; the bold promontory of the Cap-à-l'Aigle,[167] the beautiful profile of the picturesque Laurentian range to the North, purpling in the evening lights; and the spruce-clad nearer hills towering above us at the West.

The panorama in every direction gave us pictures of surpassing beauty, which no brush could ever rival or do justice to.

My husband and I passed many hours together on the Braemead verandah, drinking in the beauties of the scene, my husband often saying with a thrill of loving reverence in his voice as he thought of the Giver of "Every good and perfect gift,"[168] "I do not believe there is a more beautiful spot on God's earth."

The French Canadian natives (or *habitants*) greatly interested my husband. The ingenuity which, notwithstanding their meagre opportunities, they displayed in really skillful work in certain directions was a source of never-ending wonder to him.

THE MURRAY BAY CHURCH

Among his interests at Murray Bay, the welfare of the unique Union Church there, which was started some fifty years ago under the comprehensive title of "The Murray Bay Protestant Church," was especially near his heart.[169]

The title to the beautiful river-side lot on which the church still stands came from Madame Nairne,[170] the widow of the owner (at that time) of one of the old Quebec Seignories which reach back to the French Feudal days.

Her deed of gift required that the affairs of the church should be entrusted to the care of two trustees, one of whom was to be an Anglican and the other a Presbyterian; and that, as far as possible, the services of the church should alternate between the Anglican and Presbyterian forms of worship.

For fifty years the Anglicans and the Presbyterians (and other non-Episcopal visitors at Murray Bay) have worshipped together in beautiful unity, forgetting (as they could so easily do during the summer months) all of the differences that divide and vex us in our churches at home. The Presbyterians and other non-Episcopalians in the little Union Church have heartily participated, at the alternate services, in the forms prescribed by the Anglican Book of Common Prayer, an undenominational Hymnal being used at both kinds of services, while the Presbyterian and Anglican clergyman have alternated in the conduct of the services.

During the nineteen years of our experience at Murray Bay, the clergyman officiating for both services have been men of marked ability, and I have often heard visitors comment on the very unusual church privileges that were to be found in that summer resort, many feeling that they were nearer heaven in that little church than anywhere else in the world.

Shortly after we began to go to Murray Bay my husband

was appointed as the Presbyterian Trustee of the Church, serving until the time of his death—first with Professor George Wrong of Toronto and afterwards with Mr. Robert Minturn of New York, as the Anglican Trustee.[171]

He soon came to love that little church at Murray Bay as his home church for the long and happy summer months. He was a regular attendant at both the morning and evening services, giving his best thought to the financial and other affairs of the congregation.

In this connection, the following extracts from an article entitled "The Country of the Dormer-Window" by Mr. H. D. Sedgwick,[172] which appeared in *The Century Magazine* for September, 1913, may be of interest:[173]—

Of course there are other things to do at Murray Bay than to drive or visit the sights. But do what you will, so long as you stay out of doors you cannot escape the view. There is golf, pursued with the regularity that characterizes all kinds of superior machinery, on a links of much variety and picturesqueness, which is associated with memories of President Taft and of the late Mr. Justice Harlan; there is tennis; there is the Sunday afternoon walk.

The great charm of Murray Bay lies even more in the character and disposition of its people than in its beautiful scenery. To everyone who has been long familiar with Murray Bay its most delicate charm lies in the memories of the men whose dignity of character and fine friendliness of manner set a special seal upon the beautiful place. Among those who will not come again to brighten the summer days by their presence are Mr. Edward Blake and Mr. Justice Harlan. These men belonged to the history of Canada and of the United States, but in matters that do not concern the Muse of History they belong to Murray Bay. No golfer can tee his ball on the links without involuntarily expecting to see Judge Harlan's noble figure striding joyously from hole to hole, and to hear his exultant, boyish glee over a good stroke or his humorous explanation of an unlikely one. No worshipper goes to the Protestant Church, the pretty stone church on the village street, without a glance at the spot where the Justice used to stand on Sunday mornings, a symbol of large-hearted, Christian hospitality, and greet the congregation as it str[a]ggled in. And if, for instance, in order to give a visual reality to one of Shakespeare's heroes, one seeks for an embodiment of dignity, grace, and high character, the image of Mr. Edward Blake comes instantly up with his handsome bearing and courtly simplicity. Indeed, Murray Bay is rich in human memories that outdo nature in her prodigal attempts to make the place delightful.

The year after my husband's death, his Murray Bay friends arranged for a beautiful memorial of his devotion to the little Union Church and of his deep interest in the community as a whole (the *habitants* as well as the summer visitors). Over the main entrance to the church and facing the public road, they placed a fine "Town Clock," the hands and hour-numbers being made of hammered Norwegian iron, painted black; and on the wall inside the church, near the main door, they placed a beautiful memorial brass tablet reading as follows:—

TO THE HONOURED MEMORY
OF
JOHN MARSHALL HARLAN
1833–1911,
A JUSTICE OF THE SUPREME
COURT
OF THE UNITED STATES
FOR MANY YEARS A TRUSTEE OF
THIS CHURCH,
SOLDIER, PATRIOT, CHRISTIAN
THE CHURCH CLOCK IS
DEDICATED.

A DRAMATIC SEQUEL OF A CIVIL WAR EPISODE

In connection with our life at Murray Bay, I must tell of a dramatic incident which occurred one evening at Braemead.

My husband's circuit, during the last years of his services on the Supreme Court, comprised the States of Ohio, Kentucky and Tennessee. Among the Federal Judges in that Circuit was Judge Horace H. Lurton[174] of Nashville. My husband and he often held court together on the Circuit and they had become greatly attached to each other, although they had served on opposite sides during the Civil War.

Hearing my husband's glowing account of Murray Bay as a summer resort, Judge and Mrs. Lurton went there in the summer of 1902 or 1903. We saw much of them, for we were anxious to make the summer pass pleasantly for them. One evening, we invited some friends to meet them at supper—the "simple life" being the rule at Murray Bay, "dinners" were rarely given.

There were perhaps a dozen people at the table, and my husband, being in the best of spirits, began to tell the company some of his experiences in the Civil War. He was describing a hurried and exciting march which he and his regiment made through Tennessee and Kentucky in pursuit of the daring Confederate raider, John Morgan. He came to a point in his story where he and the advance guard of the pursuing Union troops had nearly overtaken the rear-guard of Morgan's men, who had just crossed a little stream near Hartsville, Tennessee, and were being fired upon by the Union men from the opposite shore.

Suddenly, Judge Lurton (who was sitting at my right at the opposite end of the table) laid down his knife and fork, leaned back in his chair, his face aglow with surprise and wonder, and called out to my husband in a voice of great excitement, "Harlan, is it possible I am just finding out *who* it was that tried to shoot me on that never-to-be-forgotten-day?"

In a tone of equal surprise and wonder my husband said, "Lurton, do you mean to tell me that *you* were with Morgan on that raid? Now I know *why* I did not catch up with him; and I thank God I didn't hit *you* that day."

The whole company was thrilled by the belated but dramatic sequel to my husband's story, as they realized afresh how completely the wounds of that fratricidal war had been healed; for there were those two men, fellow citizens of the one and united country, serving together as Judges on the Federal Bench. It was as if there had been no Civil War.

A few years after that interesting occasion, Judge Lurton was promoted to the Supreme Court, when the ties of friendship that had united them became still more closely knit together.

THE TAFTS

I think that the family of Mr. William Howard Taft[175] began to spend their summers in Murray Bay about 1895, two years before my husband and I began to go there. At that time, Mr. Taft was the Chief Federal Judge in the Ohio Circuit.[176] Upon his return from the Philippines, in 1904 or 1905[177] (as nearly as I can remember), he resumed his place in our summer colony, greatly to the pleasure of his hosts of friends at Murray Bay.

That summer (I think it was on the occasion of his birthday), a surprise party was arranged for him, beginning with a torch-light procession of his men friends, who with a number of outsiders (many of whom were ladies), finally "fetched-up" at a cottage occupied by warm friends of the Tafts, into which the Judge and his wife had been decoyed in advance.

One of the features of the evening was a dance, in which Judge Taft, greatly to my surprise, asked me to join as his partner. I had heard how accomplished he was in that line and I said, "Oh, you must excuse me; I have not danced for many, many years and I could not at all interest or keep up with you as a dancer."

"But," he replied, "it is only the Virginia Reel." Looking round I saw my husband being led out by Mrs. Taft to take the head of the line. Thinking to myself, "Well, if *he* can dance, *I* can," I reconsidered the matter and quickly took my place with Mr. Taft at the end of the line.

It was understood that "no one *under* forty should be eligible for the reel;" and we dancers had much fun to ourselves over the comparatively small number that were willing to confess to being *over* forty, although all looked on with longing eyes, while we old boys and girls renewed our youth. It was a most delightful and jolly occasion.

A VISIT TO THE QUEBEC CITADEL

One of the most delightful experiences connected with our summers at Murray Bay was a visit which we made (in 19___) to Lord and Lady Grey[178] at their residence in the Quebec Citadel, when he was the Governor General of Canada. They had invited us to come to them for a weekend visit, and a Government boat was sent to Murray Bay for us. The weather was fine and we had a most delightful trip up the river. A carriage was waiting for us at the Quebec Pier, conveying us in a short time to the Citadel, where a most cordial welcome was given us by Lord and Lady Grey and their two most charming daughters.

I well remember an afternoon tea in an open pagoda on the cliff, where we had a fine view of the Plains of Abraham, where Wolfe and Montcalm[179] fought out the question between Britain and France for the ascendancy on this continent. The place where Wolfe's bold troops climbed up what was then supposed to be an impregnable cliff was pointed out to us.

In the hundred and fifty years that had elapsed since that momentous battle, the two races had gradually learned to co-operate in the building of a united Canada, which, in this Year of our Lord (1915), is now playing its glorious part, with the rest of the British Empire, in the effort to free the world from the menace of Teutonic militarism. And as Britain is to-day fighting alongside of its ancient enemy and now its cordial Ally, France, the brave Canadians, both of French and English birth, are now giving their best and their dearest to the defense of the great Empire to which both races belong.[180]

On the evening of our arrival at the Citadel, a beautiful dinner was given, at which the Mayor of the city, with his wife, and my husband and I were the special guests. I was seated at Lord Grey's right. The gentleman at my right had not been introduced to me—the custom of "introducing" at such functions not being the rule, as it is with us in the United States. As the dinner progressed, my own escort to the table having to divide his attentions with the lady on his left, I felt I must do my part in the feast of reason and the flow of soul,[181] by conversing with the gentleman to my right. I therefore took the card bearing my name which had marked my place at the table and presented it to my neighbor and asked for his card. I afterwards learned that he was one of the leading physicians in Quebec, though I do not now recall his name. We had a very pleasant time together.

Another delightful experience we had at about that period was a trip up the Saguenay, on which we were the guests of Sir Charles Fitzpatrick,[182] the Chief Justice of Canada, whose summer home is at Murray Bay. A Government yacht was put at our disposal and we chose our own hours as to coming and going, as well as our own speed. We were thus given the opportunity of seeing that sublimely wonderful river from both sides and in the full light of day, and altogether the trip was most enjoyable.

"Jackson"

It has always been the custom for the Government to furnish a messenger or personal attendant for each Justice of the Supreme Court. These messengers are always coloured men, and have been chosen with great care, being men of exceptionally good character, good manners and intelligence. Of the three messengers that served my husband during his 34 years on the Bench, I must mention one in particular, James Jackson, who for twelve or fourteen years was not only a most faithful attendant, but served my husband with an affectionate loyalty that endeared him to every member of our family. He was with my husband when he died, and he shared our grief as one who was in a real sense a member of our household.

"Jackson" (as we always called him) was by nature a man of fine character and kindly feelings. The dignified and courtly manners which characterized him were undoubtedly acquired from the fine "Old Maryland" family in which he was brought up as a slave in the ante-bellum days.

While he was on peculiarly friendly and even affectionate terms with his employer, he never for one moment forgot his place, nor the respect that was due from him to all the members of the family.

By the time Jackson had been in the service of my husband for two or three weeks, he had so thoroughly identified himself with my husband and all our family interests, that, whenever he spoke to others about my husband or addressed him personally, he always used the pronouns "We," "Us" and "Ours."

His loyalty to "The Judge" and his pride in all matters affecting "The Family" may be seen from the following stories that will always be treasured by us as among our most delightful recollections.

After a very serious attack of grippe, which left my husband's heart in a rather bad condition, the Doctor ordered him to use just half of the small quantity of whiskey in the toddy which he was in the habit of taking once a day during the latter part of his life. Jackson was present when the Doctor gave these orders, and my husband instructed him to bear these orders in mind. But when, the next day, in bringing my husband his toddy he faithfully carried out the Doctor's instructions, the small amount of whiskey, when added to the ice and water in the glass, gave the toddy such a "pale and ineffectual" look, that my husband, forgetting what had been the Doctor's orders, turned upon Jackson rather savagely and said, "What do you *mean* by bringing me a toddy like that? It is nothing but water and ice." Jackson, grinning most respectfully, said "Why, Judge, I thought we were taperin' off."

I may mention two more delightful and very characteristic stories of Jackson:—

One summer, a certain Mr. S., who was a guest of my son Richard at Tamarack Top, challenged my husband to a game of golf. Mr. S. had two weaknesses:—he took his game of golf very seriously; and he was rather sensitive on the subject of his age, for although he was at that time on the shady side of sixty (my husband being then about sixty-eight), Mr. S. played with the "boys of forty." When Mr. S. returned to my son's cottage at the close of the match with "The Judge," my son asked him, "Well, S. how did you get on?"

"O, Richard, he's a wonder. He beat me seven up and six to play."

The next morning, Jackson went over to my son's cottage, ostensibly for the purpose of inquiring after Mr. S.'s health, but really for the purpose of respectfully gibing at Mr. S. on the subject of his game of golf.

"How are you feelin' this mornin', Mr. S.?"

"O, I am feeling very well, Jackson. Why?"

"O, nuthin', *We* were only wonderin' how you were feelin' after the game yestiddy. 'Cause *We* have made up *Our* minds that after *this* season *We* will only play with the young men, with the men of *Our* class."

Though such a vicarious message from a man of sixty-eight to an "old boy" of sixty (who had prided himself on his game of golf, and whose friends never referred to his age) touched him on the raw in two places, Mr. S. was a good enough "Sport" to tell this good story on himself to all of his friends in Rochester.

Jackson took so much pride in all the members of "The Family" that he had a naive confidence in the ability of my boys to do anything, or win any contest, if they really thought it worth while. On one occasion, my youngest son

(John Maynard) won the cup at a Handicap Tournament held at the Murray Bay Golf Club. Knowing how keenly interested Jackson was in the outcome of the Tournament, my son came up to our cottage for the special purpose of seeing what this loyal partisan of "The Family" would have to say. The news of the "Family's" victory had reached the cottage, before my son got there. When my son entered the room and before he could say a word, Jackson, with his kindly, ebony countenance fairly shining with affectionate pride, grasped my son's hand in both of his hands and said, "Mr. John, *when* will *these people* around here understand what kind o' stock *We* come from?"

Unlike most of his race, Jackson, when he first entered my husband's service, had little or no interest in church-going. Later on, however, he became a communicant in a coloured Methodist church in Washington and, as he was far above the level of intelligence and education of most of his people, he became at once a prominent figure in his congregation.

He became greatly interested in the work of his Church, and he often came to my husband for advice as to reading and explanations of the Scripture Lessons in his Church Service—a duty that was often assigned to him by his pastor. With great care and much interest my husband would direct him—showing what lessons could be drawn from certain passages. My husband was never so busy that he could not put aside the study of the lesson that he was preparing for his own Bible Class, that he could not stop long enough to give Jackson a helping hand.

Banquet Commemorating Twenty-Five Years of Service on the Supreme Bench

In December 1902, the Bar of the Supreme Court of the United States gave my husband a dinner to celebrate the twenty-fifth anniversary of his appointment to that Bench.

Mr. Philander [C.] Knox,[183] who was then the Attorney General of the United States, and Mr. Elihu Root,[184] the Secretary of War, took a great interest in the occasion and gave much time and thought to the arrangements for the dinner, which proved to be a very notable one.

Two hundred and forty prominent lawyers and other leading men from all parts of the country were present, Mr. Wayne MacVeagh presiding. The speakers included President Roosevelt,[185] Chief Justice Fuller and Justice Brewer, Senator Hoar,[186] the Hon. Edward Blake, K.C., of Toronto, who was then a member of the British Parliament, Assistant Attorney General James Beck,[187] while Mr. Alexander P. Humphrey of Louisville represented the Bar of my husband's native State. In the course of his speech, President Roosevelt said:—

It is not an idle boast of this country when we speak of the Court upon which Mr. Justice Harlan sits as the most illustrious and important Court in all of the civilized world. It is not merely our own people who say that—it is the verdict of other nations as well. Mr. Justice Harlan has served for a quarter of a century on that Court. During that time, he has exercised an influence over the judicial statesmanship of the country of a kind such as is possible only under our own form of government. For the judges of the Supreme Court of the land must be not only great jurists, but they must be great constructive statesmen. And the truth of what I say is illustrated by every study of American statesmanship, for in not one serious study of American political life will it be possible to omit the immense part played by the Supreme Court in the creation, not merely the modification, of the great policies through and by means of which the country has moved on to its present position.

One of the balconies overlooking the speaker's table was put at the service of myself, my daughters and daughters-in-law, and several friends were invited to enjoy the evening with us, among whom was my very dear friend, Mrs. Edward Blake.[188]

I must mention one incident in connection with this dinner, which, when I learned its real significance, was naturally very pleasing to a mother's heart. My son James was at the time the Attorney General of Porto Rico.[189] Certain matters that were before him, in connection with the beginnings of the American administration of that Island, had created some friction among some of the native officials. Attorney General Knox, who was of course in full touch with Porto-Rican affairs, unexpectedly cabled my son to come immediately to Washington. He and his wife at once sailed for the United States. The day after his arrival in Washington, he went to pay his respects to the Attorney General, who, as my son imagined at the time, received him rather formally. Somewhat troubled by his apparently cool reception, he began to wonder if his conduct of Porto-Rican matters had in some way met with the disapproval of the Attorney General; and, as diplomatically as possible, he finally made bold to inquire if that there was anything unusual that needed attention. The Attorney General, with a most genial smile, replied:—"A banquet is being given in honour of your father next Saturday night and I wanted you to be present. We will talk business afterwards." And I may add that the "business" proved to be not very pressing and it was in no way embarrassing to my son, who always suspected that the "business" could just as easily have been cleared up by the interchange of a few letters, but that the Attorney General's real purpose in cabling him to come to Washington was that he might be present at the dinner given in his father's honour.

The Attorney General's kindly thought for us touched me very much, for it gave us the pleasure that we had longed for but had not thought possible, namely, the presence of all three of our sons on an occasion of such interest to our family.

A full account of this dinner was afterwards issued in pamphlet form, giving the list of the guests present, the personnel of the committees and all the speeches in full.

The following year, on the evening of the twenty-third of December, 1903, which was the forty-seventh anniversary of our marriage, a committee of distinguished lawyers representing the Bar of the Supreme Court of the United States, headed by Mr. MacVeagh and Senator Hoar—came to our house for the purpose of presenting me with a beautiful copy of the pamphlet, bound in soft green morocco, with my initials (MFH) in silver on the cover. To me and my children, the book is a most precious heirloom. Its exquisitely illuminated frontispiece bears the inscription:—

PRESENTED TO
MRS. JOHN MARSHALL HARLAN,
BY THE BAR OF
THE SUPREME COURT OF THE UNITED STATES.

On that occasion, also, Mr. MacVeagh was the Chairman and he made a delightful and very kind presentation speech as follows:—

Mrs. Harlan, by the undeserved kindness of my brothers of the Bar, I have been asked to represent them in bringing to you a memorable volume containing the proceedings upon that memorial occasion, on December 9th, 1902, when the Bar of the Supreme Court of the United States honoured themselves in honouring Mr. Justice Harlan on his completion of a quarter of a century of service upon the bench of that great tribunal.

We thought it very fitting to present this book to you on the anniversary of your wedding day, for, as he has doubtless told you how often *we* have tried *his* patience, this day may serve to remind him how often *he* has tried *your* patience; for we are sure that the weakness he has displayed in his judicial career must also have found expression in the domestic circle. (Laughter) I allude, of course, to his lack of positiveness, his disposition to "wobble," alike in forming and expressing his opinions. (Laughter)

But, jesting aside, twenty-five years of useful and distinguished service in one of the highest stations in the world is a record of which you and your children may be justly proud. As for myself and my associates at the Bar, I can only say that we honour him as a judge and we love him as a man; and both feelings find expression, although inadequate expression, in the memorial volume I now hand to you.

It was my first appearance as a speaker and I think my husband was very nervous as he realized it, for he knew that I had made no preparation for such an ordeal. But Mr. MacVeagh's genial and ironical reference to my husband's want of firmness gave me my cue, and I replied as best I could, on the spur of the moment. My words must have been taken down by someone and I am able to record them here:—

Mr. Chairman and Gentlemen:—Forty-seven years ago today, I threw a halter about my husband's neck and I have, he says, dominated him ever since. (Laughter) But, as from your remarks you seem to know him so well, I do not mind telling you in confidence that I have found him very difficult to manage at times. I can feel him now pulling at my sleeve; he wants to do all the talking this afternoon. (Laughter) But I shall not allow it; I shall speak for myself, though I wish for the moment I were the "New Woman," with her eloquent tongue, that I might thank you in fitting manner and language, for this book. But I am not, you see;

so you must let me tell you, in my own simple fashion, how much I shall prize it, both for the event it commemorates, and for your lovely thought in presenting me with this special and most beautiful copy.

I thank you from my heart, gentlemen, not only for myself, but for my children and grandchildren; for I feel sure that, as long as one of the name survives, this book must always be most carefully and affectionately guarded, as a treasure far beyond price. Again, let me thank you with all my heart.

The Presbyterian General Assembly

In the spring of 1905, my husband was appointed a delegate to the General Assembly of the Presbyterian Church, which was held at Lake Winona, Indiana. Neither of us had ever attended a meeting of our great Church Court, and we were, therefore, greatly delighted by this appointment.

The Winona Auditorium, seating (as I remember) about 4,000 people, was crowded to the door. The delegates occupied the body of the hall, and the galleries were filled with the interested spectators.

At the first business meeting of the august body, which was most interesting and stirring, my husband was elected as the Vice-Moderator, and often through the week of the sessions of the Assembly he was in the chair.

The Interior (the leading Presbyterian Church paper of the middle West) in its issue of June 8, 1905,[190] made the following reference to my husband's deep interest in the work of the Assembly:—

Among religious people in private life there prevails a suspicion that men engrossed for a long time in public affairs are biased thereby to a secular view of world problems and lose some part of their sense of the importance of the Church.

That there is no necessary consequence of that sort pursuing a statesman was most certainly evidenced by Justice Harlan's place and part in our late Assembly.

No legislator of the Church sitting in that body manifested keener interest in pending Church questions than this great jurist, whose attention might be supposed to be wholly occupied with the tremendous civic issues considered daily in the "most august tribunal among men." His remarks on Foreign Missions, on Presbyterian Unity, on the right of our Church to the public recognition, on Liberty of Worship, and especially on the obligations of Christian justice to the Negro race were self-evidently out of his life and not expressions concocted for the occasion.

The so-called "Cathedral" project for Washington City came as directly out of Judge Harlan's inborn Presbyterianism; it was not a momentary fancy, but the slowly wrought-out answer of his own mind to a condition of things which has hurt him for years. He indicated it all by a single flash-light when he said that he had never known a Presbyterian Clergyman to be called on to offer prayer at a public function since he resided in Washington.

To a man who is conscious of what part the Presbyterian influence has played in the formation and development of our national institutions, this eclipse of Presbyterianism by other orders of Christian polity in the National Capital is painfully anomalous. And Justice Harlan, knowing what kind of things impresses Washington, has simply proposed to the denomination at large a means of recalling the Capital to a proper consideration of the Presbyterian Church.

It is an idle misunderstanding to suppose that in this idea there is any longing for stately formalism. The difficulty in the way of the project is not any danger of ritualism, but the practical difficulty of planting in Washington a church of such commanding character, without doing harm to the Churches already existing there. And this practical problem the Justice recognizes so squarely that he declared he would not press the idea if the Washington Presbytery did not heartily agree thereto.

A "STORY" THAT MADE VOTES

One of the burning questions before the Meeting of the Assembly was "The Book of Common Worship" that had been compiled and reported to the Assembly by a special Committee, of which the Rev. Dr. Henry van Dyke[191] of Princeton University was the Chairman. Intense feeling was aroused, and a very heated discussion ensued. One man, brandishing the proposed Prayer Book aloft in his clenched left hand and pointing scornfully to it with his right, declared that "the book smelt of Popery." Another delegate threatened to throw "Jenny Geddes' historic stool"[192] at the head of the Chairman of the Committee.

For a few minutes, it looked as if the liturgical and anti-liturgical parties in the Assembly would get into a Kilkenny fight.[193] My husband, as Vice-Moderator, was in charge of the meeting on that occasion. Finding that the discussion was waxing too hot, he rose to his feet for the purpose (as was soon evident) of pouring a little oil on the troubled waters.

He was always full of fun and, like Lincoln, he often resorted to a good "story" as a means of enforcing his point. But, in order to disarm any suspicion of his intentions or of his own attitude on the question, he began, as it seemed to me, miles away from the subject in hand. Then, making a short cut around Robin Hood's barn (during which I was much puzzled as to what he was driving at) and looking very solemn as he made that journey, he soon came out into the open and (still without cracking a smile) he then referred, in a very earnest manner, to the fact that even so small a matter as the pronunciation of a word often brought about a most unlooked-for and strange result.

Then, as it were a question of serious importance, he described a discussion which he said had once taken place as to the correct pronunciation of a certain word, which he then proceeded to spell out to the solemn-looking delegates to our General Assembly, C-A-S-T-O-R-I-A.[194]

He told the delegates that some of the people in his story emphasized the second syllable, while others insisted that the emphasis should be upon the third syllable; and that no agreement was reached until a physician, who happened to be present, rose to his feet and said, "*I* pronounce Castoria *harmless.*"

The joke is now an old "chestnut" but it was new at the time and there was no need for my husband to apply it to the question then before the Assembly. He took his seat as soon as he landed his joke. He had not so much as *mentioned* the question of the proposed Prayer Book; but the delegates saw the point and application of his "story" and the Assembly broke in a roar of laughter. The Book of Common Worship, without further debate, was pronounced "harmless," being adopted by an overwhelming majority, and the Assembly proceeded with the rest of the morning's programme.

Many of the delegates afterwards said that my husband's little "story" probably turned the tide—at least, to the extent of reducing, to neglible dimensions, the minority that was opposing Dr. van Dyke's report.

A PRESBYTERIAN MINSTER AT WASHINGTON

The chief interest my husband had at that meeting of the General Assembly was the personal Memorial which he had prepared and which he then presented to the Assembly in favour of establishing a Presbyterian "Cathedral," or Minster at the National Capital.

In February and March of that same year (1905) from his home in Washington, he had sent out a Circular Letter on the subject to a number of Presbyterian clergymen and laymen throughout the country. The letter formed a part of the Memorial which he presented to the Assembly.

The plan which he then proposed to our American Presbyterian Church was marked by such a statesman-like breadth of view and was characterized by such a prophetic hope as for the part he longed for his beloved Church to play in the history of the country that I have yielded to the temptation of inserting here the following extracts from the Circular Letter above mentioned:

A Presbyterian Cathedral

Twenty-seven years' residence in this City has brought me to the conclusion that the time has come when the Presbyterian Church as a whole ought to establish in Washington a church which would represent our denomination at the National Capital in a more impressive and effective way than could be done by the ordinary *parish* church.

My interest in this matter moves me to send this letter to a large number of Presbyterian ministers and laymen throughout the country in order to get their judgment upon the general idea. And it may be added that this is written entirely upon my individual responsibility as a layman.

If the general plan herein suggested should commend itself to the Church at large and my services should be needed in helping to work out its details I would take pride in devoting a large part of the time remaining to me in co-operating with others throughout the country, in the effort to establish what, for want of a better word, might be called the "Cathedral Church," or "Minster," of our Denomination at the National Capital.

Speaking accurately, there is of course no place in a non-prelatical system like ours for the historic "Cathedral." I simply use the phrase "Cathedral Church or Minster," in order to indicate a church of such dimensions, as well as of such impressiveness and equipment (both as to the numbers of its ministers and workers and general facilities), that it would have a larger and more influential relation to this great City as a whole than is possible in the case of what our Scotch brethren call a mere "Parish Church," with only one clergyman and ministering on a modest scale to a single section of the City.

The latter case is the condition which, in the main, now prevails in Washington, and must always prevail more or less in other large cities of the country.

Washington is an unique city, and is the Capital of the nation. In a degree not true of any other city, its life is concentrated; and my long connection with official affairs and public officers here convinces me that in Washington, of all cities, there is a place for a great Presbyterian Church, by means of which our denomination could make its influence felt more effectively in the Capital of the Nation. . . .

There should be, on some commanding site near the real centre of the life of the Capital, a large and impressive edifice, thoroughly churchly in character, nobly suggestive of the best periods of our Church, in fact a real "Presbyterian Minster," that would be the striking architectural symbol of our great communion; able to command the attention of this unique city, filled, as it is, with people from all over our country and from the other nations of the world.

Attached to or connected with the proposed "Cathedral Church" should be a work-building or "Parish House," with all the conveniences and appliances that are required for the most practical and effective forms of modern church work.

With the thousands of young men and women in the Government Departments here, there are numberless ways which would suggest themselves to every pastor and experienced Presbyterian layman, by which a Church thus equipped could perform a most beneficent mission to those whose only anchorage is the ordinary boarding house, and who therefore are open to great peril on account of having broken away from home ties and the helps of their own communities.

In other words, the church proposed to be erected should have some features of what is called the "Institutional Church." On some such plan a church could be established here that would stand "four-square"[195] to this remarkable city and the superb opportunity it presents for serving the Master.

Adjoining the main edifice there should be also a fitting manse for its chief Minister; and for the work I have in mind there should be a staff of assistant-ministers and lay workers, and in addition, a small Clergy House in which those assistants could live.

These details are suggested only in the out-line, but they are sufficient to give some idea of the proportions of the work which such a church might undertake.

Of course, the establishing of such a church as is here proposed would involve the purchasing of a large block of land, and the erection of expensive buildings; and, in my judgment, it would demand a fund for the partial endowment of the enterprise, in order to ensure its success on a large and permanent scale....

The strategic importance of Washington is being recognized by other Churches. Our Episcopalian brethren are far-sighted enough to see this, and they are already carrying out plans for a great Cathedral here, as the rallying point of their denomination at the Capital. The Methodists entertain great hopes of a university in Washington. And what the Roman Catholics have done and are planning to do in the same connection is well known.

My husband felt that a Church which, at the beginning of the Revolutionary War, gave to Thirteen Colonies such a man as John Witherspoon;[196] a Church, some of whose laymen afterwards played a leading part in the evolution of our Constitution and the formation of our National Government—that such a truly *national* Church as the Presbyterian ought to be especially represented at the Nation's Capital by a church of stately and impressive architecture, which would, in addition, be so centrally and attractively located, so strongly endowed and so efficiently manned, that it could do a much larger and more influential work than would be possible for *any* "Parish Church"—not only for Washington itself, but indirectly, for the whole Nation.

To this Circular Letter my husband received a hundred or more interesting replies from prominent Clergymen and laymen throughout the country. With very few exceptions, they expressed a hearty and even an enthusiastic approval of his plan.

The so-called "Cathedral" Memorial was duly referred by the General Assembly to a Special Committee; but—in view especially of the parochial jealousies that showed some signs of appearing in some of the Washington congregations in regard to the development of a great "Presbyterian Minster" at the National Capital—the time did not appear to be ripe for taking up the plan; so that nothing came of it.

It is to be hoped, however, that some day a sufficiently large number of earnest and broad-minded Presbyterian laymen of large means may make it possible to realize such a statesman-like project.[197]

LOUISVILLE BANQUET

From Lake Winona we went directly to Louisville, where the Bar of the city were to give a large dinner in honour of my husband's seventy-second birthday. We were the guests of Mr. and Mrs. Augustus E. Willson.[198] Mr. Willson, as I have said elsewhere, had been my husband's law partner, and as the friendship that existed between them had grown in all the years that followed, we felt as much at home with them as we would have been with kindred, Mrs. Willson and I being almost as mother and daughter, or as older and younger sisters.

The birthday dinner, given at the Galt House[199] on June 1st, was a most enjoyable affair, many of my husband's old friends taking part in it. Our two sons, Richard and John Maynard, were among the guests, and at the urgent demand of some of the company, they led the crowd in singing some college glees at the close of the dinner.

[Here Malvina intended to insert "an account of reunion with the survivors of the 10th Kentucky Regiment."]

Our Golden Wedding

In the winter of 1906, the three survivors of my six brides-maids, Mrs. Samuel Bayard[200] and Mrs. James M. Shanklin (the widow of my oldest brother), both from Evansville, and Mrs. John Wymond of Chicago—came to make us a visit in Washington.

The fiftieth anniversary of our wedding came on December twenty-third of that year and invitations had to be sent out for a large reception, my husband having insisted that we must make it a day long to be remembered by our children and grand-children. As the twenty-third fell on a Sunday, our invitations were for Saturday the twenty-second. The visiting bridesmaids were not able to stay, each one having reasons for being at home for Christmas; so, greatly to our regret, we had to let them go.

It was a cold crisp day; but our friends came in great numbers, crowding the reception room of our Euclid Street house, from four to seven o'clock. The room was filled with flowers, and lovely gifts in great variety came in all day long.

My husband, as he stood beside me to receive our guests, looked (to me) very little changed from that happy day fifty years before. He had remembered a bouquet which I carried on my wedding day (though he could not describe it in the old-fashioned way, the roses having green leaves for their bed, and being mounted on white lace paper, in a round shape), and our daughter-in-law, Mrs. John Maynard Harlan, of Chicago, had ordered one made as nearly as she could from my husband's rather vague description. The Bridal Bouquet of fifty years before was of white roses and was a very modest affair compared with the gorgeous one of yellow "Golden Gate Roses" which I carried on our Golden Wedding Day. Its form and general make up, however, seemed quite novel to many of the visitors and attracted much attention. After admiringly it extravagantly, one lady said, "Where in the world did it come from?" I replied, "An old sweetheart ordered it for me." She looked askance, and upward, at the tall figure beside me and asked, "How did the Judge like it?" I answered, "Oh, *he* likes it the best in the world, for *he* was the old sweetheart," which greatly amused the lady.

The President and Mrs. Roosevelt honoured us with their presence, as did many other distinguished people. Two dear friends of the old Kentucky days, Governor and Mrs. Willson, came on for the occasion, adding greatly to our pleasure.

Fifty years before (a few days after our wedding), an old-fashioned daguerreotype had been taken of us—I in my bridal dress, standing at my young husband's left, my right hand lightly resting in his strong and protecting right, and he in the dress coat, black velvet waistcoat, and with the old-fashioned stock which I have described in an earlier chapter in exactly the same positions as we had occupied when we stood before my Pastor and repeated our marriage vows. Though my husband was only twenty-three at the time, yet in that daguerreotype he looks over thirty. My eldest son used always to say that "it was impossible for anyone to be *half* as wise as his father *looked* in that picture."

Shortly before our Golden Wedding, a clever Japanese photographer in Washington had managed to make a modern negative from the elusive daguerreotype, and the photographic copy of the old-time picture excited no little interest among the guests at our Golden Wedding.

On the occasion of our fifty-third anniversary, in presenting to each of my children a copy of the same photograph, I was moved to write the following lines, addressed to them:—

December 23, 1909

Just three and fifty years ago,
One bright December night,
This Man and Maid did pledge their love,
And life-long troth did plight.
You children, looking on, have thought
The way, at times, quite dreary;
But we two, looking back, still find
It sweet and short and cheery.
Then follow on, you dear loved ones;
And, when we're gone, remember
This picture, showing how we looked
In our dear young December.

After the guests at our Golden Wedding had dispersed, all of our children, including our three daughters-in-law, and the grand-children—together with the Willsons and Mr. Charles Henry Butler[201] (the Reporter for the Supreme Court and the brother-in-law of Mrs. John Maynard Harlan, Mrs. Butler being at that time in Europe)—sat down to a "Family Supper." It was served in the drawing-room, the table being arranged in the form of a horseshoe. My husband and I sat in the middle, with Governor and Mrs. Willson, on either side of us, as the guests of honour.

Some lines written especially for my "Golden Wedding" by Mrs. Clara Ophelia Bland were read. She was the daughter of Mary Wiley (afterwards, Mrs. Chas. J. Harris, of Macon, Ga.), who was one of the special school-girl friends I had made, at the age of fourteen, during the year (1853) which I had spent at "The Misses Gill's School" in Philadelphia—a well-known Presbyterian institution of that region and period. I never saw Mary Wiley again; I was therefore all the more touched thus to be remembered by her daughter, after the lapse of so many years. The lines were as follows:—

1856

A Bride is starting—crowned with hope,
Starting to read her horoscope;
Life's promises are sweet.
A Wife is standing, crowned with love
And motherhood—both from above;
Life's promises complete.

Some delightful and appropriate verses of his own composition were then read by Mr. Butler, and also the following quaint "Wedding Song of Pioneer Kentucky Days," which was sent on for the occasion by some of my husband's Kentucky kindred:—

When Adam was created, he dealt in Eden's shade;
As Moses had related, a bride then soon was made,
Ten thousand times ten thousand of creatures formed around,
Before a bride was formed, or Man a Maid had found.

He had no conversation, but seemed as one alone,
'Till, to his admiration, he found he'd lost a bone,
Great was his exultation, when first he saw his bride;
Great was his elevation, so to see her by his side.

He spoke as in a rapture, "I know from whence you came;
From my left side extracted, and WOMAN is your name."
There seems to be one reason, why man should love his bride:—
A part of his own body, the product of his side.

The Woman was not taken from Adam's head we know;
So she must not rule over him—'tis evidently so.
The Woman was not taken from Adam's feet we see;
So he must not abuse her—the meaning seems to be.

The Woman was extracted from under Adam's arm;
So she must be protected from injury and harm.
The Woman was extracted from near to Adam's heart;
By which we are directed that they should never part.

And now, most noble Bridegroom, to you we turn with pride;
Be sure the Sacred Volume you never lay aside;
The book we call the Bible, be sure you don't neglect;
For, in every scene of duty, it will you both direct.

After the table had been taken away, my husband, much to our surprise, ordered the rugs to be taken up and, to the music of one of the children, we finished the evening with an old-fashioned, rollicking Virginia Reel, my husband and I leading the dance.

"The Kentuckians" Dinner

In the winter of 1907, "The Kentuckians" residing in New York City expressed a wish to give a dinner in honour of my husband. Having been offered the choice of the date, he suggested the 23rd of December, marking the 51st anniversary of our marriage. To me and to the members of my family, the occasion was naturally one of peculiar interest.

The dinner was given at the beautiful Plaza Hotel, which was then quite new. There were present a hundred or more "Kentuckians" with quite a number of distinguished special guests.

Two of our sons, Richard and John Maynard, were there with their wives, my son James being detained by an injury to his knee that disabled him for the time being. My youngest daughter, Ruth, and I represented the immediate family in the crowd of ladies that looked on from the gallery surrounding the beautiful Dining Hall. My son Richard was asked to say grace, and to offer a special prayer appropriate to the occasion. It was taken down by a stenographer at the time and, as it seems to me so full of the spirit that had always animated my husband's life and that is so much needed in this awful period of the world's history (1915), I give the Grace and the Prayer in full:—

For good health and good cheer for good company and good friends, for home and for Country, may the Giver of all good things make us thankful.

O Lord of Hosts, Who didst guide our fathers out of the house of bondage; Who didst bring their children's children through the Red Sea of a brother's war, and Who didst afterwards bind up the Nation's wounds and make us whole again; Who has granted to us the heritage of glorious sufferings and the strength of chastening trials; and Who hast given us a potent ministry to all mankind—do Thou enable us who are privileged to be actors in this age of the world to do our full part in helping to close up all chasms between the strong and the weak, the rich and the poor.

To that end may we cast away all pride and prejudice, all luxury and lust, all envy and covetousness, the insolence of riches and the rancour of poverty, that so we may build up a highway for the King of men to pass over and for all the people to walk therein together.

Enable the younger generation of Thy servants, upon whom must fall the burden and heat of the battle, to quit ourselves like men. As true lovers of Liberty, may we likewise be obedient servants of the Law. Help us ever as wise stewards of the gifts of Freedom, to be soldiers of the Common Good, so that in all things we may show ourselves worthy of the fathers and of our high calling as citizens of this favored land.

Thus may we establish the Republic upon a Rock and build in America the Holy City, foretold and dreamed of by the prophets and sages of all races since the world began.

We ask it for the sake of Him Who maketh men to be of one mind in the house, Who giveth integrity to states, Jesus Christ, the desire of all nations, the memory of whose birth among men fills the heart of the world, this night, with gladness and immortal hope. Amen.

The speech delivered by my husband on that occasion called forth numerous and approving comments from the Press and, in the following Spring, it was given a permanent place in the Congressional Record by a Senator who spoke of it as embodying what to him seemed so important a message to the American people that it should be sown broad-cast throughout the land.

CHILD'S WELFARE CONVENTION

In the Autumn of 19[08] the International Child's Welfare Congress[202] met in Washington. Our dear friend, Augustus E. Willson, was the Governor of Kentucky at that time. In the mail one morning I received a long official envelope, postmarked Frankfort, Ky. I had other letters that morning and, in my hurry, the only thing that I had found in this particular one was a short personal note from Governor Willson, in which he said he wished me to be Kentucky's Delegate to the Convention.

Knowing the Governor's love of fun, especially when "done up" in rhyme, I very hurriedly scribbled off the best jingle I could muster as my answer in accepting the honour thus offered to me. I showed the lines to my husband, for I always leaned upon his approval in everything I did or said. After reading them, he said, "send them along; they will make him laugh"—which was something much to be desired at that time, for the Governor's hands were full of trouble on account of the wild doings of the "Night Rid-

ers," in the struggle then going on over the tobacco question.[203] My acceptance ran as follows:—

> *Ye'd scarce accept one of my age*
> *To speak in public on the stage;*
> *But while I think ye'd better wait*
> *And make a "New Woman" your diligate,*
> *I'll try to be there, my Governor dear,—*
> *Though for Kentucky t'will not seem quite clear*
> *She'll be ripresinted at all to her mind,*
> *The choice of your old friend is considered kind;*
> *And she'll do her best (of that ye'll be sure)*
> *And signs herself, "Yours till death."*
>
> *Katie O'Moore.*

Hurriedly slipping the lines into an envelope, I sent
words to our messenger Jackson to post it at once. Upon
looking over the morning's mail more carefully, I found to
my great surprise that the envelope from Frankfort contained a beautifully engraved document, bearing the Seal of
the State of Kentucky, formally naming me as Kentucky's
Delegate to the Congress. That I should have sent such a
trivial reply to a "State Paper" filled me with horror. Hur-
rying to the speaking tube, I called down to the kitchen and
ordered my reply to Governor Willson to be brought back
at once. The cook answered, "La, Madam, it's done gone; I
done gib it to de postman." So there was no help for it.

Curiously enough, that very afternoon my husband had
a telegram from Governor Willson, saying that he was just
starting for Washington for a day or two of business. When
he arrived, he asked me if I had received his letter. I told
him that I had, and had already given a favorable reply,

which must have crossed him on the way. His wife meanwhile had already forwarded it to our house, and it reached him the day after his arrival. Going to my husband's study, he shut himself up with the Muse of Rhyme for a little while and shortly afterward, he handed me a long envelope saying, "Here is a Valentine for you" (for it was the 14th of February). Upon opening it, this was what I found:—

> *I am glad ye've accepted, 'twill make us all proud.*
> *'Tis the loike of your goodness, I'm thinking aloud;*
> *Ye'll stand for our best thought, our dearest and kindest;*
> *In insight and foresight, Ye'll not be the blindest.*
>
> *'Tis Katie O'Moore, the colleen of our choice;*
> *Be aisy, 'tis she that's Kentucky's rale voice.*
> *The top o' the mornin' to Katie O'Moore;*
> *While* She's *on the bridge, 'tis not we'll run ashore.*
>
> *For intilligence, kindliness and sympathy too,*
> *We'll love her and praise her, and* that's *nothing new;*
> *She's to us more than part of us, our Diligate;*
> *Be jabers, we think she's the best in the State.*

I attended the sessions of the Convention, morning and afternoon for a week, and was much interested, the Delegates from the different countries giving an account of what had already been done for the children throughout the world.

At Governor Willson's earnest request I gave a full report of the meetings, which he had published in the *Louisville Courier-Journal.*

THE GARFIELD HOSPITAL

Outside of his judicial duties and his church work, my husband's chief interest in Washington was in the Garfield Memorial Hospital. During the last years of his life, he was the President of its Board of Directors. He was never too busy to attend its meetings and was always on time. He was keenly interested in everything that concerned it. Each year he presented the claims of the hospital in person to the Appropriations Committees of the House and Senate and he always succeeded in getting a most generous appropriation in response to his appeals on its behalf. He had great faith in the future of the Hospital and he gave a great deal of his time and thought to its affairs.

During the last summer of his life, a rather imposing iron fence, with a stone wall for its base, had been put round the grounds of the Hospital. Just before he was suddenly stricken with what proved to be a fatal illness, he took me over to the Hospital in order that I might share the great pleasure he took in the new fence and the imposing entrance to the grounds.

The last work he did was for the Hospital. In the forenoon of the very day in which he was stricken (only four days before his death) and before he went to Court, he spent over an hour with two prominent members of the Board of Directors in discussing its work and its needs.

LAST DAYS

The last summer of my husband's life (1911) was spent at our beloved "Braemead," and was a most delightful one. Although a little weaker and less active than he had formerly been, he was in good health and excellent spirits. On most days in good weather he had his game of golf, generally playing the full eighteen holes and sometimes entering the various tournaments, and enjoying it all to the full.

The younger children of our son John Maynard, in the charge of a competent nurse, were in Tamarack Top next door, so that in effect we were one household. My husband greatly enjoyed the company of the younger grandchildren—his namesake, John Marshall, Jr.,[204] Janet and little Edith. Towards the end of the summer their father came on from Chicago for his vacation at Murray Bay and in September we were joined by their mother and eldest sister, Lysbeth, who had been spending the summer abroad, the two cottages being quite equal to the pleasant task of sheltering them all.

Our son Richard and his wife were abroad during that summer and my son James and his wife were at their summer home on Lake Champlain. At the vacation's end—which was always a sad time after these partial family re-unions—our son John Maynard went with his father to New York, where they spent a happy week together at the Hotel Belmont, my daughter Ruth and I joining them for the last few days of their stay.

My husband's friend, Mr. McReynolds[205] (who since then has been made a Justice of the United States Supreme Court) was most kind to him during that visit to New York, giving him a luncheon at one of the Clubs.

On that occasion, Judge Roger A. Pryor[206] happened to enter the reception of the club. My husband had not seen him since the days of the Civil War, in which they took opposite sides; but he recognized him instantly, accosting him with characteristic cordiality, and indulging, as he frequently did, in a joke. Said he, "The last time we met we were *slightly at odds;* but we are good friends now, I hope."

Judge Pryor, although equally cordial in his manner, was evidently racking his memory in his effort to identify my husband. Finally he said, "May I ask who it is with whom I have the pleasure of speaking?" My husband then gave his name and told him how much pleasure I had recently had in reading Mrs. Pryor's charming book about the old days in the South.[207] After responding to inquiries as to her health, Judge Pryor with great pride said that she was writing a love story—adding with fine humour, "but *I* am not in it."

After the luncheon, Mr. McReynolds took my husband to the Riverside Drive, to see Grant's Tomb, which my husband had never seen. He was so profoundly interested in it, that the next day he insisted upon my going to see it with him.

It was a gray afternoon, not chilly, but invigorating. After a delightful drive through Central Park and along Riverside Drive, we sat together on one of the benches near the Tomb. My husband recalled to me the story of Grant's great service to the country. And, then, his thoughts running on to what were the occupations and interests of those in the "Great Beyond" (as was often his habit when speaking of those "upon whose day of life the night has fallen"),[208] he wondered "whether the memories of their active life on earth entered into their thoughts in the life beyond the veil."

I can never forget his face as he talked upon these high themes, as we sat together in the quiet of the beautiful spot—so near to the great city with its noise and turmoil. As I recall it afterwards, he seemed in imagination to have entered already into the peace and rest of the Great Hereafter.

We got back to Washington a few days before the Court opened for its Autumn and Winter Sessions; and as was his invariable custom, his study table was made ready, with all its appointments for his work, which he seemed so ready and eager to begin. Though he had taken a severe cold while in New York, yet he was present on the opening day of the Court, on Monday October 9. Everyone remarked upon his apparently good health.

But, on the afternoon of the second day, while at Court, he was taken sick and was brought home under the tender care of one of his brethren, with a high fever which proved to be the forerunner of pneumonia. He suffered little, and after four nights and three days the great summons came, and he "fell asleep" on Saturday, October 14th, at about six o'clock in the morning. His noble life on earth was finished and the new life in "the glad Homeland, not far away," had begun.

My eldest son Richard was abroad at the time; but we were comforted by the presence of our two younger sons, who were with him when he breathed his last.

His funeral was held in New York Avenue Church which he had for many years served as an Elder. The Pastor, the Rev. Dr. Wallace Radcliffe,[209] preached the sermon. Among the hymns that were sung was one by Oliver Wendell Holmes,[210] which was a special favorite of my husband's:—

> *O Love Divine, that stooped to share*
> *Our sharpest pang, our bitterest tear,*
> *On Thee we cast each earth-born care,*
> *We smile at pain while Thou are near.*

> *Though long the weary way we tread,*
> *And sorrow crown each lingering year,*
> *No path we shun, no darkness dread,*
> *Our hearts still whispering, Thou art near.*

> *When drooping pleasure turns to grief,*
> *And trembling faith is changed to fear,*
> *The murmuring wind, the quivering leaf,*
> *Shall softly tell us, Thou art near.*

> *On Thee we fling our burdening woe,*
> *O Love Divine, forever dear,*
> *Content to suffer while we know,*
> *Living or dying, Thou art near.*

At my request, one of the prayers used at the service was the beautiful evening prayer written by John Henry Newman,[211] which my husband greatly loved to hear:—

O Lord, support us all day long of this troublous life, until the shadows lengthen and the evening comes, and the busy world is hushed, and the fever of life is over, and our work is done. Then in Thy mercy grant us a safe lodging, and a holy rest, and peace at the last; through Jesus Christ our Lord.

Amen.

HARLAN FAMILY TREE

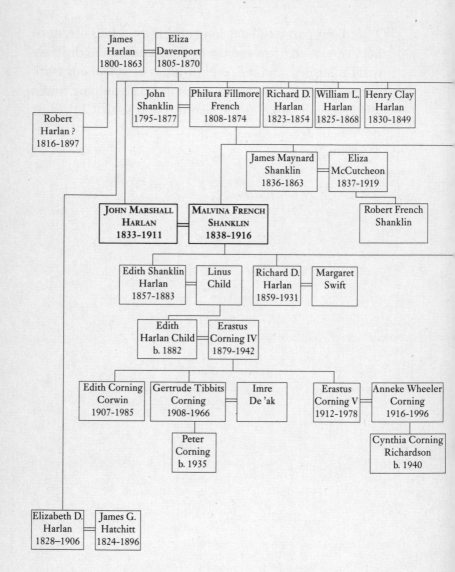

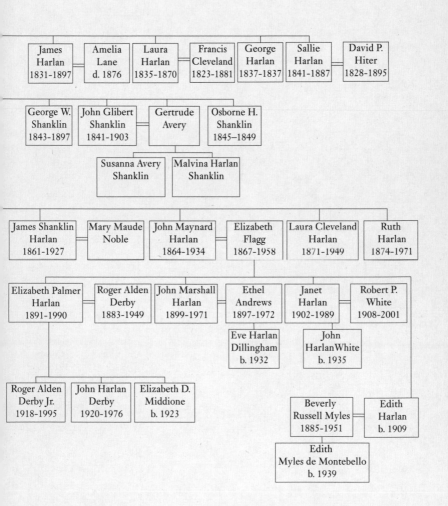

EPILOGUE

A SECOND HARLAN ON THE BENCH

Amelia Newcomb

Malvina Harlan took great pleasure in her family. Her marriage to John transformed her into a committed Kentuckian, and she effortlessly—or so it seemed—adopted her new family's interests and its close ties between generations. The Harlans returned the favor, embracing Malvina as one of their own. She would reminisce in later years that the "hospitable and cordial atmosphere of my father-in-law's house made life there exceedingly pleasant for me," no small achievement considering the physical and psychic distance she traveled to join John Harlan in marriage at seventeen.

John and Malvina would never house so many under one roof as did their Kentucky elders. But they would gather family in places that echoed the trappings familiar to Malvina as a young bride: the expansive embrace of her "beloved Braemead," the family's Canadian summer retreat in Murray Bay, or the large home they built in Washington, D.C. And it was in such places that they would try to emulate not only the Harlan inclusiveness but the "love and perfect trust" of Malvina's childhood home, laying out as much by example as by precept traditional family customs and values.

As John saw the family legacy, contributions to society that would live on after one's death were a preeminent goal—and law was particularly high on his list as a means to that end. Like his father before him, who had named his son after John Marshall for a reason, Harlan wanted his sons to follow in his professional footsteps. He saw to it that they were well-educated, as equipped as any to take full advantage of "the active stirring civilization" of their young adulthood. But if the world and its opportunities were expansive, the path to reaching them was narrow: "Labor, unremitting labor, study, serious constant study, is essential to great success," John Harlan wrote to his son James in 1880.

Two of his boys would indeed follow him into the law, and the third into an institution Harlan also held dear: the ministry. But the most striking continuity in the family would emerge in John Maynard Harlan's grandson. The similarities in career path and personal choices between John Marshall Harlan II (1899–1971) and John Marshall Harlan I (1833–1911) would reach so far beyond the name that it would seem the younger John had taken notes at his grandfather's knee.

Of course, if young John had a high standard to follow in his grandfather, he also had the record of three uncles who had done well for themselves. All attended Princeton University, though with varying records of achievement. Richard was valedictorian of his class, while youngest son, John Maynard, Harlan II's father, was expelled twice, once for hazing, before finally graduating. But he overcame his collegiate missteps and went on to become politically influential in Chicago, running twice for mayor and once for governor of Illinois, though losing all three times.

John and Malvina's three daughters would escape the pressures for public achievement, but their role in the family was significant nonetheless. The oldest, Edith, became a favorite, along with her parents, at the Hayes White House, where she would often play the piano at hymn sings. She married, but died of typhoid fever not long after bearing a daughter; her distraught father wrote to one son that "Wherever I go, & whatever I may be doing, her presence will be recognized in its influence upon me. She was to me not simply child, but companion." The other two daughters, Ruth and Laura, never married, and would share a home first with their parents, then with each other, for the duration of their lives. Laura served as social secretary to the wives of Presidents Harding and Coolidge, and later became a successful real estate agent in Washington, showing signs of becoming that "new woman" of whom Malvina spoke in such awestruck tones.

John Maynard, with his wife, Elizabeth Flagg, would shift the locus of the Harlan family's next generation to Chicago, a city at the center of the "stirring civilization" that fascinated John Harlan, but distant physically and atmospherically from the Kentucky ties that framed his background. Yet even as change shifted the family toward northern climes and a less multigenerational lifestyle, the well-established values of the Harlans persevered. There continued to be a sense of pride in the serious endeavors of most family members. And while professional expectations were still directed only at male children, given the traditional values of the era, Malvina would probably have been pleased to see the achievements of her granddaughters. The oldest, Elizabeth, was an accomplished musician who studied piano in Paris. Janet graduated Phi Beta Kappa from Smith College by age twenty. Edith, who got her degree from Vassar College and also graduated Phi Beta Kappa, went on to develop a thriving career as a financial adviser.

As these children were growing up, Murray Bay became the new base for ensuring the link between generations. The summers were not as idyllic for the grandchildren, perhaps, as they were for Malvina; her son John Maynard was known as an irascible man who was inclined to keep his children at a distance while vacationing there. But they were times for visiting with relatives and socializing with other families who sought out the commanding views of the St. Lawrence River and the familiarity of a close-knit community.

The second John Marshall Harlan, therefore, would have been well acquainted with his famous grandfather, even though he died when John was twelve. A regular at Murray Bay, young John took up the tennis and golf that were such a regular feature of life there. Golf, in fact, was a bond between the two while John Harlan I was still alive: young John would often prop up his less surefooted grandfather from behind, for example, when he had to stand on an incline to get a good shot.

As the second child and only boy, John was much adored. If his father was temperamental, John was steady and thoughtful, and possessed of a good sense of humor and fun. As he matured and work widened his world, the circle of those who valued him as a good friend and wise counselor—not to mention an inveterate practical joker—grew quickly.

At age eight, John was sent to boarding school in Canada. His final year of preparatory school, designed to give him more connections with American boys, was spent at the Lake Placid School in New York. From there, John followed in his father's footsteps to Princeton, where he was president of his class and chairman of the *Daily Princetonian*. His foray into producing the newspaper was something that might well have pleased John Harlan I, who had harbored his own interests in the field. (Once, while on the Supreme Court, the senior Harlan cut a deal with a Louisville reporter. The journalist had passed a note to the Justice saying he couldn't figure out who had won a particular case from Harlan's summary of it. Harlan offered to write the reporter's article for him if he would run out and buy the Justice some tobacco. The reporter ended up filing the dispatch verbatim, though not using Harlan's byline, of course.)

The younger Harlan then went on to study law as a Rhodes Scholar at England's Oxford University, and upon his return three years later, entered his grandfather's favored field for a rising star. John Harlan became an associate at the New York firm of Root, Clark, Buckner, and Howland, despite the initial feelings of senior partner Emory Buckner that Harlan should attend an American law school before joining the firm. But Harlan impressed Buckner enough to get hired, and he attended New York Law School in the afternoons to fill in his knowledge of American law and to prepare for the bar exam, which he passed the following year.

John Harlan II did not share his grandfather's missionary views about his role in assuring the progress of the Republic. But his outlook nonetheless was based on the same values: Work was to be done to the highest possible level of excellence. Service was important, willingness to sacrifice a given.

Like his grandfather, he was a handsome man, and hard to miss at six feet two inches. John Harlan II carried himself with a high degree of self-assurance. Throughout his life, however, those who knew him would comment on his unusual blend of confidence and modesty. In introducing him to the law firm, Buckner described Harlan as "poise in motion" and "persistence embodied." Michael Boudin, Chief Judge of the United States Court of Appeals for the First Circuit and a former law clerk, recollects that he was "master of his own passions; more ready to listen than to speak; calmly self-confident, not about answers but about his capacity to find answers; and in all things, dignity without pretension."

As a young adult, John Harlan II cut much the same kind of figure that had caught Malvina's eye when her husband-to-be walked into sight in Evansville, Indiana, in 1853. In the younger Harlan's case, it was Ethel Andrews who would take notice. Her brother, John, brought her to a Christmas party one year at Root Clark, where he and Harlan were both associates. Ethel had attended Bryn Mawr College and was the daughter of Pulitzer Prize–winning historian Charles McLean Andrews and his wife, Evangeline. After a courtship of several months, John Harlan proposed to Ethel while she was confined to a sickbed—though only after they talked for two hours about trout fishing.

Her affirmative response not only set him up with a life partner to whom he was devoted, but gave him new reason to be glad that the family touchstone was Murray Bay. Ethel Andrews, who was nearing thirty years old, was strikingly beautiful, intelligent, and artistic—the kind of prospective daughter-in-law that any mother would cherish for her son. But she was also a divorcee. Concerned that his Victorian mother would sense scandal, Harlan judiciously waited until she was firmly ensconced for the summer in Canada, perhaps to enforce a considered response, and then put his full power of persuasion and charm to paper: "Dearest Mother," he wrote. "Prepare yourself for a shock. I'm engaged to be married. The lady is Ethel Andrews, and of course she's the most wonderful girl in all the world. You'll love her as much as I do when you meet her."

After introducing her family members and detailing her education, he continued:

> When she was 21, she married a man over 40, one Henry Murphy, an architect in New York. She lived with him for two years and then of course such a match proved impossible and they separated. She finally concluded to get a divorce which she did last year. The rest of it is she's a perfect darling, and there you have it. . . . We both feel very much the same way about getting married—namely that if we can avoid it we're not going to do it. . . . I may say that at present we are both agreed that we can't possibly avoid getting married.

On November 10, 1928, the couple exchanged vows at the house of her aunt, Ethel Walker Smith, in West Hartford, Connecticut.

The senior John Harlan once circled in his Bible the verse from Proverbs 12: "A virtuous woman is a crown to her husband." Malvina and he could not have foreseen the good fortune of the grandson they knew only as a young boy in finding so compatible a companion as Ethel. The particulars of John and Ethel's relationship were not, of course, identical. Ethel was twelve years older than Malvina when she married, albeit for the second time. Malvina spoke of her youth and innocence at the time of her marriage. Ethel, by contrast, was a seasoned world traveler and a devotee of the sophisticated life of New York who would bring into her husband's life acquaintances from the theater and the arts. John had already made a name working for Buckner, who became U.S. attorney in New York. His charge was to enforce Prohibition, and he enthralled the press with a sensational case that involved a witness he dubbed the "bathtub Venus," as she had posed nude in a tub of champagne at a party.

Despite those differences, however, there were similarities between the two couples. Like Malvina and John Harlan, Ethel and John Harlan would create a country home that became the center for their life together: "Little Mountains," a stately home they built in 1937 on nineteen acres of land in Weston, Connecticut. Ethel, like Malvina, would watch her husband go to war well past the age where it would have been expected, serving in England during World War II as chief of the operations analysis section of the Eighth Air Force. And the couple would ultimately find a second home in the city where Harlan I made a national name for himself: Washington.

John and Ethel were celebrating twenty-seven years of marriage when, in November 1954, President Eisenhower made the appointment that brought Harlan to the court where his grandfather had sat just four decades earlier.

Harlan was by then the father of one daughter, Eve, and grandfather to the first of five grandchildren. He had served as chief counsel to the New York State Crime Commission that probed corruption on the New York waterfront. He was also the litigator brought in to head up a large team of lawyers representing the DuPont family in a major antitrust case until his appointment to the United States Court of Appeals for the Second Circuit in 1953. Many commentators noted that he was young: only fifty-five years old. That was eleven years older, however, than Harlan I had been when he took his seat on the bench.

Author and cultural critic Alistair Cooke described John Harlan II as "almost appallingly handsome" and "so ideally cast as to sound more like a Supreme Court Judge in a Marquand novel than one in life." Another observer said later that despite the great prestige associated with the appointment, "no rank or office can add to this man's stature. His strength comes from within and is the sort that all men trust." Harlan joined the Court in March 1955, wearing the gold pocket watch the brethren had presented to his grandfather in 1896. Just fifty-nine years earlier, Harlan I had penned his famous dissent in *Plessy* v. *Ferguson*. Just one year earlier, the Court had cited that opinion in its landmark desegregation case, *Brown* v. *Board of Education*. Harlan would hang a portrait of his grandfather in his chambers, leading a member of a visiting Japanese delegation to comment that he hadn't known the position was hereditary.

Like his grandfather, the new justice became a dissenter from many decisions handed down by the Court. Harlan I, though, diverged from a conservative court, whereas Harlan II dissented from what he saw as an increasingly liberal bench. Though they were both members of the Republican party, Harlan I concerned himself with the prospect of too much state power in the decades following the Civil War, while Harlan II focused more on whether the federal government's reach had become too long in the wake of the New Deal and World War II. Their judicial outlooks defied neat categorization, however; the younger Harlan, for example, though generally seen as conservative, supported desegregation, a stand that was an extension of Harlan I's views on civil rights.

Those who worked with Harlan during his sixteen years on the Court often drew on the same terms to describe him: integrity, good humor, courage. "Patrician" cropped up regularly as associates noted his preference for black tie at the symphony and his graciousness. To Harvard professor Philip Heymann, a former law clerk, he was "deeply and instinctively democratic; his working staff were treated with unfailing respect as well as warmth." In fact, Harlan loved to be a mentor. "[Harlan] felt like a father to his clerks," Heymann said, "yet didn't have a patronizing moment with half-grown twenty-somethings."

That familial closeness to those he worked with continued a tradition in the Harlan family. Malvina had noted her mother-in-law's willingness to "make room for one more," exhibiting a hospitality that was "most marked" and that "gladdened the hearts" of many a young person. John Harlan held annual reunions for his clerks, just part of John and Ethel's extensive entertaining of secretaries and justices alike in both Washington and Connecticut. Clerks would join the Harlans for breakfast and dinner; even when the design was to work into the evening, Harlan would invite the young lawyers for cocktails and a meal, and only then move to the work before the Court and the inevitable glass of Harlan's much loved Rebel Yell bourbon. Visiting family and guests would linger on the broad flagstone terrace of Little Mountains during the summer, and gather inside for dinner at Christmas and New Year's.

A natural hospitality threaded its way through the Harlans' lives. Ethel had a reputation as a warm and charming hostess, while the justice was known for his ability to make a guest, whether a government official or a law clerk's parent, feel as if he or she were the only matter of interest at that moment. The Justice talked weekly from Washington with John Twarda, a master gardener and caretaker who worked for Harlan for five decades—a record inspired in part, Twarda says, because "he accepted me like a member of the family." Harlan would give him the keys to his Georgetown home whenever John visited Washington. Harlan also had warm relationships with other employees in his two households, in keeping with the long-established pattern of caring for those who worked for the Harlans. The Harlans also helped employees out in times of financial trouble, and John was known to exchange inside jokes that would often send Elizabeth Middleton, his cook in Connecticut, into gales of laughter.

The formidable devotion that he inspired served him particularly well in his last years on the Court. An almost complete loss of eyesight forced him to do much of his work from memory and to rely heavily on clerks to be his eyes for him. Several remarked on the unique experience of working on pornography cases that required them to read aloud or narrate related books and films to Harlan—situations the Justice couldn't help but handle with a certain amusement. Twarda became a bulwark, as did Paul Burke,

Harlan's messenger and assistant at the Court. Harlan's perseverance through ongoing tragedy—blindness, severe pain, and illness, and Ethel's increasing loss of memory in the last decade of her life—would inspire and sustain those around him until his death in December 1971.

Ethel followed her husband just six months later, in June 1972. She was a force in her own right who had once held notions of becoming a playwright. She wrote verse for her daughter as well as occasional magazine articles. She mastered the seventeenth-century Williamsburg art of dried flower arranging, and stayed quite busy providing arrangements to the Court, where they were popular. But she would in many ways echo the role of Malvina in supporting her prominent husband's career. She commented to reporters when John took his seat on the Court that "it seems to be most unusual when a husband and wife both have successful careers and a successful marriage. I think it would be difficult . . . the husband's profession should come first."

John's high-powered career may have influenced that view somewhat; Ethel once commented to a family member that John was the battleship in their marriage, and she was the rowboat. But while she may have been making a wry comment about their relative stature, she also likely recognized her key role in helping John and periodically drawing him away from his natural tendency to work ceaselessly. Washington was not a city she particularly favored, but Ethel would carve out a niche for herself and stay well informed about the work before the Court. If Malvina produced the Taney inkwell at a critical juncture during Harlan's writing of his dissent in the Civil Rights Cases, Ethel's history of tracking her husband's cases would generate headlines, recorded in Ethel's scrapbook with amusement, like "The Wife of Justice Harlan Is a Real Courtroom Fan," and "Mrs. Harlan Lacks Only a Law Degree." "Much of the law—especially trial law—is terribly interesting," she would note in one interview. "It's sort of like going to the theater. You get so much human nature, so many fascinating situations."

It is likely, nonetheless, that Ethel would have been as surprised as Malvina to see the first woman, Sandra Day O'Connor, appointed to the Supreme Court just a decade after John resigned, shortly before his death. Equally remarkable, perhaps, would be the draw Malvina's memoir would hold some eighty years later for Ruth Bader Ginsburg, the second woman appointed to the Court. The voice of a woman coming into her own through raising six children, supporting a prominent husband, and learning to strike out independently, spoke powerfully to Justice Ginsburg. She began to seek a wider audience for the memoir, recognizing its import to the annals of American history.

It is not always the case that a voice from four generations earlier can speak to those who follow. Perhaps that's especially true when the century that spanned those generations transformed women's lives by giving them access to the voting booth, the top universities, substantial careers, and aspirations to hold the highest offices in the land. Yet Malvina succeeded. The humanity of her story, from its charming opening scene of spotting her would-be husband for the first time to her triumph in dealing with a disruptive Prussian army officer in Switzerland, drew in Justice Ginsburg. It caught the ear of Clare Cushman, managing editor of the *Journal of Supreme Court History*, in which it was published in July 2001. A note from Justice Ginsburg about the publication of the memoir spurred

Linda Greenhouse, the Supreme Court reporter for *The New York Times* to read it. During a cab ride, she in turn told Jill Abramson, Washington bureau chief for *The New York Times,* about the article she planned to write on the memoir. And Ms. Abramson, who was to be in charge of the Sunday *New York Times* front page the following week, saw a front-page story. Malvina would have marveled at all these women taking such an interest in her memoir, women who held positions of power once reserved exclusively for men.

She could not have anticipated her wedding picture and life story on Page 1 of a national newspaper. She would have delighted, though, in the publication of her account of a life both long and well lived. At that moment, Malvina might well have turned to the words she spoke when presented with a book of speeches commemorating her husband's years of service to the Court: "I shall speak for myself, though I wish for the moment I were the 'New Woman,' with her eloquent tongue, that I might thank you in fitting manner and language, for this book. But I am not, you see; so you must let me tell you, in my own simple fashion, how much I shall prize it. . . ."

———

AMELIA NEWCOMB is an editor at *The Christian Science Monitor.* She is the granddaughter of the second Justice John Marshall Harlan, and the great-great-granddaughter of John Marshall and Malvina Harlan.

AFTERWORD

Linda Przybyszewski

The first Justice John Marshall Harlan of Kentucky served on the United States Supreme Court from 1877 to 1911, where he voted in over fourteen thousand decisions. He wrote more than seven hundred majority opinions and some of the most famous words uttered from the bench on behalf of the country's black citizens. It was Harlan who dissented in 1896 from *Plessy* v. *Ferguson*, the case in which the Court decided that racial segregation in public accommodations did not violate the Thirteenth and Fourteenth Amendments, protesting that "Our Constitution is colorblind, and neither knows nor tolerates classes among citizens." He warned his brethren and the nation that "The destinies of the two races, in this country, are indissolubly linked together, and the interests of both require that the common government of all shall not permit the seeds of race hate to be planted under the sanction of law."[1] Harlan's words inspired Thurgood Marshall and others in their fight for legal equality. As a result of his long career on the Court, three full-length biographies and a dozen scholarly articles have been written about him. On the other hand, Malvina Shanklin Harlan, his wife of fifty-four years, is an unknown figure of no renown who has made only brief appearances in biographies of her husband.[2] So, you may well be wondering, why are we presenting *her* memoir?

The answer is not that Justice Harlan did not write his memoir and Malvina Harlan wrote hers. Instead, it arises from the fact that, even if we had Harlan's memoir, it would probably not reveal the glimpses of home life that Malvina's offer us, glimpses that I found essential to solving the puzzles of Harlan's public life in my book *The Republic According to John Marshall Harlan* (1999). Harlan thought of himself as a public man, and his short autobiographical writings—including a letter he wrote to his eldest son on July 4, 1911, and various undated recollections of the Civil War era—focus on his works as a politician and Union Army officer. Malvina details Harlan's public life as well, and includes extracts from his Civil War recollections.

The dates Malvina uses in her title indicate that John was her focus: 1854 was the year they first met, and 1911 was the year he died. These are her memories of *their* life together. She probably prepared this memoir for publication and then realized that her only claim to an audience was as the wife of a public man. One of her children did try to get it published: the stamp of literary agent Paul S. Reynolds appears on the first page of the typescript. However, it never found a publisher and was eventually deposited in the Library of Congress among John M. Harlan's papers.

Of course, memories need to be taken with caution. The first generation of professional historians of the nineteenth century, who prided themselves on their scientific approach, considered memoirs inaccurate sources of factual information. They rejected them as evidence if there was no outside corroboration. More recently, psychologists and biologists have determined that our brains construct our memories in an ongoing process. We create and rearrange our memories without any necessary awareness of the activity.

So, for example, when Malvina describes her conversation with John in 1861 over whether he should join the Union Army, we must keep in mind what the conventions of the time dictated about such scenes. By 1915, most Americans were familiar with the standard tableau of brave, womanly sacrifice captured in novels and images of the Civil War era. One would think from these fictional accounts that no woman ever kicked and screamed when her primary financial support went off to risk his life, leaving her with children to raise, a household to manage, and a farm or business to run. All women supposedly acted as Malvina tells us she did (all good women, anyway): when John said that he would leave the question of his enlistment "entirely" to her because "his first duty" was to her and their two young sons, she asked him what he would do if he had no family. "He said at once with great earnestness, 'I would go to the help of my country.'" Malvina bravely replied that he should go: "I could not stand between you and your duty to the country and be happy." This conversation may well have taken place, but memory and literary conventions surely simplified and dramatized it into an acceptable form. Similarly, important events have been left out. Malvina was very close to her older brother James Maynard Shanklin, yet she mentions nothing of his being taken as a prisoner of war by the Confederates or of his death shortly after his release in 1863.

Instead of depicting the full reality of the past, Malvina's memoir tells us what she chose to remember and how she wanted others to remember John. The week John was buried in 1911, Malvina wrote a letter to her children on the black-bordered stationery customary for one in mourning. The widow consoled herself with the thought that she could "truthfully say, that never knowingly did I do anything that I thought he would not approve!" She tried to follow John's wishes in the face of his death: "I am trying to be brave, as I know he would have me be, but the wakening in the morning to find him gone is heartbreaking."[3] Malvina wished to honor her life's companion in this memoir. We should think of it not as a full record of the past, but rather as a record of the stories that the "Harlan tribe" told about themselves.

Despite its limitations, the memoir contains the only depictions of John M. Harlan's personal relations with blacks during the days of slavery and after emancipation. In these depictions, we can find the solution to two puzzles in Justice Harlan's public life. The first puzzle is biographical: how did a white man born in 1833 in Kentucky to a slaveholding family become a Republican and a champion of civil rights?

John M. Harlan's father was James Harlan (1800–63), a lawyer and Whig politician who held both state and national offices. His mother was Eliza Shannon Davenport Harlan (1805–70), the daughter of Kentucky farmers. James

Harlan opposed the immediate abolition of slavery and the challenge to the Constitution that abolitionism represented, but he was an ally of Henry Clay, the leading Whig politician from Kentucky, who supported gradual emancipation. John M. Harlan followed in his father's professional and political footsteps. He attended Centre College and Transylvania University for his law degree, then joined the family law firm. (His father had not named him after Chief Justice John Marshall for nothing.)

When the Whig party collapsed under the strain of the slavery issue in the 1850s, John M. Harlan became a supporter of the anti-immigrant Know-Nothing party for a brief time. That party tried and failed to reunite native-born whites across sectional lines. By the presidential election of 1860, Harlan had aligned himself with John Bell of the Constitutional Union party. Bell won Kentucky's electoral votes, but came in third nationally behind John C. Breckinridge and Abraham Lincoln (Stephen A. Douglas came in last).

After this election, six Southern states, led by South Carolina, seceded from the Union by February of 1861 and set up a provisional government. In March, Harlan counseled Secretary of War Joseph Holt to remove federal troops from Fort Sumter and Fort Pickens or risk losing the border states like Kentucky to secessionist sentiment. He explained that "no earthly power will prevent the people" of the border states "from sympathizing and to a great extent taking part with 'their brethren of the South' against what is called an 'abolition' administration."[4] A month later, Fort Sumter was attacked and the Civil War began. Kentucky remained officially neutral until Confederate troops invaded it in August. Then Unionists like Harlan gained the upper hand in a deeply divided state. Harlan raised his own Union Regiment, the Tenth Kentucky Infantry, in September of that year. However, the longer the Union Army stayed in Kentucky, the more of the white population it alienated. Union soldiers stopped Confederate sympathizers from speaking out, and even Unionist Kentuckians found their property liable to requisition. The Emancipation Proclamation in early 1863 and the efforts of Union officers to liberate slaves infuriated many whites. Harlan may have resigned his commission in March 1863 in response to his father's death and the need to salvage the family law firm, but he was angry enough with Lincoln to support Lincoln's Democratic opponent for the presidency, General George B. McClellan, in 1864.

In political speeches delivered between 1864 and 1867, Harlan made clear his opposition to immediate emancipation. He believed that the national government had abused the trust put in it by white Kentuckians. While speaking to a crowd in Indiana in 1864, he reminded them of why the people of the Union states had risen against secession. "It was for the high and noble purpose of asserting the binding authority of our laws over every part of this land." Clearly, "it was not for the purpose of giving freedom to the Negro."[5] Harlan wrote a public letter in 1865 complaining that the national government had exceeded its powers and left Kentucky to cope with "the ruinous effects of such a violent change in our social system."[6] Although Harlan came out in support of a plan for gradual emancipation in the tradition of Henry Clay, he was willing to leave it up to white men to decide whether or not to adopt

such a plan. As Kentucky's attorney general, Harlan in-
dicted Union general John M. Palmer for his earlier efforts
to free slaves by recruiting them into the army after the
war was over. This occurred in 1866 after the Thirteenth
Amendment had freed the slaves. (Kentucky's legislators
refused to ratify the amendment at that time, and only did
so as a symbolic gesture in the 1970s.)

If John M. Harlan was willing to go this far to preserve
slavery, however, other white men were willing to go much
farther. From the late 1860s through the early 1870s,
armed gangs of white men, encouraged by the Democratic
party, roamed the countryside of Kentucky and attacked
both freed blacks and whites who had supported the
Union. A group of Frankfort blacks petitioned Congress
for protection and detailed sixty-four attacks between November of 1867 and December of 1869. Some 30,000 black
Kentuckians decided to leave, a disproportionately high
number of migrants compared to other border states.[7]

How did Harlan respond to white terrorism? He joined
the Republican party in the late 1860s. He ran unsuccessfully for governor as the Republican candidate in 1871 and
1875. In a speech in 1871, he acknowledged his political
past thus: "Let it be said that I am right rather than consistent." From then on, he was consistent. He told a Kentucky
crowd whose votes he needed, "It is true that I was at one
time in my life opposed to conferring these privileges [of
citizenship] upon [blacks], but I have lived long enough to
feel and declare, as I do this night, that the most perfect
despotism that ever existed on this earth was the institution of African slavery." Slavery damaged whites as well as
blacks. "With Slavery it was death or tribute. . . . It was an

enemy to free speech," he reminded them, "It was an enemy to a free press." Now he threw his full support behind the Civil War Amendments. He was glad that blacks "are now in possession of freedom, and that that freedom is secured to them in the fundamental law of the land, beyond the control of any state." He celebrated the end of slavery: "I rejoice that it is gone; I rejoice that the Sun of American Liberty does not this day shine, upon a single human slave upon this continent. . . ."[8]

Of Justice Harlan's checkered political career and once adamant support of slavery, neither he nor Malvina Harlan says very much. Malvina refers only generally to the fact that Kentucky whites "were slow in reaching the point where they would have been willing to fight for the freedom of the negro." Harlan's recollections of the Civil War are equally vague about his support for slavery: he admits only that, despite the victory of pro-Union men in the congressional elections of 1861 in Kentucky, "it is true that many, if not most of the men elected at that time sympathized with the people of the South so far as the preservation of slavery was concerned. . . ."[9] Both Harlans smooth over his political past in order to make it more coherent.

Neither Harlan offers a detailed explanation for Justice Harlan's conversion to Republicanism. In Harlan's recollections, he explained his vote for Republican presidential candidate Ulysses S. Grant in 1868 by saying that "There was nothing else to do; . . . I was then of the opinion that the general tendencies and purposes of the Democratic Party were mischievous, while those of the Republicans were better calculated to preserve the results of the War and maintain the just rights of the National Government."[10]

Only a handful of Harlan's letters have survived from

the late 1860s, so it is hard to know exactly what reasons— political or personal—prompted the political transformation by which he voted for Grant in 1868, joined in a law partnership with Benjamin H. Bristow, then one of the only U.S. attorneys trying to enforce the Civil Rights Act of 1866, and became Kentucky's leading Republican politician. The answer might be found in Malvina Harlan's descriptions of John's relationships with blacks in slavery and freedom.

What Malvina Harlan describes are not the sort of relationships that one would expect from a man hailed in the twentieth century as a prophet for his dissents in defense of civil rights. Instead, she describes white paternalism as the ideal of the Harlan household, long after the Civil War. The word *paternalism* comes from the Latin root word for father, and at the heart of any form of paternalism is a belief in the benevolence of the superior in the relationship. The offensiveness of the assumption of white superiority within racial paternalism is obvious today, but its claims to benevolence were stressed by nineteenth-century slaveholders. In contrast, slaveholders of the eighteenth century, much as they saw themselves as racially superior, rarely imagined themselves as fulfilling a fatherly role for their slaves. The rise of the paternalist ideal justified the institution of slavery as a whole while claiming to target its abuses. The belief in racial hierarchy premised on racial difference is apparent in many of Malvina's descriptions of the Harlans' relationships to their slaves and to former slaves. For example, describing the era of slavery, Malvina depicts blacks as having an innate gift for music and as somehow less sensitive to heat than whites. In addition, apparently only those slaves with "unusual ability" deserved the opportunity to free themselves by self-purchase. The reader may well wonder how John M. Harlan, the Great Dissenter, could spring from a home where such ideas were held.

Malvina Harlan also shows us the other aspect of paternalism: the self-restraint that was supposed to mark the good slaveholder. Far from abusing their legal power, the Harlans are depicted in her memoirs as kind people devoted to the welfare of their slaves. Malvina only remarks on the supposed insensitivity of black skin to heat while recounting John's attempt to save a young slave whose clothes had caught on fire. She also tells us how James Harlan, appalled at how other whites treated their human property, cursed a slave trader one Sunday morning: "like some old Testament prophet he seemed to be calling down Heaven's maledictions upon the whole institution of slavery." The good slaveholder was not supposed to abuse slaves, much less sell them.

Of course, the Harlan family was complicit in the whole institution of slavery. Not only did they make no attempt to free their slaves prior to the ratification of the Thirteenth Amendment, but census records dating from before the war indicate that they must have bought and sold slaves themselves.[11] For all their supposed kindness, the Harlans owned these people and could do with them as they willed. Nothing makes this clearer than finding the names of Bob, Lewis, Henry, Sarah, Jenny, Silva, Maria, and Ben listed on the 1863 inventory of James Harlan's estate along with his furniture, horses, and law books and valued at $1,490.[12] In addition, for a long time James Harlan stood accused of the ultimate act of white hypocrisy: fathering a child by a slave woman. The written evidence is suggestive but incomplete. Robert James Harlan was reputed to have been seven-eighths white in ancestry, meaning he was the result of three generations of racial mixing. Born in 1816, Robert would have been fathered by James when he was only a boy of fifteen years, before his marriage to John's mother. An 1887 biography explains that Robert, a native Virginian, had been allowed "unusual freedom" when he arrived in James's household as a boy. When the local public school expelled him because of his race, he was "taught the elements of an education by Mr. Harlan's older sons." Malvina refers obliquely to Robert in her memoir only as a slave whom James allowed to buy his freedom because of his extraordinary abilities. Robert made a fortune during the Gold Rush in 1848 and settled down to a business and political career in Cincinnati, Ohio, where he was a leader of the black community. The *Cincinnati Daily Gazette* of October 15, 1881, wrote that he, "on the paternal side, is a son of one of the best Kentucky families."[13] Robert and John remained friends and Republican allies, but no evidence of Robert's origins is revealed in the Harlan family letters. Robert's son, Robert Jr., once complained to William Howard Taft about the race prejudice visited upon him by "a moral lapse made by my grandfather."[14] And Robert Jr.'s son, Robert Jackson, a lawyer, met with John's grandson, the second Justice John Marshall Harlan, in 1956.[15] Oral history, so often essential to the preservation of black history, is mixed. The descendants of Robert Jr.'s wife's family tell a story which sounds more like that of Thomas Jefferson and Sally Hemings: that James was a planter who took up with Robert's mother after his first wife died.[16] Following the advice of Dr. Eugene Foster who organized the DNA tests of the Jefferson and Hemings descendants, I asked Robert's and John's families if they would help me try to settle the issue. Two men, distant cousins of John's from all-male lines of descent, and the sole descendant of an all-male line of descent from Robert's family, were tested. John's cousins' Y chromosomes matched one another closely, but neither matched that of Robert's descendant. This still leaves open the possibility that James believed Robert to be his son or the son of some other Harlan male.

To many white Southerners who had owned slaves, stories of paternalism served to acquit them of their responsibility for the evils of slavery and to fashion the myth of the Old South, a world of devoted slaves, kindly masters, and proper racial hierarchy disturbed by the Union victory. John M. Harlan did something else with this remembered past. Because political circumstances after the Civil War had effectively separated the two halves of white paternalism—racial hierarchy and self-restraint—from each other, Harlan was faced with a choice: he could become a Democrat who approved of lawlessness and white supremacy, or a Republican who defended the new legal order and racial equality. Harlan decided that avoiding the abuse of power was more important than championing white supremacy. By elevating the story of James Harlan's cursing of the slave trader and forgetting other stories, the Harlan family fashioned a myth of paternalism that emphasized above all the duty of white men to condemn violence against the powerless.

Drawing on the Founding Fathers' ambivalent attitude toward slavery, Justice Harlan fashioned a similar myth for the whole nation. Under the terms of this myth, the Civil War was not so much a disruption of the nation's course as it was the fulfillment of earlier generations' wishes to remove the stain of slavery from the nation's history. Harlan came to consider emancipation and the Civil War amendments as the fulfillment of the promise of the Declaration of Independence. Malvina Harlan's frequent mentions of Justice Harlan's religious beliefs make clear how much it meant when he called the Declaration "our political bible."[17] He spoke of Washington, Jefferson, Lincoln, and Grant as "Providences" and said of the *Dred Scott* decision, "I think I may say that that case was a work of special Providence to this country, in that it laid the foundation of a civil war which, terrible as it was, awful as it was in its consequences in the loss of life and money, was in the end a blessing to this country in that it rid us of the institution of African slavery."[18] The United States had a God-given mission to forward the legal equality of the races. This mission required that white men oppose violence directed at the former slaves and appreciate that "it is not enough 'to help the feeble up, but to support him after,' " as Harlan put it (quoting Shakespeare) in his dissent from the Civil Rights Cases in 1883.[19]

Justice Harlan was supposed never to have forgotten that Sunday morning when his father cursed a man who traded in slaves, but he also never forgot that his race, that of the Anglo-Saxon, had a claim to some superiority—if not the superiority of blood, then that of tradition. Malvina's memoir offers evidence that the Harlan family's belief in racial paternalism did not disappear with the end of slavery. She describes one of John's black Court messengers, James Jackson, a former slave, in language similar to what she uses to describe the Harlan family's slaves. Like the slaves, Jackson was supposed to have recognized the respect that he owed each member of the Harlan family. The two races are still described at the turn of the century as bound together in an affectionate household hierarchy. Malvina tells us how quickly Jackson adopted the habit of referring to the judge and his family as "we," "us," and "ours." She describes Jackson, who worked for the Justice during the last fourteen years of his life, as mourning alongside the family at John's death. By offering us proof of the survival of racial paternalism, Malvina's memoir also helps to explain the doctrinal puzzle of Harlan's life.

Harlan is well known for his dissents in *Plessy* and the Civil Rights Cases. He also dissented from other decisions where the Court approved of segregation in public accommodations.[20] Harlan gave an impassioned dissenting opinion from *Berea College* v. *Kentucky* in 1908. The state had banned interracial teaching in private schools, and the Court decided that the corporation of Berea College had to comply. Harlan thundered in protest, "The capacity to impart instruction to others is given by the Almighty for beneficent purposes and its use may not be forbidden or interfered with by Government—certainly not, unless such instruction is, in its nature, harmful to the public morals or imperils the public safety."[21] He also condemned the practice of debt peonage, whereby white landowners bound poor black workers to a new form of servitude.[22]

However, there are two decisions that have troubled Harlan admirers. *Pace* v. *Alabama,* 106 U.S. 583 (1882) involved a law punishing interracial adultery more harshly than same-race adultery. A unanimous Court declared that this did not violate the Equal Protection Clause of the Fourteenth Amendment because both members of the interracial couple received the same punishment! Clearly, this law violates the rule of constitutional color-blindness. Harlan delivered the opinion in another troubling case,

Cumming v. *Richmond County Board of Education*, 175 U.S. 528 (1899). Here the school board had shut down the local black high school in order to devote more funds to the black grammar school, and Harlan took this decision as an honest effort to serve black students. Because the black public high school had charged tuition and nearby private high schools enrolled blacks for the same costs, Harlan wrote, "so far as the record discloses, both races have the same facilities and privileges of attending them."[23] The situation and the pleadings made it possible for Harlan to avoid confronting the issue of segregation in the public schools, a subject he had also passed up the chance to say anything about in *Berea College*. There Harlan stated, "Of course what I have said has no reference to regulations prescribed for public schools, established at the pleasure of the State and maintained at the public expense. No such question is here presented and it need not be now discussed."[24]

The persistence of paternalism, as recorded in Malvina Harlan's memoir, accounts for the limits of Justice Harlan's civil rights jurisprudence as demonstrated in these instances. Paternalism relied on a belief in racial identity, and Harlan continued on some level to believe in it himself. Even in *Plessy*, his most renowned dissent in favor of civil rights, he declares, "Every true man has pride of race, and under appropriate circumstances when the rights of others, his equals before the law, are not to be affected, it is his privilege to express such pride and to take such action based upon it as to him seems proper."[25] We need to keep in mind that a belief in racial identity did not always amount to racism—the idea that certain races are biologically incapacitated. It could also be an expression of nineteenth-century romantic racialism—the idea that races have various characteristics.[26] For example, Africans were supposed to make especially good Christians because of their "meek, long-suffering, loving virtues."[27]

Harlan believed not only that blacks had the capacity to join in the American experiment of self-government but that Anglo-Saxons had a duty to make sure that they could. Harlan openly mocked the white man who claimed superiority based solely on the color of his skin. He told his constitutional law class at Columbian (now George Washington) University in 1898, "You occasionally meet with a [white] man, as I did about a year ago, who never did an honest day's work in his life, and who never earned the salt that he ate on his food. That was his only aim in life, to live upon somebody else." Yet this white man of no accomplishment "was greatly disturbed at the probability, that that race would come into contact with the Whites in this country." The message to the students was clear: no white of ability wasted time on racism. Harlan offered himself as a better example for his students: "I am ready to say that if there is a black man who can get ahead of me, I will help him along, and rejoice, and his progress in life does not excite my envy." He was "glad to feel and know that it is the desire of the white people in this country, that that race shall push themselves forward in the race of this life."[28]

Plessy demonstrates how Harlan expressed racialism and yet recognized that race might have little to do with behavior. He appealed to white racial pride in order to defend legal equality of the races. Just before the famous words quoted in my opening paragraph he wrote, "The white race deems itself to be the dominant race in this country. And so it is, in prestige, in achievements, in education, in wealth and in power. So, I doubt not, it will continue to be for all time, if it remains true to its great heritage and holds fast to the principles of constitutional liberty." Only then did he write the passage for which he is best known: "But in view of the Constitution, in the eye of the law, there is in this country no superior, dominant, ruling class of citizens. There is no caste here. Our Constitution is color-blind, and neither knows nor tolerates classes among citizens."[29] Whites had to yield legal superiority in order to fulfill their racial heritage.

If Anglo-Saxons were better than other people, then, it was because they obeyed their Constitution. When they failed to do so, Harlan reminded his brethren of their obligations. For example, when Justice Henry Billings Brown contended in the Insular Cases, 182 U.S. 1 (1901), that the inhabitants of Puerto Rico did not need the Bill of Rights applied to them by the Court because "There are certain principles of natural justice inherent in the Anglo-Saxon character which need no expression in constitutions or statutes to give them effect," Harlan practically snorted at him in dissent.[30] Harlan wrote that "the patriotic people who adopted [the Constitution], were unwilling to depend for their safety upon . . . 'certain principles of natural justice inherent in Anglo-Saxon character . . .' They well remembered," as Brown had forgotten, "that Anglo-Saxons across the ocean had attempted, in defiance of law and justice, to trample upon the rights of Anglo-Saxons on this continent."[31] The mirror image of this rejection of an essentialist definition of race is found in Harlan's insistence in his dissent from *Elk* v. *Wilkins,* 112 U.S. 94 (1884), that an assimilated, tax-paying Native American had "become a part of the people of United States" included in the Constitution's preamble. Elk acted like a citizen; his race could not disqualify him.[32]

These decisions indicate that Harlan thought the measure of human virtue was behavior, not racial heritage. Still, traces of a belief in the kind of set racial identity central to the myth of paternalism survived in Harlan's jurisprudence and caused him to violate the color-blind rule he had voiced in *Plessy.* Although Harlan acknowledged elsewhere that immigrants should be judged by their behavior and could learn American ways, he refused to concede in *United States* v. *Wong Kim Ark,* 169 U.S. 649 (1898), that the Fourteenth Amendment applied to a Chinese-American whose parents could not be naturalized because of a racist law. Harlan's continued belief in racial identity is probably responsible for his failure to attack the sophistry of *Pace* v. *Alabama* and his avoidance of the issue of segregation in the public schools in *Cumming* v. *Richmond County Board of Education.* Tacit concern for the preservation of racial identity is also evidenced in Harlan's unwillingness in his dissent from *Plessy* and the Civil Rights Cases to confront the issue of interracial public schools or marriage. He stuck to other public spaces and transportation.

Despite Harlan's declaration of the color-blind rule, his route to this rule was through three traditional ideas that undermined it. As I wrote in my book, "Harlan did not come to proclaim a commitment to the equality of all men before the law because of some abstract Enlightenment ideal of a universal human identity. He defended legal equality in the name of three traditions. One was familial, one historical, and one racial: his father's paternalism, Unionism cleansed of the stain of slavery, and a romantic

Anglo-Saxonism which made him a hereditary protector of a precious form of liberty."[33]

Malvina Harlan's account of her traditional marriage comprises another indication of the enduring appeal of paternalism to the Harlans. Just as the two races were supposed to live in a happy hierarchy based on mutual affection, so too were husband and wife. Racial paternalism and male paternalism reinforced one another. Malvina's accounts of her mother's advice, her help as legal copyist, her social obligations as the wife of the justice, the poems read on her fiftieth wedding anniversary, all show us that she saw her role as that of a helpmate to John who represented the family before the world. Malvina knew other possibilities were opening up for women. She twice refers to the "New Woman," who was college-educated, active in public life, and far more independent than was she.

Malvina Harlan remained in the shadows cast by her husband, yet she thought of her marriage as a partnership in which her quiet role was essential. In her memoir, she indicates that she approved of the sentiments voiced by James M. Barrie in his 1908 play *What Every Woman Knows*. In the play, a politician's success turns out to depend on his wife's brilliant but unacknowledged advice, although the husband never quite realizes it. The wife does not mind this. Her last speech reads: "Every man who is high up loves to think that he has done it all himself; and the wife smiles, and lets it go at that. It's our only joke. Every woman knows that."[34]

The most remarkable example of Malvina's influence on John's public life is her decision to offer an inkwell that once belonged to Chief Justice Roger B. Taney as an inspiration for John when he was having trouble drafting a dissent from the Civil Rights Cases. By doing this, Malvina reminded her husband of Taney's *Dred Scott* decision and how the Civil War amendments were in some sense a rebuke to the Court for expressing the idea that a black man had no rights that a white was bound to respect. The legal briefs placed before the Court had not brought up *Dred Scott*, yet Harlan's dissent dwelled on its meaning for understanding the war and its constitutional outcome. Malvina Harlan had helped make history.

This story reminds us of the importance of appreciating the links between private and public life. Proud as she was of John's public accomplishments, Malvina thought of him in the end as a private man. When John made arrangements to be buried in Arlington National Cemetery, Malvina objected and was reassured by him that there would be room there for her as well. When he died, however, she made her own arrangements: she had him buried in Rock Creek Cemetery in Washington, D.C., in a family plot where there was enough room for herself and all their children. To Malvina, John was not a public servant in the end, but a husband and father.

———

LINDA PRZYBYSZEWSKI is an associate professor of history at the University of Cincinnati. She is the author of *The Republic According to John Marshall Harlan* (The University of North Carolina Press, 1999).

A NOTE ON THE AFTERWORD

I would like to thank the Supreme Court Historical Society and Justice Ruth Bader Ginsburg for making the publication of this memoir possible. Clare Cushman's work as managing editor of the Journal of Supreme Court History *has been essential. I would also like to thank my research assistants at the University of Cincinnati: Stephen Rockenbach, Kelly Wright, and Gregory Long. And thanks to Stanley Karnow for first alerting Justice Ginsburg and myself to our mutual interest in justices' wives.*

AFTERWORD NOTES

1. *Plessy* v. *Ferguson,* 163 U.S. 537, 559, 560 (1896).
2. The exception that proves the rule is Ruth Bader Ginsburg and Laura W. Brill's "Remembering Great Ladies: Supreme Court Wives' Stories," *Journal of Supreme Court History* 24 (1999): 255–68.
3. Malvina Shanklin Harlan to her children (October 27, 1911), John Marshall Harlan Papers, Library of Congress, Manuscript Division, Washington, D.C.
4. John M. Harlan to Joseph Holt, March 11, 1861, Joseph Holt Papers, Library of Congress, Manuscript Division, Washington, D.C.
5. Quoted on p. 651 in Alan F. Westin, "John Marshall Harlan and the Constitutional Rights of Negroes: The Transformation of a Southerner," *Yale Law Journal* 66 (April 1957): 637–710.
6. Quoted on pp. 29–30 in Louis Hartz, "John M. Harlan in Kentucky, 1855–1877: The Story of His Pre-Court Political Career," *Filson Club Historical Quarterly* January 14, 1940: 17–40.
7. *See* pp. 254–56 in W. A. Low, "The Freedmen's Bureau in the Border States," in *Radicalism, Racism, and Party Realignment: The Border States during Reconstruction.* Richard O. Curry, ed. (Baltimore, Md.: Johns Hopkins Press, 1969), 245–64.
8. All quotes in this paragraph from editorial, "General Harlan's Republicanism," *Louisville Daily Commercial,* November 1, 1877, typed copy. John Marshall Harlan Papers, Library of Congress, Manuscript Division, Washington, D.C.
9. "Civil War of 1861 . . . ," n.d., autobiographical essay, John Marshall Harlan Papers, Library of Congress, Manuscript Division, Washington, D.C.
10. "The Know Nothing Organization . . . ," n.d., autobiographical essay, John Marshall Harlan Papers, Library of Congress, Manuscript Division, Washington, D.C.
11. James W. Gordon, "Did the First Justice Harlan Have a Black Brother?" *Western New England Law Review* 15 (1993): 159–238, 160.
12. Estate of James Harlan, John Marshall Harlan Papers, Library of Congress, Manuscript Division, Washington, D.C.
13. Quotations from Linda Przybyszewski, *The Republic According to John*

Marshall Harlan (Chapel Hill: University of North Carolina Press, 1999), 23–24.

14. Quoted in Tinsley Yarbrough, *Judicial Enigma* (New York: Oxford University Press, 1995), 15.

15. Robert Jackson Harlan to John Marshall Harlan the Younger, May 22, 1956, John Marshall Harlan II Papers, Seeley G. Mudd Manuscript Library, Princeton University.

16. Roger Lane, *William Dorsey's Philadelphia and Ours* (New York: Oxford University Press, 1991), 301–302.

17. John M. Harlan, Constitutional Law Lectures, October 21, 1897, John Marshall Harlan Papers, Library of Congress, Manuscript Division, Washington, D.C. This is another remarkable yet neglected document. Two students took Harlan's lectures down in shorthand, then typed them out, producing a verbatim transcript. Decades later, one of these men sent his copy to John Marshall Harlan the Younger when he was sitting on the Court.

18. John M. Harlan, Constitutional Law Lectures, March 12, 1898, John Marshall Harlan Papers, Library of Congress, Manuscript Division, Washington, D.C.

19. *Civil Rights Cases,* 199 U.S. 3, 61 (1883).

20. *Louisville, New Orleans, and Texas Railway Company* v. *Mississippi,* 133 U.S. 587 (1890); *Chiles* v. *Chesapeake and Ohio Railway Co.,* 218 U.S. 71 (1910).

21. *Berea College* v. *Kentucky,* 211 U.S. 45, 67 (1908).

22. *Clyatt* v. *U.S.,* 197 U.S. 207 (1905), and *Bailey* v. *State of Alabama* (1), 211 U.S. 452 (1908).

23. *Cumming* v. *Richmond County Board of Education,* 175 U.S. 528, 542 (1899).

24. *Berea College* v. *Kentucky,* 211 U.S. 45, 69 (1908).

25. *Plessy* v. *Ferguson,* 163 U.S. 537, 554 (1896).

26. As David Levin once explained, "The Frenchman was mercurial; the Spaniard, romantic, haughty, sometimes chivalrous, often cruel, fanatical; the Italian, subtle and crafty; the Dutchman and the Englishman, frank, manly, self-reliant, enterprising, vigorous." David Levin, *History as Romantic Art: Bancroft, Prescott, Motley, and Parkman* (Stanford, Calif.: Stanford University Press, 1959), 74.

27. Quoted in George W. Fredrickson, *The Black Image in the White Mind: The Debate on Afro-American Character and Destiny* (1971; reprint: Middletown, Conn.: Wesleyan University Press, 1987), 106.

28. John M. Harlan, Constitutional Law Lectures, May 7, 1898, John Marshall Harlan Papers, Library of Congress, Manuscript Division, Washington, D.C.

29. *Plessy v. Ferguson,* 163 U.S. 537, 559 (1896).

30. *Downes v. Bidwell,* 182 U.S. 244, 280 (1901).

31. *Downes v. Bidwell,* 182 U.S. 244, 381 (1901).

32. *Elk v. Wilkins* 112 U.S. 94, 121 (1884).

33. Linda Przybyszewski, *The Republic According to John Marshall Harlan* (Chapel Hill: University of North Carolina Press, 1999), 121–22.

34. James M. Barrie, *What Every Woman Knows,* in *Representative Plays* (New York: Charles Scribner's and Sons, 1914), 288.

NOTES

1. In 1848, Dr. J. G. Hatchitt (1824–96) had married John's sister Elizabeth Harlan (1828–1906).
2. Malvina's mother was Philura Fillmore French (1808–74), a schoolteacher from Vermont; she named her daughter after her sister Malvina French who married the Rev. Calvin Butler. Malvina's father was John Shanklin (1795–1877) who emigrated from Ireland in 1815 and became a successful merchant and an elder at the Walnut Street Presbyterian Church. They were married in 1834.
3. Malvina's eldest brother was James Maynard Shanklin (1836–63), a lieutenant colonel in the Union Army, taken prisoner in 1863 and held at Libby Prison in Richmond, Virginia, for several months. He died shortly after his release, and the *Evansville Journal* reported that the funeral procession, which John and Malvina participated in, "was one of the largest that ever marched through the streets of our city." His letters are collected in *"Dearest Lizze": The Civil War Letters of Lt. Col. James Maynard Shanklin*, edited by Kenneth P. McCutchan (Evansville: Friends of Willard Library Press, 1988). His wife, Eliza McCutcheon

(1837–1919), never remarried. Malvina's brother John Gilbert Shanklin (1841–1903), who married Gertrude Avery, named one of his daughters Malvina French. He was at one time the owner of the Evansville *Courier* and later became head of its editorial department along with his brother George William Shanklin (1843–97), who served in the Union Army during the Civil War. Malvina's youngest brother, Osborne Henry Shanklin (1845–49), did not survive childhood.

4. This is a quotation from the poem "Young Lochinvar," by Sir Walter Scott (1771–1832).

5. It is not clear to whom Malvina Harlan was referring, but her father John Shanklin was friendly enough with African Americans in Evansville to sell them property for a church for $1.00.

6. This is a paraphrase of Ruth 1:16.

7. The married son was James Harlan (1831–97), who married Amelia Lane (d. 1876); the two unmarried daughters were Sally (1841–87) and Laura (1835–70); and the married daughter was Elizabeth Hatchitt.

8. The slave census of 1850 lists James Harlan (the father) as owning fourteen slaves, who ranged in age from three months to seventy years.

9. Malvina Harlan is referring to Robert Harlan (1816–97), who was seven-eighths white in ancestry and was rumored to be James's son. He did indeed make a fortune during the Gold Rush, moved to Cincinnati later in life, and pursued a career in business and politics.

10. Established in 1819, Centre College was primarily a Presbyterian institution aimed at educating teachers and clergy. In 1901 the college consolidated with Central College.

11. Save for James, none of John's brothers lived past their forties. Their dates are: James (1831–97), Richard Daven-

port (1823–54), William Lowndes (1825–68), Henry Clay (1830–49), and George Harlan (1837–37).

12. This was probably John Mann Harlan (1808–55).

13. John Marshall (1755–1835) served as a captain in the American Revolution. He became the third chief justice of the United States in 1801 and spent thirty-four years on the bench. He wrote many important opinions, including *Marbury v. Madison,* 5 U.S. 137 (1803), and *McCulloch v. Maryland,* 17 U.S. 316 (1819).

14. Transylvania University was founded in 1780 as the first college west of the Allegheny Mountains. It no longer has a law school, but in its early years the school had a good reputation, boasting Henry Clay as one of its professors.

15. This is from Isaiah 55:1.

16. Sir James Barrie (1860–1937), Scottish playwright and novelist, is best remembered for his 1904 production of *Peter Pan or The Boy Who Wouldn't Grow Up.* Barrie wrote the play *What Every Woman Knows* in 1908.

17. The New York Avenue Presbyterian Church was one of Washington's prestigious churches, boasting the attendance of many presidents and politicians. John M. Harlan presided over the church's centennial celebration in 1903.

18. Information appearing in brackets throughout these memoirs has been added by the editor for the purpose of clarification.

19. Malvina's eldest two children were Edith Shanklin (1857–83) and Richard Davenport (1859–1931).

20. Richard was an ordained Presbyterian minister, and the president of Lake Forest College from 1901 to 1906. The letter can be found in the John Marshall Harlan Papers, Library of Congress, Manuscript Division, Washington, D.C.

21. Thomas Jefferson (1743–1826) was the author of the Declaration of Independence and president of the United States

(1801–09). He was an advocate of decentralized government and of a strict construction of the Constitution.

22. Daniel Webster (1782–1852) and Henry Clay (1777–1852) were both lawyers and leaders of the Whig party. Webster served in both houses of Congress and as secretary of state. He was a nationalist and proponent of business interests. Henry Clay also served as a congressman and senator, and was nominated twice as the Whig presidential candidate. Clay earned the title the Great Compromiser because of his role in the Missouri Compromise, the Compromise Tariff of 1833, and the Compromise of 1850.

23. Zachary Taylor (1784–1850) served in the U.S. Army from 1808 to 1847, rising to the rank of major general in 1846. He was elected president of the United States in 1848, but died before the end of his term.

24. James G. Blaine (1830–93) began teaching at the Western Military Institute at the age of seventeen. Blaine helped found the Republican party in 1850 and was a leading candidate for the party's presidential nomination in 1876. He was nominated again in 1880 and won the nomination in 1884, only to lose to Grover Cleveland. Blaine remained a strong presence in the Republican party until his death.

25. Charles S. Morehead, of the American party, defeated the Democratic gubernatorial candidate, Beverly L. Clarke, in 1855. The American party gained control of both houses of the Kentucky legislature, only to lose the house to the Democrats in 1857. The party itself emerged in the 1850s as an outlet for anti-immigrant sentiment. Its members, "Know-Nothings," were to disavow any knowledge of nativist connections. The party gained strength in 1854 only to split over the slavery issue in 1856, severely hampering the efforts of its presidential candidate, Millard Fillmore (1800–1874), who, as Zachary Taylor's vice president, had become president when Taylor died in 1850. The party fell

apart after 1856, and most Know-Nothings joined the Republican or Democratic party.

26. The election of 1856 reflected rising sectional conflict. The Kansas-Nebraska Act and the violence in Kansas split the parties. The Republican party ran its first presidential candidate, John C. Fremont, unifying Whigs, Democrats, and Know-Nothings in favor of free labor, and was a formidable presence thereafter. The Democratic party contained much of the proslavery South, but selected Pennsylvanian James Buchanan, who won with 45 percent of the popular vote.

27. Andrew Jackson Donelson (1799–1871) was the political adviser of his namesake. He also served as a diplomat, facilitating the annexation of Texas in 1845. Donelson was a Southerner and a slave owner, but his Unionist sentiments caused him to leave the Democratic party in 1855 and accept the position of Millard Fillmore's running mate.

28. William E. Simms (1822–98) was a lawyer and congressman. Simms, a Democrat, fought in the Mexican War and served in the Kentucky House of Representatives in 1849. He defeated Harlan by only sixty votes. During the Civil War, Simms joined the Confederate army and served in the Confederate Congress. He was pardoned by President Andrew Johnson.

29. John Bell (1797–1869) and Edward Everett (1794–1865) were presidential and vice-presidential nominees for the Constitutional Union party. The party was made up of members of the Whig and American parties who opposed sectionalism, secession, and abolition. Bell did well in border slave states, but the Republican candidate, Abraham Lincoln (1809–65), succeeded in winning eighteen free states and the popular vote. Lincoln was reelected in 1864, but was assassinated the next year. The Democratic party split in 1860, running Stephen A. Douglass (1813–61) as the

Northern candidate, while Southern Democrats nominated
John C. Breckenridge (1821–75).

30. John Marshall Harlan to Richard Davenport Harlan, July 4,
1911, John Marshall Harlan Papers, Library of Congress,
Manuscript Division, Washington, D.C.

31. James Buchanan (1791–1868), a Democrat, was president of
the United States from 1856 tó 1860. Buchanan favored
compromise over the abolition of slavery, even though he
thought slavery immoral.

32. The Southern states feared the antislavery platform of the
Republican party. South Carolina was the first state to secede on December 20, 1860. Six other lower Southern states
followed between January 9 and February 1, 1860. These
states formed the Confederate States of America, and declared independence. There was some resistance to secession, especially in Virginia, North Carolina, Tennessee, and
Arkansas, which did not secede until after April 15, when
Fort Sumter fell to South Carolina troops.

33. Malvina Harlan's account is correct. Beriah Magoffin
(1815–85) was elected governor of Kentucky in 1859. By
August 1861, the Unionists had gained a majority in the
state legislature, ending Kentucky's neutrality. Magoffin resigned from his position on August 18, 1862.

34. In May 1861, the Civil War broke out in Missouri, as factions rallied behind Unionist general Nathaniel Lyon
(1818–61) and pro-Confederate governor Claiborne F. Jackson (1806–62). A series of battles followed, eventually ending in Union victory. Although the Union was officially in
control of the state, guerilla warfare continued thereafter.

35. By telegraph on April 15, 1861, Secretary of War Stanton
called upon Kentucky for four regiments of troops. Governor Magoffin immediately telegraphed his response.

36. William F. Bullock (1807–89) was an established Louisville
lawyer who had served as judge on the Louisville circuit

court between 1846 and 1855. Like Harlan, Bullock was a Unionist.

37. John Marshall Harlan to Richard Davenport Harlan, July 4, 1911, John Marshall Harlan Papers, Library of Congress, Manuscript Division, Washington, D.C.

38. James Speed (1812–87) was a prominent Louisville attorney who served in the Kentucky Senate from 1861 to 1863. In 1864, Speed was appointed attorney general of the United States by Abraham Lincoln, his longtime friend. He served in that position until July 1866, when he resigned in opposition to the policies of Andrew Johnson.

39. Zouaves were volunteer regiments modeled after French colonial infantry units. Their uniforms were brightly colored and often consisted of a turban, a fez, a short jacket, and baggy trousers. Zouave units were popular at the beginning of the Civil War, but proved impractical in actual campaigns. Thomas L. Crittenden (1819–93) was the son of John Jordan Crittenden (1787–1863), governor of Kentucky from 1848 to 1850, who promoted compromise between the North and the South. Thomas L. Crittenden subsequently rose to the rank of major general in the Union Army.

40. The quote is from the poem "Lincoln, the Man of the People" by Edwin Markham (1852–1940), published in 1901.

41. George D. Prentice (1802–70) was editor of the *Louisville Journal* from 1831 to c. 1868. The *Journal* was founded in order to support Whig Henry Clay's presidential campaign. With the demise of the Whig party, Prentice became a supporter of the American party in 1855 and, subsequently, an advocate of the Constitutional Unionist party in 1860. He supported Kentucky's neutrality.

42. Horace Greeley (1811–72) was cofounder and editor of the *New York Tribune,* a leading Whig newspaper.

43. Henry J. Raymond (1820–69) was one of Greeley's employ-

ees until 1851, when Raymond founded his own paper, *The New York Times.*

44. Samuel Bowles (1797–1851) was founder of the *Springfield Republican,* a Massachusetts newspaper. The newspaper was a platform for the Whigs in the 1830s, and Bowles continued as editor until his death.

45. Joseph Medill (1823–99) was the editor and principal owner of the *Chicago Tribune.* Medill was heavily involved with the Republican party.

46. The quotation is from John James Piatt, ed., *The Poems of George D. Prentice, Edited, with a Biographical Sketch* (Cincinnati: Robert Clarke & Co., 1876), xxxvii. Henrietta Benham of Cincinnati (d. 1868) married Prentice in 1835. Their sons Clarence Joseph and William Courtland (d. 1862) enlisted in the Confederate Army.

47. Robert R. Letcher (1788–1861) was a Whig politician and a congressman from 1822 to 1835. James Harlan managed his congressional campaign in 1833 and then was appointed secretary of state from 1841 to 1845.

48. Colonel John Mason Brown was a Whig and a radical candidate for attorney general.

49. Paul R. Shipman was assistant editor and business manager for the *Louisville Journal.* He was an easterner and a loyal Unionist. During the war he penned several pro-Union editorials with the assistance of John M. Harlan.

50. In mid-September 1861, Brigadier General Simon Buckner, a Kentuckian, led Secessionist home guard troops to Lebanon Junction, thirty miles outside of Louisville. Harlan's Home Guard and the Fifth Kentucky Volunteers, under the command of William T. Sherman, went out to engage the Confederate troops, only to find that the enemy had withdrawn.

51. George H. Thomas (1816–70) was repudiated by his Virginian family for remaining loyal to the Union when the

Civil War began. He was made brigadier general in 1861 and major general in 1865.

52. John Marshall Harlan to Richard Davenport Harlan, July 4, 1911, John Marshall Harlan Papers, Library of Congress, Manuscript Division, Washington, D.C.

53. John's only remaining brother, James, suffered from alcoholism and was supported by John during his last years.

54. William Stark Rosecrans (1819–98) graduated from the U.S. Military Academy in 1842. During the Civil War, Rosecrans served in several theaters, including in Tennessee and Kentucky with the Army of the Cumberland. He moved to California in 1880 and served two terms in Congress.

55. James A. Garfield (1831–81) was a native of Ohio. His antislavery views drew him to the Republican party in the 1850s. At the beginning of the Civil War, he raised an infantry division in Ohio and was commissioned as its colonel. In 1863, he resigned his commission to take a seat in the U.S. House of Representatives. He was elected president of the United States in 1880, only to be assassinated the next year.

56. The Emancipation Proclamation did not affect Kentucky, since it specifically targeted states in open rebellion. During the war Secessionist Kentuckians faced the Union Army's confiscation of their slaves, but loyal slaveholders such as the Harlans were not required to free their slaves. Slavery remained legal in Kentucky after the war, with some exceptions, until December 18, 1865, when adoption of the Thirteenth Amendment officially ended slavery.

57. This was a raid into Kentucky led by Confederate raider General John Hunt Morgan (1825–64). In June 1864, Morgan led his detachment of Confederate cavalry through central Kentucky until he was defeated by Union troops at Cynthiana on June 11, 1864. Morgan was killed in battle in September 1864 by Union forces at Greenville, Tennessee.

58. In 1877, "Aunt" Charlotte wrote a letter to John M. Harlan asking for some winter clothes and sending her love to the Harlans' children (she addressed him as "Mr. Mars John"). Aunt Charlotte to John Marshall Harlan, November 5, 1877, John Marshall Harlan Papers, Library of Congress, Manuscript Division, Washington, D.C.

59. The Hewitt house was on the corner of Broadway, across from the Capitol Building.

60. This church was founded in 1815; the present church building dates from 1849.

61. Judge John E. Newman (1819–73) was a Constitutional Unionist during the war, and afterward embraced the Republican party.

62. Benjamin J. Bristow (1832–96) was a lawyer, a colonel in the Union army, and a statesman, well known for his Unionist sentiments and his opposition to postwar attacks on the blacks and Union men in Kentucky. He served as secretary of the treasury from 1874 until he resigned and became a Republican presidential nominee in 1876. His friendship with Harlan broke down over Harlan's appointment to the Court.

63. Augustus E. Willson (1846–1931) became a fervent Republican under John Marshall Harlan's influence. After five unsuccessful campaigns, Willson was elected governor of Kentucky in 1907. During his time as governor, he dealt with the temperance issue and a price war over tobacco. After leaving office in 1911, he returned to law in Louisville.

64. The four children were Edith Shanklin, Richard Davenport, James Shanklin (1861–1927), and John Maynard (1864–1934).

65. Henry Ward Beecher (1813–87), son of theology professor and abolitionist Lyman Beecher, attended Lane Theological Seminary in Cincinnati, Ohio. Like his sister Harriet

Beecher Stowe, he was a writer. He advocated the abolition of slavery, and during the Civil War he championed the Union effort.

66. Ulysses S. Grant (1822–85) was given supreme command of the Union forces in 1864 and forced Confederate General Robert E. Lee's surrender at Appomattox, Virginia, in 1865. He was elected president in 1868 and 1872. His terms were marked by several scandals, over which Benjamin Bristow resigned as secretary of the treasury in protest.

67. Harlan set a record for Republican votes in Kentucky in 1871, and he got 41 percent of the vote in both elections.

68. Preston H. Leslie (1819–1907) became a Democrat after Henry Clay's death and held Southern sympathies during the Civil War. He became governor in 1871 after John W. Stevenson resigned. Leslie's 1871 gubernatorial campaign centered on states' rights and opposition to the Fourteenth and Fifteenth Amendments.

69. James B. McCreary (1838–1918) was a colonel in the Confederate Army during the Civil War, and was a Democrat with strong ties to the South. He served as the governor of Kentucky from 1875 to 1879. After serving as a senator, McCreary ran for governor again in 1911 as a Progressive.

70. Rutherford B. Hayes (1822–93) was a Republican who served in the Union Army during the Civil War and in Congress directly afterward. Hayes was governor of Ohio from 1868 to 1876, when he won the Republican party's presidential nomination in 1876. During the election, Hayes's advisers challenged the validity of ballots from South Carolina, Florida, and Louisiana, culminating in the Tilden-Hayes affair. A bipartisan commission was appointed to decide the election, and Hayes's Republican allies succeeded in winning over several Southern Democrats in secret negotiations. Hayes's presidency is best known for the official end of Reconstruction and national noninterference

in the South, both promises made during the secret negotiations.

71. Isaac Wayne MacVeagh (1833–1917), lawyer and diplomat, joined the Republican party because of his opposition to slavery. He was President Garfield's attorney general in 1881, and ambassador to Italy from 1893 to 1897. He served as chief counsel at the Hague Tribunal in 1903.

72. John Calvin Brown (1827–99) was a Confederate veteran in spite of his opposition to secession, and postwar governor of Tennessee.

73. Charles B. Lawrence (1820–83) served as a justice on the Illinois Supreme Court from 1865 to 1870 and was made chief justice in 1867. He went on to support Harlan's nomination to the Supreme Court.

74. Joseph Roswell Hawley (1826–1905), an antislavery crusader turned soldier-politician, helped organize the Republican party in Connecticut. Hawley was a colonel of Union volunteers who distinguished himself in battle, at one point leading African-American troops in Virginia. He served four terms in the Senate.

75. John Sherman (1823–1900) founded the Republican Party in Ohio and served as a congressman and senator, as well as secretary of the treasury under Hayes and secretary of state under McKinley. Sherman made several attempts at the Republican presidential nomination.

76. William Eaton Chandler (1835–1917) supported Ulysses S. Grant's presidential campaign as secretary of the Republican National Committee. He was disenchanted by corruption in the Grant administration. He helped swing the Florida electoral vote to Rutherford B. Hayes in 1876.

77. Stephen B. Packard fought in the Civil War and became Louisiana's U.S. marshal in 1871. After the collapse of his gubernatorial claims in Louisiana, he was made the U.S. consul in Liverpool.

78. Francis Redding Tillou Nicholls (1834–1912) a West Poin
graduate, served in the Confederate Army. In 1877, Nicholls
became governor of Louisiana in a controversial election.
He quickly replaced the state supreme court judges appointed by the Reconstruction government. His administration imposed racial segregation laws that were upheld in
Plessy v. *Ferguson,* 163 U.S. 537 (1896).

79. Charles Deven (1820–91) rose to the rank of general during
the Civil War. President Hayes initially offered him the position of secretary of war, but Deven accepted the post of
attorney general instead. He was a judge on the Massachusetts Supreme Court before and after his stint in the cabinet.

80. David Davis (1815–86) practiced law in Illinois, becoming
involved in Whig party politics in 1840. President Lincoln
appointed Davis to the Supreme Court in 1862.

81. William Henry Smith (1833–96) was a newspaperman in
Cincinnati and became general manager of the Western As-
sociated Press in 1869 and of the Associated Press in 1883.
He was instrumental in boosting Hayes's political career.

82. James B. Beck (1822–90) practiced law in Kentucky and
sympathized with the South during the Civil War. A Democrat, he abstained from holding office until 1866, when he
served in Congress until 1876, and in the Senate from 1882
to 1890.

83. Lucy Ware Webb Hayes (1831–89) led a vibrant and visible
public life. She supported her husband's campaigning and
worked for the welfare of children, women, and veterans.

84. In fact, four other justices were younger than Harlan at the
time of their appointments: Bushrod Washington was thirty-
six, James Iredell was thirty-eight, and Benjamin Curtis a
John A. Campbell were both forty-one.

85. Morrison R. Waite (1816–88), Melville Weston Clif-
(1833–1910), Edward D. White (1845–1921), Nnuel F.
ford (1803–81), Noah H. Swayne (1804–8

Miller (1816–90), Stephen J. Field (1816–99), William Strong (1808–95), Joseph P. Bradley (1813–92), William B. Woods (1824–87), Lucius Quintus Cincinnatus Lamar (1825–93), Horace Gray (1828–1902), Samuel Blatchford (1820–93), Rufus W. Peckham (1838–1909), George Shiras (1832–1924), Henry B. Brown (1836–1913), William H. Moody (1853–1917), Oliver Wendell Holmes (1841–1935), Joseph McKenna (1843–1926), Horace H. Lurton (1844–1914), William R. Day (1849–1923), Joseph R. Lamar (1857–1916).

86. Harlan actually served alongside twenty-eight justices; Malvina missed Stanley Matthews, David J. Brewer, Ward Hunt, Howell E. Jackson, Charles Evans Hughes, and Willis Van Devanter.

87. Although Lucy Hayes was a Methodist teetotaler, it was Rutherford B. Hayes who made the decision not to allow alcohol in the White House, in order to gain the temperance vote for the Republicans.

88. Charlotte Augusta Gibbes married John Jacob Astor III in 1846. The Astors gave generously to various charities, but critics denounced their lavish spending.

89. William T. Sherman (1820–91) served in the Union Army and proved his abilities in leading his "March to the Sea" in 1864. He succeeded Ulysses S. Grant as commander of the army from 1869 until his retirement in 1885.

90. Belva Ann Bennett McNall Lockwood (1830–1917) had to force Congress to pass a law allowing her to be admitted to the bar of the U.S. Supreme Court, and was the first woman admitted, in 1879. The following year, she argued *Kaiser* v. *Stickney,* 131. U.S. clxxxvii Appx. (1880), the first of several cases she brought before the Supreme Court.

Charles Nordoff (1830–1901), a native of Germany who migrated as a child, wrote for *Harper's Magazine* and the *Atlantic Monthly.*

92. John Goode, Jr. (1820–1909), a lawyer, served in the Confederate Army and Confederate Congress and in the United States House of Representatives from 1875–1881. He was the solicitor general of the United States in 1885–86.

93. Vinnie Ream Hoxie (1847?–1914) was a sculptor and artist who began her career in Washington, D.C. The Senate granted her a commission to sculpt a full-length model of Abraham Lincoln to place in the U.S. Capitol rotunda. In 1878 she married Naval Lieutenant Richard Leveridge Hoxie.

94. Jean Margaret Davenport (1829–1903), an English-born actress, married Frederick West Lander (1821–62), a topographical engineer and a brigade commander during the Civil War.

95. Frances Hodgson Burnett (1849–1924), author and playwright, left England in 1865 and moved to the United States. She wrote stories for *Godey's Lady's Book* and *Harper's* and also wrote novels, including *Little Lord Fauntleroy* (1886).

96. Vicomte Ferdinand Marie de Lesseps (1805–94) was a French diplomat who was instrumental in the building of the Suez Canal. He was president of the French company that began working on the Panama Canal but failed.

97. *The Coming Crown* by Henry Grattan Donnelly (1850–1931), was a pamphlet that protested a third presidential term for Ulysses S. Grant in 1880. It purported to be a series of extracts from 1882 newspapers describing the activities of "His Imperial Majesty, the Emperor Ulysses I."

98. Henry Watterson (1840–1921) was a soldier, journalist, and politician. He moved his family to Louisville, Kentucky, in 1868, where he joined the *Journal* and merged the paper with the rival *Louisville-Courier*, forming the *Courier-Journal*.

99. William Clafin (1818–1905) was a founder of the Free Soil party in Massachusetts. Elected to the first of three terms as governor in 1868, he supported women's suffrage, prohibition, and social welfare programs.

100. William Siddons was the grandson of Sarah Kemble Siddons (1755–1831), the celebrated English actress.

101. "From Greenland's Icy Mountain" was written in 1822 by Bishop R. Heber (1783–1826) in response to a royal letter for the furtherance of the eastern operations of the Society for Propagating the Gospel. The hymn is one of Heber's best-known.

102. James Shanklin Harlan graduated from Princeton University in 1883, apprenticed law with the firm of Melville W. Fuller in Chicago from 1884 to 1888, and joined the bar in 1886. He worked in the firms of Gregory, Gould & Harlan and Harlan & Harlan. President McKinley appointed him attorney general of Puerto Rico from 1901 to 1903. He was appointed to the Interstate Commerce Commission in 1908 by Roosevelt and reappointed by Taft in 1911. He became chairman of the ICC in 1914.

103. John Maynard Harlan graduated from Princeton University in 1884. He practiced law in Chicago with the firm of Harlan & Harlan and married Elizabeth Palmer Flagg in 1890. Their children were Elizabeth Palmer (b. 1891), John Marshall (1899–1971), Janet (b. 1902), and Edith Harlan (b. 1909).

104. Harlan became an associate justice in 1877; John G. Nicolay, one of Abraham Lincoln's two presidential secretaries, was marshal of the Supreme Court from 1872 to 1887.

105. Justice Roger B. Taney (1777–1864) was chief justice of the United States Supreme Court from 1836 to 1864.

106. In *Dred Scott* v. *Sanford,* 60 U.S. 393 (1857), a majority of the Court declared that a slave could not be a citizen and that the Missouri Compromise of 1820 was unconstitutional because Congress did not have the power to ban slavery from the territories.

107. George H. Pendleton (1825–89) was a congressman, sena-

tor, and a minister to Germany. In 1846 he married Mary Alicia Lloyd Nevins Key ("Alice"), the daughter of "The Star-Spangled Banner" author Francis Scott Key.

108. The Civil Rights Cases were five suits alleging denials of public accommodation by blacks in violation of the Civil Rights Act of 1875. The Supreme Court, with only John M. Harlan dissenting, decided that the Fourteenth Amendment applied only to state action and not to private owners. The Civil Rights Act of 1875 guaranteed equal rights in public places without regard to color.

109. Charles Sumner (1811–74) was a Massachusetts senator, antislavery activist, and radical Republican.

110. This is a paraphrase of *Dred Scott* v. *Sanford*, 60 U.S. 393, 407 (1857).

111. Indeed, Harlan's dissent in the Civil Rights Cases identifies Taney's decision in *Dred Scott* as what Congress meant to undo by passing the Thirteenth and Fourteenth Amendments.

112. Linus Child was a Chicago attorney. Linus and Edith had one child, also named Edith Harlan, born in 1882.

113. On July 2, 1881, President James A. Garfield was waiting at Baltimore's Potomac Station when a religious fanatic named Charles J. Guiteau shot him. Garfield was president only six months, and died September 19, 1881.

114. According to the Harlan family genealogy, Edith and Linus were married on October 15, 1881, not the 20th. John M. Harlan taught a Sunday school class at the church and served as an elder.

115. John R. Paxton (1843–1923) graduated from Princeton Theological Seminary in 1870 and served as the pastor of the New York Avenue Presbyterian Church in Washington, D.C., from 1878 to 1882.

116. John M. Harlan telegraphed Mrs. Hayes that Edith died of

typhomalarial, which then meant a fever exhibiting both the symptoms of typhoid, including intestinal inflammation, and malaria.

117. George Washington University was previously known as Columbian University. Harlan taught there for twenty years, and he wrote a friend that he "regarded my connection with the University as a part of my life-work—and the most interesting part." Harlan to Walter C. Clephane, August 4, 1910, John Marshall Harlan Papers, University of Louisville, School of Law, Law Library, Louisville, KY.

118. Harlan's annual salary was $10,000 when he joined the Court, increased to $12,500 in 1903, and was $14,500 in 1911, the year of his death.

119. The dinner was probably held by Augustus H. Garland, attorney general in Grover Cleveland's first administration (1885–89).

120. According to Genesis 9, Japheth is one of Noah's sons.

121. George Boyd Harlan (1829–89) married Margaretta Keerl in 1867.

122. Daniel Boone's son Israel was killed at the battle of Lower Blue Licks, which took place on August 19, 1782.

123. Donnybrook Fair was an annual Irish event that was abolished in 1855 because of continual brawls.

124. Thomas Lord Fairfax (1692–1782) was a cousin of Colonel William Fairfax. William gave Washington his start in surveying in 1747 and early 1748, when Washington was not quite sixteen. In 1749, he became surveyor for Culpepper County, the entirety of which lay within Thomas Lord Fairfax's estate.

125. President Benjamin Harrison (1833–1901) was the grandson of President William Henry Harrison. He was elected president in 1888, but lost the 1892 election to Grover Cleveland and returned to his law practice in Indiana.

126. The Arbitration Tribunal met in Paris in 1893. The Bering

Sea Fur Seal Commission Arbitration involved a dispute among the U.S., Canada, and Great Britain involving sealing rights on the Pribilof Islands, a small group of islands that served as the breeding grounds for fur seals. Justice Harlan was the only American arbitrator to side with the majority against four of the U.S. claims of jurisdictional rights over the Bering Sea. In the end, the U.S. was ordered to pay damages to Great Britain, but open-sea hunting was forbidden within sixty miles around the islands for a specified period each year.

127. This was the spelling used at the time.

128. Laura Cleveland Harlan was born in 1871.

129. David J. Brewer (1837–1910) was the son of a missionary father and a mother who was a sister of Supreme Court justice Stephen J. Field. He searched for gold at Pike's Peak before settling in Leavenworth, Kansas Territory, where he lived for thirty years working as a railroad and corporate lawyer. Brewer served on the United States Supreme Court from 1889 to 1910.

130. Ruth Harlan was born in 1874.

131. They were traveling through Switzerland.

132. The Vices "make night hideous" for the virtuous man in "The Duellist" by Charles Churchill (1731–64).

133. John Tyler Morgan (1824–1907) was a brigadier general in the Confederate Army. He became a U.S. senator from Alabama in 1877 and was reelected five times. He married Cornelia Willis, and they had five children.

134. Tiziano Vecellio (1477–1576) was an Italian painter, one of the masters of the Venetian school. His *Assumption of the Virgin* of 1518 is housed in the Church of Santa Maria dei Frari in Venice.

135. The reference is to *History of John Gilpin* by William Cowper (1731–1800): "That though on pleasure she was bent, / She had a frugal mind."

136. Thomas Jefferson Coolidge (1831–1920) was a businessman and diplomat who amassed a fortune in railroads and banking before being named minister to France in 1892.

137. Marie-François Sadi Carnot (1837–94) was a French statesman and a civil engineer. In 1887, Carnot was elected president of the Republic of France.

138. *Salammbo* was by Italian composer Errico Petrella (1813–77).

139. Alphonse Chodron, Baron de Courcelle (1835–1919), was a French diplomat who held a variety of posts, including ambassador to Germany in 1881.

140. Lord James Hannen (1821–94) was a British judge.

141. Sir John Sparrow David Thompson (1844–94) was premier and attorney general of Nova Scotia. He served as a Supreme Court judge from 1882 to 1885 and prime minister from 1892 until his death in 1894.

142. William Strong (1808–95) was a prominent railroad lawyer who was elected to the Pennsylvania Supreme Court in 1857. He was appointed to the Supreme Court in 1870 and retired ten years later. A very religious man, he supported the movement to add a dedication to Jesus Christ to the preamble of the U.S. Constitution.

143. Charles Russell, First Baron of Killowen (1832–1900), was a life peer and British attorney general. He went on to represent Great Britain in the Venezuela and Guiana boundary question in 1899.

144. Richard Everard Webster, First viscount Alverston (1842–1915), was British attorney general, lord chief justice, and then a peer. He went on to serve as arbiter in the Venezuelan and Guiana boundary question (1898–99), and then in the Alaska boundary dispute (1903).

145. Edward John Phelps (1822–1900) taught law at Yale University in the 1880s, and was the minister to Great Britain from 1885 to 1889.

146. James Coolidge Carter (1827–1905) was an American lawyer.
147. Frederic René Coudert (1832–1903), an American lawyer, was a member of the international conference at Berne (1880) and also represented the United States during the Venezuelan boundary dispute.
148. Queen Alexandria Victoria (1819–1901) was queen of the United Kingdom of Great Britain and Ireland from 1837 to 1901 and empress of India from 1876 on.
149. In the mid-seventeenth century, modern tapestry weaving was born in Paris. Tapestries of this period (Louis XIV) became known by the name "Gobelin."
150. Alexander Felix Joseph Ribot (1842–1923) served in a variety of positions in the French cabinet and as premier.
151. Robert T. Lincoln (1843–1926) was the eldest son of Abraham Lincoln. He served as secretary of war (1881–85) and minister to Great Britain (1889–93).
152. John Duke Coleridge, Baron (1820–94), was an English justice from 1835 to 1858. Coleridge was knighted in 1868. He served as attorney general (1871–73), lord chief justice of the Court of Common Pleas (1873–75), and lord chief justice of England (1880 until his death).
153. William Baliol Brett, First Viscount Esher (1815–99), was a leader in the Court of Admiralty and Court of Passage, Liverpool. Knighted in 1868, he became a judge of the Common Pleas Division of the High Court of Justice in 1875, and was then promoted to the Court of Appeal in 1876. He became master of the rolls in 1883.
154. Charles Synge Christopher Bowen (1835–94) was Judge of Queen's Bench in 1879, became a judge of the Court of Appeal in 1882, and served as a lord of appeal from 1893 until his death.
155. Michael, Lord Morris (b. 1827), was a lawyer and judge. He

served as queen's counsel in 1863, in the British Parliament, and as solicitor general and attorney general for Ireland. He was made lord chief justice in 1867 and a lord of appeal in 1889.

156. Honorable James Bryce, Viscount Bryce (1838–1922), was a British jurist, historian, and diplomatic member of several arbitration tribunals. He served as ambassador to the United States (1907–13).

157. There is a statue of Oliver Cromwell near the entrance to St. Stephen's Hall, but it is by Sir Hamo Thorneycroft.

158. William Ewart Gladstone (1809–98) was a statesman and four times prime minister of Great Britain (1868–74, 1880–85, 1886, 1892–94).

159. Home rule was a movement to secure internal autonomy for Ireland within the British Empire. Prime Minister Gladstone was converted to home rule by 1885, but his First Home Rule Bill was rejected by Parliament in 1886. Malvina is referring to Gladstone's Second Home Rule Bill, introduced in 1893. This second bill was defeated in the House of Lords.

160. Frederick Temple Hamilton-Temple-Blackwood, first Marquess of Dufferin and Ava (1826–1902), held numerous international governmental positions for Great Britain between 1849 and 1896, including ambassadorships to Italy and France. He married Hariot Hamilton in 1862.

161. In 1722, the Duke of Charost built the house, known as the Hôtel de Charost (located in the Faubourg Saint-Honoré, Paris), under the direction of architect Antoine Mazin. In 1803, the Charost family sold it to Bonaparte's sister, Pauline Leclerc. The Duke of Wellington, then British ambassador to France, purchased the house in 1814, and it has remained the residence of the ambassador since then.

162. Napoléon Joseph Charles Paul Bonaparte (1822–91) was

recognized as a French prince in 1852 and an heir to the French throne. He was said to bear a striking resemblance to his uncle.

163. Chicago World's Columbian Exposition in 1893 was a World's Fair at which more than fifty countries exhibited.

164. Murray Bay is the American name for La Malbaie ("the Bad Bay"), surrounding Pointe-au-Pic along the St. Lawrence River. The villages of Murray Bay, with buildings of gabled roofs and dormer windows, and the area's spectacular views of the mountains made the bay a popular resort among the American elite.

165. The Honorable Edward Blake (1833–1912) was a prominent equity lawyer and authority on the Canadian constitution. He became prime minister of Ontario in 1871–72 and minister of justice in 1875. From 1879 to 1887, he led the Liberal party.

166. The grandchild was Edith Harlan Child (b. 1882). Richard Davenport Harlan was married to Margaret Prouty Swift. James Shanklin was married to Maude Noble. John Maynard married Elizabeth Palmer Flagg in 1890. Their children were Elizabeth Palmer (b. 1891), John Marshall (1899–1971), Janet (b. 1902), and Edith Harlan (b. 1909). Daughters Laura Cleveland Harlan and Ruth Harlan never married.

167. Situated on the bluffs overlooking the Murray River, the town of Cap à-l'Aigle's most notable pilgrimage site was Mount Murray Manor, the seigniory awarded at the same time Nairne (see note 170) came into possession of his seigniory on the opposite side of the river.

168. The quotation is from James 1:17.

169. Mr. and Mrs. Harlan attended what was then known as the Union Church in Pointe-au-Pic (now the Murray Bay Protestant Church), an Anglican and Presbyterian church

that catered to Murray Bay's summer residents. Harlan served as the Presbyterian trustee from 1900 until 1911.

170. Madame Nairne, born Christiana Emery, was a native of Scotland who married John Nairne in 1766. Nairne was commissioned to the Seventy-eighth Regiment (Frasier's Highlanders) who, after the captures of Louisbourg (1758) and Quebec (1759), bought the seigniory of Murray Bay in 1761.

171. Reverend George MacKinnon Wrong (1860–1948) was a Canadian historian who taught in the University of Toronto's history department from 1894 until 1927. He served as Union Church trustee from 1900 to 1916. Robert Shaw Minturn served as trustee from 1908 to 1916. The overlap in the years of their service with Harlan is accounted for by Wrong's service as church treasurer part of the time.

172. H. D. Sedgwick (1861–1957) was an author and attorney.

173. These excerpts are from "The Country of the Dormer-Window," which appeared in *The Century Illustrated Monthly Magazine* 86 (May–Oct., 1913): 720–29.

174. Judge Horace H. Lurton (1844–1914) was a justice of the Supreme Court of Tennessee from 1886 to 1893, and became an associate justice of the U.S. Supreme Court in 1910.

175. William Howard Taft (1857–1930) was a Republican from Cincinnati, Ohio, who served as president of the United States from 1909 until 1913 and as chief justice of the United States Supreme Court from 1921 until his death.

176. Taft served on the Sixth District, which included Ohio.

177. Taft returned in 1904 in order to become secretary of war under President Theodore Roosevelt.

178. Albert Henry George Grey (1851–1917) was the governor-general of Canada from 1904 until 1911. He was made an earl in 1894, and served as administrator of Rhodesia from

1894 to 1897. He married Alice Holford, the daughter of Robert Stayner Holford, M.P., in 1877.

179. James Wolfe (1727–59) led the British expedition against Quebec in 1759. After scaling the heights, he was mortally wounded while leading the attack across the Plains of Abraham against French field marshall Marquis de Montcalm (1712–59), who was also mortally wounded there.

180. Malvina Harlan is, of course, referring to World War I.

181. "The feast of reason and the flow of soul" is from Alexander Pope, (1688–1744), *Satires, Epistles, and Odes of Horace,* Satire I, Book ii, line 127.

182. Sir Charles Fitzpatrick (1851–1942) held a number of governmental positions and was chief justice of the Canadian Supreme Court from 1906 to 1918.

183. Philander Chase Knox (1853–1921) was a corporate attorney who became attorney general under William McKinley and Theodore Roosevelt. He also served as President Taft's secretary of state.

184. Elihu Root (1845–1937) was a lawyer and a senator from New York from 1895 to 1899. He was secretary of war under William McKinley from 1899 to 1904 and secretary of state under Theodore Roosevelt from 1905 to 1909. Root won the Nobel Peace Prize in 1912 for his work toward international peace.

185. Theodore Roosevelt (1858–1919), twenty-sixth president of the United States, served as assistant secretary of the Navy from 1897 to 1898, fought in the Spanish-American War, and became president in 1901 upon the assassination of William McKinley. He was reelected in 1904.

186. George Frisbie Hoar (1826–1904) was a founder of the Free Soil party and organizer of the Massachusetts Republican party. He served as a congressman from 1869 to 1877, and a senator from 1877 until his death.

187. James Beck (1861–1936) held the positions of attorney general, assistant attorney general, and solicitor general (1896–1925) and served as a congressman from 1927 to 1934.

188. Mrs. Blake was Margaret Cronyn, daughter of the Bishop of Huron. She married Blake in 1858.

189. The Treaty of Paris made the misspelling "Porto Rico" official until 1932.

190. Harlan's photograph graced the cover of this issue.

191. Dr. Henry Van Dyke (1852–1933) graduated from Princeton Theological Seminary in 1877 and was a professor of English literature from 1900 to 1923 at Princeton University. He was the chairman of the Special Committee on Forms and Services.

192. Jenny Geddes was a seventeenth-century woman who protested against the introduction of English liturgy into Scotland. She supposedly started a riot by throwing a stool at the bishop.

193. Alfred Perceval Graves (1846–1932) wrote of "The Kilkenny Cats," who ate each other up in the fierceness of their fighting.

194. Castoria was a patent medicine.

195. The reference is to the "Ode on the Death of the Duke of Wellington" by Alfred, Lord Tennyson (1809–92), who described Wellington as "That tower of strength / Which stood four-square to all the winds that blew."

196. John Witherspoon (1723–94) was a delegate to the Continental Congress and signed the Declaration of Independence. He was president of the College of New Jersey (now Princeton University).

197. The General Assembly of 1905 referred this memorial to the Committee on Bills and Overtures and then made John M. Harlan the chairman of a special committee on the memorial. A commission to gather funds for the project was formed in 1923. In 1947, with the approval of the Washing-

ton presbytery, the National Presbyterian Church was established. In 1969, it moved to its current location on Nebraska Avenue in Washington, D.C.

198. Augustus E. Willson (1846–1931) married Mary Elizabeth Ekin in 1877.

199. Originally one of the South's finest hotels, the Galt House was beginning to decline by the time the Harlans stayed there.

200. Martha Orr (1836–1909) married Samuel Bayard (d. 1898).

201. Mr. Charles Henry Butler was Supreme Court reporter from 1902 to 1916. Butler was Elizabeth Flagg Harlan's brother-in-law.

202. The official name of this convention was First International Congress in America for the Welfare of the Child. It was held under the auspices of the National Congress of Mothers, which evolved into the Parent-Teacher Association.

203. Civil unrest developed in western Kentucky as independent growers attempted to dismantle the "tobacco trust" headed by the American Tobacco Company. The night riders were members of tobacco cooperatives, who used intimidation and violence to extort participation in the cooperatives from local growers. Willson was criticized by both sides. Informally known as the Black Patch War, hostilities took place between 1904 and 1909.

204. John Marshall Harlan (1899–1971), like his grandfather, became an associate justice of the Supreme Court of the United States. He served from 1955 to 1971.

205. Justice James Clark McReynolds (1862–1946), known for his conservative opinions, served as U.S. attorney general under Woodrow Wilson and then served on the Supreme Court from 1914 until he resigned in 1940.

206. Judge Roger Atkinson Pryor (1828–1919) was a lawyer and a Virginia slaveholder and advocate of states' rights while publisher of the newspaper *South*. After the war, Pryor

moved to New York, where his strong connections to the Democratic party landed him a seat on the New York Court of Common Pleas in 1891.

207. Sara Agnes Rice Pryor (1830–1912) authored many books of popular history, including *My Day: Reminiscences of a Long Life* (1909), a work that sentimentalized the antebellum South and seems to have inspired Malvina's title.

208. The quotation is from John Greenleaf Whittier's poem "At Last" (1882).

209. Wallace Radcliffe (1842–1922) graduated from Princeton Theological Seminary in 1866 and became pastor at the New York Avenue Presbyterian Church in 1895.

210. Oliver Wendell Holmes Sr. (1809–94) was a professor of anatomy at Dartmouth and Harvard Universities. His real fame came as the author of stories, essays, and poems.

211. Cardinal John Henry Newman (1801–90) wrote this prayer. The original is slightly different.

PHOTO CREDITS

DISCUSSION GUIDE

1. Throughout history, there have been women such as Malvina Shanklin Harlan who possess little public power but are able to influence society through their husband's positions and their own values. What instances of this are evident in *Some Memories of a Long Life*, and what are the limitations of this power?

2. Harlan alludes to her conservative attitudes about gender relations, twice contrasting herself to the "New Woman." In what sense does Harlan's act of writing and her choice of subject matter contradict her stated views on gender, and in what sense does it confirm them?

3. Before Malvina wed John Marshall, her mother advised her, "Remember, now, that *his* home is YOUR home; *his* people, YOUR people, *his* interests, YOUR interests—

you must have *no other*." In her Foreword, Ruth Bader Ginsburg writes, "Malvina valued that advice, but did not follow it in all respects. She continued to pursue her interest in music; she eventually sojourned abroad on her own; and even, after forty-seven years of marriage, spoke for the first time on a public platform." What other evidence in the text suggests that Malvina either conformed to or challenged traditional gender roles?

4. Discuss the picture of the Civil War and its aftermath that Harlan offers through her personal account and anecdotes.

5. The *New York Times Book Review* claims that "From antebellum Kentucky to twentieth-century Washington, [Harlan] observes customs, manners, clothing, people, places, and events with the skills of a gifted storyteller." Describe the social customs and culture(s) that Harlan re-creates through her writing.

6. Discuss the symbolic significance of objects in *Some Memories* such as the inkstand and the pamphlet from Justice Harlan's twenty-fifth anniversary dinner.

7. Religion is important to the Harlans' lives and to Malvina's memoir. Describe the complex relationship between religion and government in both the Harlans' personal lives and in the public sphere.

8. In her Afterword, Linda Przybyszewski points out some of the benefits and drawbacks of reading history through the lens of a personal memoir. Comment on this in light of your reading of *Some Memories of a Long Life*.

9. Justice Harlan was involved in a number of ground-breaking political decisions, either directly—through his carefully reasoned vote—or indirectly—through his powerful influence (which he often employed in creative ways). Discuss the role Harlan played in the most historically significant decisions of the memoir, such as Kentucky's allegiance to the Union and the Plessy *v.* Ferguson case, as well as the role Harlan played in more minor political and religious debates.

10. Malvina Shanklin Harlan's work is a unique gateway into her husband's (and her time's) views on race and slavery. In her Afterword, Przybyszewski explains the evolution of the Justice's beliefs about slavery and describes his actions as instances of "white paternalism." Do you agree or disagree with this assessment of Justice Harlan's racial beliefs?

11. In her comment "Instead of depicting the full reality of the past, Malvina's memoir tells us what she chose to remember and how she wanted others to remember John," Przybyszewski cautions Harlan's readers to keep in mind the author's personal conscious and unconscious prejudices. To what degree is this caution particular to reading a memoir, and to what degree is it helpful to consider when reading any historical work?

ABOUT THE AUTHOR

MALVINA SHANKLIN HARLAN (1838–1916) was the wife of Justice John Marshall Harlan. She wrote this memoir of her years with her husband in 1915. It went unpublished until 2001, when the *Journal of Supreme Court History* first brought Harlan's words to the American public.

A NOTE ON THE TYPE

The principal text of this Modern Library edition
was set in a digitized version of Janson, a typeface that
dates from about 1690 and was cut by Nicholas Kis,
a Hungarian working in Amsterdam. The original matrices have
survived and are held by the Stempel foundry in Germany.
Hermann Zapf redesigned some of the weights and sizes for
Stempel, basing his revisions on the original design.

MODERN LIBRARY IS ONLINE AT
WWW.MODERNLIBRARY.COM

MODERN LIBRARY ONLINE IS YOUR GUIDE
TO CLASSIC LITERATURE ON THE WEB

THE MODERN LIBRARY E-NEWSLETTER

Our free e-mail newsletter is sent to subscribers, and features sample chapters, interviews with and essays by our authors, upcoming books, special promotions, announcements, and news.

To subscribe to the Modern Library e-newsletter, send a blank e-mail to: **sub_modernlibrary@info.randomhouse.com** or visit **www.modernlibrary.com**

THE MODERN LIBRARY WEBSITE

Check out the Modern Library website at
www.modernlibrary.com for:

- The Modern Library e-newsletter
- A list of our current and upcoming titles and series
- Reading Group Guides and exclusive author spotlights
- Special features with information on the classics and other paperback series
- Excerpts from new releases and other titles
- A list of our e-books and information on where to buy them
- The Modern Library Editorial Board's 100 Best Novels and 100 Best Nonfiction Books of the Twentieth Century written in the English language
- News and announcements

Questions? E-mail us at **modernlibrary@randomhouse.com**
For questions about examination or desk copies, please visit
the Random House Academic Resources site at
www.randomhouse.com/academic